Gerrit Haas
Ficto/critical Strategies

Lettre

Gerrit Haas was awarded a joint PhD from FU Berlin and UWA. His post-doctoral research interests comprise constellations, hacking literature, and discursive iconicity. Born and bred in Düsseldorf, he currently lives and works in Berlin.

Gerrit Haas

Ficto/critical Strategies

Subverting Textual Practices of Meaning, Other, and Self-Formation

[transcript]

This dissertation was presented in partial fulfilment of the requirements of the degree of Doctor of Philosophy under a joint award PhD program between Freie Universität Berlin and The University of Western Australia in April 2014.

I wish to express my deep gratitude to the following people for their kind help: Hannah, for being who you are and with me, no matter what; Barbara and Ulrich, for all the support one could possibly hope for from their parents; Birthe, for fiddling about with the thesis mobile and your sisterly succour; Becky, for our mutual research presentations, your creative writing initiative, as well as all the coffee and banter that went with it; Lyam, for your stimulating report from the academic conference; Russell West-Pavlov, for initiating and embracing the original thesis project; Philip Mead, for sustaining and salvaging it as a presentable PhD thesis; Jennifer Wawrzinek and Alison Bartlett, for your respective efforts and supervision; Stephen Muecke, Heather Kerr, Helen Flavell, and Anne Brewster, for taking the time to discuss ficto/criticism in Berlin, Adelaide, Perth/Fremantle, and Sydney.

The following institutions and scholarships have financially supported this project and enabled my sojourn at UWA: Elsa-Neumann-Promotionsstipendium / NaFöG (2009/10); FUB Centre for International Cooperation (2010); DAAD Jahresstipendium für Doktoranden (2010/11).

Printed with the kind assistance of both Siblings Boehringer Ingelheim Foundation for the Humanities and Ernst-Reuter-Gesellschaft der Freunde, Förderer & Ehemaligen der Freien Universität Berlin e.V.

Bibliographic information published by the Deutsche Nationalbibliothek
The Deutsche Nationalbibliothek lists this publication in the Deutsche Nationalbibliografie; detailed bibliographic data are available in the Internet at http://dnb.d-nb.de

Cover layout: Kordula Röckenhaus, Bielefeld
Cover illustration: Gerrit & Birthe Haas, Berlin, 2012
Printed in Germany
Print-ISBN 978-3-8376-3704-5
PDF-ISBN 978-3-8394-3704-9

Contents

1. Introducing the Ficto/critical

Advance on the thesis: academic and literary writing intersect in *literary* theories. The newly resultant textual form is therefore distinguished by the simultaneity of academic non-fiction and fiction – or: criticism and literature, theory and fiction. This artificially wrought unity of allegedly separate and institutionally opposed textualities and their means presents a curious syzygy. In a word: fictocriticism. Such at least has been the idea for some time now.

But then, sometimes, theoretical fictions of this kind incorporate textual or conceptual frictions that make perceptible the stuff and processes from which they are wrought, while at the same time giving enlightening and instructive direction to these performatively experiential insights. Now *that* shall be the theory. Outside of which remains of primordial importance only the practice of our reading and writing – ficto/critically, as it were. As always, the crux of the matter consists in its intersections. Here most significantly in the *between* that is both the textual relation and our wider discursive relating through it. So much, perhaps, up front, as an advance on the (slashed) ficto/critical to come.

Antecedently, I will offer you here only a rather rough sketch of the fictocritical, to begin with. The name "fictocriticism" is often evoked to subsume motivated experimental writing practices that confound, and thereby problematise, the generic distinctions between fiction and criticism, between fiction and non-fiction, between philosophy and literature. Fictocritical texts are usually playful in tone and experimental in attitude. At the same time, fictocritical writing is often ethically motivated as well as heavily in/formed by, mostly poststructuralist, theory. Bringing fictional means into the realm of generic academic writing, for example, fictocriticism augments the conceptual relation of such – often anaemic – nonfictional texts with the more affective relation of a literary reading. But the literary aspects in fictocritical texts not only contribute an experience that is generically excluded from academic writing. In fact, their literary imagery often subtly acquires conceptual significance for the academic discourses thus addressed. Even more profoundly, in so doing the fictocritical sometimes perceptibly stages the fictional premises of non-fictional writing. Arguably, fictocriticism thus aspires to present a critique via form – which, as I later want to establish, is most effective where the per/form/ative aspects of textual form enter the equation self-reflexively.

Fictocriticism first emerged under this name in the 1990s at the fringes of the Canadian art-scene (Flavell 2009) and within – albeit at the (perceived) margins of – the Australian academy, where the introduction of postgraduate degrees combining units in creative writing and literary theory provided a productive institutional environment that has propelled such writing (Brewster 1996a). Since then, fictocritical textual practices have become increasingly prolific internationally – if not always under that name[1] – and gained further institutional currency, especially in Australia. Importantly, in the university context fictocritical writing has originated and proliferated in proximity to the fertile grounds of contemporary feminist, post/colonial, queer, and other marginal/ised discourses which, at that historical moment, acutely experienced a lack of academic speaking positions available to them. One frequently offered narrative explains that a different kind of textual form was required in order to narrow the gap between the official academic voice and these respectively situated personal speaking positions. The rationale of this story is that writers with such personal motivational backgrounds and equipped with the theoretical wherewithal broke the generic textual structures in their respective academic subjects in an attempt also to break with the wider discursive structures that kept their respective speaking positions marginal/ised, not only at the academy.

Indeed, much fictocritical writing focuses on the intersecting discursive relations between the differentially structured linguistic, corporeal, social, and environmental fields, all of which, firstly, impact on an individual's formation of self in relation to the world and other and, secondly, are usually heavily mediated through text-discursive formations. Thus, I want to suggest, the nucleus of fictocritical writing practices can be marked as a form of textual resistance – in theory and practice – to common generic distinctions *in combination with* an ethical motivation against linguistic-discursive practices of marginalisation and domination.

1 There is a plethora of applicable and related labels in use. To name but a few: creative non-fiction, fiction-theory, paracriticism, autobiographical non-fiction, critifiction, crypto-friction, writing-between, etc.

The point of interest here is that in conflating generically separated textual approaches, fictocritical writing performatively directs attention to our dominant textual practices and the particular functions they often serve within our wider discursive practices, such as differential identity formation in relation to the world and others. In many ways the precise connection between these two aspects of fictocriticism – between genre-subversion and marginal/ised speaking positions, between the text-discursive and the wider discursive, between the fictional and the ethical, theory and criticism – is the main subject of this thesis. In pursuit of this question the careful study of marginal fictocritical texts and writing practices can still yield significant insights into our textual practices in general if we only dare to re/examine, on a *systemic* level, the mechanisms and constellations that fictocritical texts deploy differently.

Alternatively, a helpful introduction to fictocriticism can be assembled by quoting three influential passages that sketch an enticing little history of the idea via the practice, the concepts behind it, and the term hovering above it. This triad of references often features in introductory passages on the topic (e.g. Robb 2001: 5) – a fact that has since itself become the object of some critical investigation (e.g. Flavell 2009).

Firstly, as early as the mid-eighties, in her text "Poststructuralism and the Paraliterary", Rosalind Krauss has perceptively observed the following development:

> "[S]tudents, having experienced the collapse of modernist literature, have turned to the literary products of postmodernism, among the most powerful examples of which are the paraliterary works of Barthes and Derrida. If one of the tenets of modernist literature had been the creation of a work that would force reflection on the conditions of its own construction, that would insist on reading as a much more consciously *critical* act, then it is not surprising that the medium of a *post*modernist literature should be the critical text wrought in a paraliterary form. And what is clear is that Barthes and Derrida are the *writers*, not the critics, that students now read." (1986: 292, original emphases)

This pivotal shift in perspective, which recognises the literary value of critical and theoretical works and allows for a *reception* attitude of productive generic confusion, certainly functions as a precursor to fictocritical writing practices. Coming from a focus on theory and criticism, Krauss uses the term "paraliterary" to good effect but, changing direction, "paracritical" or "paratheoretical" might have been just as apt. For the present study, two things are especially remarkable: firstly, how Krauss already senses a creative relation between (modernist) meta-reflections and (post/modernist) experimentation and, secondly, how she also references "*reading* as a much more consciously critical act" (ibid, my emphasis), for which the writerly and critical acts almost converge on the page – as the quotation's last sentence would suggest.

Secondly, in an interview with Derek Attridge for *Acts of Literature*, Jacques Derrida effectively corroborates Krauss's assessment of the generic boundaries with this statement:

> "I don't feel at ease either with a rigorous distinction between 'literature' and 'literary criticism' or with a confusion of the two. What would the rigorous limit between them be? [...] Yet I would not say that we can mix everything up and give up the distinctions between all these types of 'literary' or 'critical' production (for there is also a 'critical' instance at work '*in*' what is called the literary work). So it is necessary to determine or delimit another space where we justify relevant distinctions between certain forms of literature and certain forms of ... I don't know what name to give it, that's the problem, we must invent one for those 'critical' inventions which belong to literature while deforming its limits." (1992a: 52, original emphasis)

On the one hand, there is palpable anticipation here to thoroughly deconstruct – theoretically and performatively – the dichotomy "between 'literature' and 'literary criticism'" (ibid: 52). The generically in-between space that Derrida envisions as the place from which to reflect and change fixed generic patterns also opens, on another level, the designated aporetic realm that would succeed such deconstructive processes. On the other hand, Derrida perhaps already sensed the systemic difficulty of putting a quasi-generic label to something paraliterary that could be so formally unpredictable and diverse – coming, as it would, with the same force and justification from both sides of a divide that it aims to put under erasure. Possibly then, he knowingly did not actually provide the name he called for, granting these practices just a little longer in their quasi edenic state *avant la lettre*, because a name, any name, would hasten in, from an unexpected angle, the very forces of genre these practices aim to exorcise. In any case, each of these aspects will become relevant for the theory of the (slashed) ficto/critical that the present study shall eventually advance.

Thirdly, Stephen Muecke has prominently referenced this Derridean challenge for a name in his exemplary fictocritical essay "The Fall" (2008b), which was first published under the more definitionally ambitious title "The Fall: Fictocritical Writing" (2002): "Once Jacques Derrida, the French Philosopher, asked us for a name [...]. The name we would have given him was 'fictocriticism', but he went on anyway to write, and perform, critically, and sometimes fictionally, for instance by telling stories while making his philosophical arguments." (2008b: 18) By thus cleverly indicating that the lack of a name has never harmed the practice, Muecke still appears to establish the ingenious term "fictocriticism" in direct response to Derrida for what Krauss called a paraliterary criticism. Notably, Muecke here adapts the collective markers "us" and "we", presumably speaking for the loose conglomerate of writers operating under the name fictocriticism at the time. However, this general gesture was soon to be offset by different more specific and more motivationally inflected perspectives that individual writers have since assumed together with the name.

In any case, this introductory triad of quotes, each of which contributes to a useful definition of fictocriticism, constructs only one – albeit powerful – narrative. It has the obvious advantage of delivering a history of the idea that is closely linked with the term: fictocriticism emerged at a point in time when the critical text was increasingly wrought in paraliterary form. In theory, it marks the consequential space where critical inventions that belong to literature as well as literary inventions that pertain to criticism become interventions as they proceed to deform the respective limits of their genres from an undefined space somewhere in-between. One ready way to figure fictocritical textual practice, in this sense, is the intersection, on the page, of storytelling with philosophical arguments – making the two indistinguishably reliant on each other. This figurative aspect, too, will become centrally important for the refined model of the (slashed) ficto/critical that the present thesis later proposes. However, although this second rough sketch, again, captures central traits of the fictocritical fairly well, it may still not tell the whole story. There are certainly other legitimate and important narratives, which emphasise different aspects of the fictocritical that need to be taken into account.

In her study *Writing-Between: Australian and Canadian Ficto-Criticism* Helen Flavell has made the effort to retrace the historical itinerary of the neologism "ficto-criticism", which she hyphenates, via Frederic Jameson, to the Canadian artist and art critic Jeanne Randolph (2004: 193-203). Against this background, she could then critically respond to Muecke's version of the naming narrative in "Who Killed Jeanne Randolph? King, Muecke or 'Ficto-Criticism'" (2009). Significantly, Flavell contextualises her historical research with reference to the genesis of fictocritical writing practices as a form of experimental *feminist* writing (2004: 140-90, esp. 158-70). Thus, on top of historical accuracy, Flavell also echoes the strategic move to claim fictocriticism not so much as a feminist thing (ibid: 163-5) but, figuratively, as a feminine *space between* in writing. Such are the origins of the fictocritical that Flavell's extensive research between Canada and Australia reveals. On this basis, however, it should already be noted here that her specific conception of (hyphenated) ficto-criticism emphasises its cross-cultural signature as a hybrid form of writing in equal measure – as is evident in her reading of Fred Wah's *Diamond Grill* (1996), for example (Flavell 2004: 62-7).

Importantly, Flavell thus both highlights and exemplifies something that is not as prevalent in Muecke's "The Fall", namely a positioned involvement, in terms of personal interest, that in/forms fictocriticism. In this sense, Flavell's academic thesis also marks a feminist intervention in the perpetuation of narratives surrounding the fictocritical – and in this sense her academic work is *not* disinterested for good reason. Most importantly, from the perspective of the present study, Flavell thus recognises an *ethical* motivation as central in both her conceptualisation of the term and her theorisation of the writing practices. Furthermore, her approach does not merely mention this additionally, but rather makes it central to her theory of the (hyphenated) ficto-critical.

Arguably, while both of these narratives are valid – up to a point – and important, they also both have their weaknesses. While Muecke's Derrida narrative suggests an evocative and almost explanatory scenario, which yet falls short of including the central motivational aspect of fictocritical writing, Flavell's genealogical narrative emphasises an ethical dimension, yet tacitly participates in claiming a principally open writing practice for particular positioned backgrounds and traditions – first and foremost, feminism and hybrid identities. Somewhat paradoxically, such moves claim the special brand of fictocritical openness in a gesture with exclusive tendencies. In fairness, though, Muecke has much to say on ethical motivation for fictocritical writing elsewhere,[2] and Flavell's theorisation – which is one of the best available to date – is much more inclusive than my short and necessarily reductive sketch would imply.

In contrast to the diachronic perspectives of Muecke's short history of the idea and Flavell's historical survey, I would now like to embark on developing a more synchronically inclined view in order to re/conceive of the fictocritical over the course of this thesis. The intersection of fiction and criticism as well as the theoretical and ethical dimensions of textual discourse, I want to argue, need to be made central to a *systemic* conceptualisation of fictocriticism that can hope to capture its various historical strands as well as possible forms to come without stifling its subversive potential. What is yet to be achieved, I want to suggest, is a theorisation of the fictocritical that captures a defining general pattern at work in all the different fictocritical strands and their various unpredictable textual formations.

---

2 E.g. "A Chance to Hear a Nyigina Song" is just one recent of many possible references that testify to Muecke's sustained, ethically motivated, fictocritical engagement with inter-cultural and post/colonial concerns (2008c).

1.1 WHAT'S IN A NAME?

Ambivalently, both Muecke's and Flavell's narratives of the fictocritical focus centrally on the name, which is at least partly surprising because they both acknowledge the reservation frequently encountered among fictocritical writers that providing a name – and thus a quasi-generic label – for texts as genre-resistant and purposively slippery as those subsumed under the name "fictocriticism" risks turning these practices into just another genre. While Muecke tacitly concedes this in his response to Derrida quoted above (2008b: 18), Flavell more acutely focalises the problematic implications in her "General Introduction – Fix-criticism" (2004: 1-2). In the following section, however, I would like to refute such fears and instead outright celebrate the ingenuity of the name "fictocriticism" by re/conceiving of it from the slightly tilted angle of a fresh approach. In other words, where both Muecke and Flavell anchored their approaches in the historical incident of the naming, while yet remaining ostensibly suspicious of its generic implications, I would now like to reverse direction. My synchronous and systemic re/conceptualisation of fictocriticism shall produce the virtues of the term in a manner that, firstly, prevents the perceived dangers of generic re/territorialisation and, secondly, accommodates both Muecke's and Flavell's different core emphases. Let us, therefore, dwell on this intriguing and telling name a little longer.

The Performative Compound

Among all the diverse contenders for a name, I want to argue, "fictocriticism" presents a particularly fortunate composition because the term displays what the writing practices it designates do. Wrought as one from the two constituent parts fiction and criticism, "fictocriticism" functions as a performative compound already illustrating orthographically what it denotes. The hyphenated spelling variant "ficto-criticism" even adds typographical emphasis. Anne Brewster has expressed the nominal and generic amalgamation in her essay "Fictocriticism: Undisciplined Writing" thus:

> "The portmanteau neologism invokes two oppositional constitutive terms, fiction and criticism. If there is a generic division or opposition which fictocriticism seeks to mediate, it is the demarcation inscribed in academic production of the genres of high art (fiction, poetry, drama) and the essayistic modes which purport to study them (commentary, criticism, analysis, theory). The opposition between these two genres is figured in the way we characterise criticism, for example, as neutral and disinterested and literature as expressive of a personalised subjectivity. Another figuring of this opposition is the notion that criticism trades in ideas; literature in states of emotion and feeling." (1996b: 29)

Brewster's point is that the institutionalised generic polarity of fiction and criticism, in all its multi-faceted aspects, is already figured as overcome by the term. But the terminologically incorporated combination of literary and non-fictional discourse can also be re/phrased productively on various other levels. Consider, for example, how the term similarly evokes the following oppositions:

Fiction	Criticism
Fiction	Theory
Literature	**Philosophy**
Aesthetics	Poetics
Aesthetics	Ethics
Fiction	**Non-fiction**

The most fundamental distinction here is between fictional texts that purport to constitute a world in their own right (literature, fiction) and non-fictional texts that purport to represent our world which exists prior to their making reference to it (philosophy, science, theory, criticism). This distinction between truth-constituting and truth-representing discourses anticipates a central text-epistemological dimension in fictocriticism. Note that *in writing* these two kinds of discourse converge on the page, where they are paradigmatically indistinguishable. Fictocritical writing, as I am going to argue throughout this thesis, makes much of this discursively unsettling textual insight.

Before advancing too far too early, however, it is perhaps worthwhile re/phrasing and expanding one insight from Brewster's passage in particular. In the context of my home institutions – the *Institut für Englische Philologie* at *Freie Universität Berlin* (FUB) and the English and Cultural Studies department at the University of Western Australia (UWA) – a fictocritical text, thus understood, would blur the line between the kind of primary texts we read (literature, fiction) and the kind of secondary texts we are taught to write on them (criticism, theory, non-fiction). In particular, it would shift the institutionalised generic practice from writing non-fiction on fiction to the fictocritical practice of writing fiction on fiction, *albeit endowed with non-fictional import.* In this sense, fictocritical texts are valid fictional contributions to non-fictional debates – sometimes even to non-fictional debates on fiction. Such fictocritical turns in perspective and practice cause the all-too familiar elements of everyday reading and writing to spin in an academically unheard-of manner.

Fictocritical effects of this kind, however, are not achieved by simply placing narration and argument side by side. They need to become indistinguishable, inextricably the same thing. Here is how Heather Kerr, in her essay "Sympathetic Topographies", describes that strange polar unity which fictocriticism implies:

> "The academic's assertion of meaning and the narrator's performance are paired as opposites: 'either you fail to be moved by the text (by asking what it means, you don't let it work), or the text moves you (by not asking what it means, you let it work). The fictocritical effect is to combine the fantastic transformations of fiction with critical theory." (2001: 113)

In this sense, such texts function like picture puzzles in which both figures are simultaneously on display and at work. Juxtaposing their respective parameters and orientation, the figures bring each other into a paradoxical relief that requires us to take a step back if we are to make sense of the bigger picture, rather than taking only one of their (generic) sides. From Kerr's perspective the fictocritical effect and challenge thus lies in a mutually dependent generic both/and rather than a decidable either/or. She certainly prefers the insights of an *aporia* over either one-sided decision.

As a consequence of this perception, fictocriticism not only intersects generic opposites but, in so doing, makes them excessive. Amanda Nettelbeck has expressed this pointedly in her "Notes towards an Introduction" for the seminal collection *The Space Between: Australian Women Writing Fictocriticism*:

> "Fictocriticism might most usefully be defined as hybridized writing that moves between the poles of fiction ('invention'/'speculation') and criticism ('deduction'/'explication'), of subjectivity ('interiority') and objectivity ('exteriority'). It is writing that brings the 'creative' and the 'critical' together – not simply in the sense of placing them side by side, but in the sense of mutating both, of bringing a spotlight to bear upon the known forms in order to make them 'say' something else." (1998: 4)

Thus, fictocritical texts conflate elements of these genres and their characteristic aspects in order to create something *else*, that is in order not only to say something different but to say it differently as well. Fictocriticism, and this echoes Derrida's point, thus creates something that can no longer be contained within the erstwhile generic structures on which it yet feeds – a *something* that, in fact, ultimately necessitates a reassessment of the entire generic field and its conditions of possibility.

Nettelbeck's suggested understanding of fictocriticism as hybrid writing has even found typographical expression. Sometimes, as we have already seen, the performative term is hyphenated to visually emphasise the generic hybridity of the form it designates: "ficto-criticism". Especially against motivational background concerns that arise from hyphenated identities and their hybrid speaking positions, this textual performativity of the hyphenated spelling variant transports more than just the generically hybrid style of fictocritical writing practices.

It will be worthwhile, in any case, to keep reminding and questioning which oppositions are at play in the fictocritical and which are real oppositions. If ficto-criticism situates itself *between* fiction and non-fiction, making the two indistinguishable, its value can hardly consist in bringing the alleged virtue of either side into the realm of the other. Where fictocriticism has surplus value on offer, this would certainly lie in aspiring to *a different level entirely*.

Further Fictocritical Self-Perceptions

Apart from hybridity, an entire spectrum of self-perceptions is explicit in fictocritical literature, some of which can provide further introductory characterisation of fictocritical writing at this early stage. From the many self-stylising perceptions that can be found in different texts, I am now going to mention only a few of those that are frequently evidenced, have proved influential, and can furthermore serve as first reference points to anticipate a number of shifts in perspective that my approach will fully introduce further down.

First of all, fictocriticism is often said to create a marginal space between dominant generic forms. The notions and terminology of the space between and the gap have been influential for some time now – testament of which is the formative essay collection *The Space Between* (Kerr/Nettelbeck 1998). More than a decade on, the space between is still the trope most readily associated with fictocriticism. Its figurative potential has been put to good use on a number of levels, too, bringing together inter-cultural realities, inter-generic forms, and ascribing female form to writing. But while the notion of a space between generic centres naturalises the fictocritical at the margins, I want to maintain that this does not at all condemn it to only marginal relevance. Quite to the contrary, theorising these deviant writing practices may actually cast a different light on our writing practices in general. While fictocriticism takes its historical motivation from the academic margins and presents a generically marginal form, it may yet provide insights of central importance into our textual practices and textual culture in general. In this vein, I would like to reinterpret the figures of the gap and the space between in such a way that their potential for marginal writing practices can be perceived at work on the constitutive level of our textual practices – not least, because such awareness among textual agents would greatly enhance the radical potential, momentum, and edge of the fictocritical.

At the same time, fictocriticism has been hailed as genre-crossing, genre-subverting, and genre-defying writing that is not itself a textual genre but a writing practice. It is thus not only about writing in the sense of the written, but about writ*ing* as a process, as a kind of textual performance. According to this view, fictocriticism is not a fixed textual form at all, but a performative writing practice, whose outcomes are therefore unpredictable on the textual level. Therein lies the genre-defying strength of fictocriticism, which has been characterised, in Deleuzian terms, as "deterritorialising" (Flavell 2004: 42-3) because it breaks (with) supposedly fixed structures, makes them move, and thus opens a realm of potential to re/structure known fields. This is a revolutionary impetus in fictocriticism that cannot easily be explained away in the dominant terms it ventures to critique. And yet, I want to maintain, there is also a sense in which it is problematic to call something as territorially rigid and fixed as an inscribed textual structure de/territorialising. If fictocritical writ*ing* is de/territorialising, the resulting fictocritical text as the trace of that process is, by contrast, a thoroughly territorial structure. Note that this is a constitutive feature of the textual medium. Hence, different, better, and even fictocritical writing cannot get around this fact. What we need therefore is a complementary understanding of how fictocritical texts can elicit de/territorialising read*ing*s. Ultimately, our theorising of the fictocritical needs, firstly, to narrow perspective from a general genre-defying tendency to the paradigmatic acts that create this force and thus, secondly, to expand perspective from the inscribed structures of the textual work to include our textual acts of read*ing* and writ*ing*.

Fictocritical writing is also frequently characterised as self-reflexively aware of the practices it engages. Importantly, fictocriticism not only includes some other forms of writing in the critique it mounts but also its own writ*ing*. As a result, this kind of self-reflexivity is usually circumspectly aware of its own practices and their consequences when criticising others – which brings to mind my parent's advice to always think twice before finger-pointing because in the event three of my hand's fingers would be pointing right back at me. Fictocriticism makes a virtue of this awareness as its kind of critique engages in finger pointing only through a self-reflexively inclusive gesture. Note that this circumspect kind of self-reflexivity is also just one example of a certain post-critical attitude sometimes ascribed to fictocriticism, which avoids the moral high ground of philosophy (Muecke 2008a: 14). By contrast, the post-critical aim is to not simply assume a privileged speaking position from which to judge, but to at least reflect this assumption in the act. Similarly, much fictocriticism avoids claims to generality and objectivity, proposing partial and situated knowledges instead. A non-transcendental tendency and prioritisation of the local can often be discerned as well. Not so much despite as in harmony with these perceptions I will later argue that there is also a different kind of self-reflexivity wrought by fictocritical texts that *does* give general import to their critique of our textual practices.

A broader post-critical attitude in fictocriticism also follows from the insight, often grounded in experiences at the margins, that even the assumed academic objectivity is not wholly disinterested. In fact, where the academic claim to objectivity has been experienced or perceived as a mechanism of domination, the fictocritical reaction has often been to acknowledge one's own situated position while still critiquing the mechanisms one deploys, in order to avoid replicating them as mechanisms of domination. Thus, quite to the contrary, fictocriticism often follows a strong emancipatory impetus and agenda from the respective marginal positions that have engendered it. While there is a strong feminist strand of fictocritical writing for which the term will have specific connotations, there is also a broader enlightenment element in fictocritical emancipatory tendencies that goes hand in hand with a non-colonising and empathetic attitude towards its subject (Flavell 2004: 296). Additionally, I want to argue, we need to understand such tendencies as also relating to the mediating agent who is at work on the fictocritical text – notably both reader and writer. There is thus an emancipatory impetus that pertains to the agent position of textual relat*ing*.

Another common perception of fictocriticism emphasises its saturation with theory. In this view, the fictocritical is a kind of writing that feeds theoretical, and mostly poststructuralist, thought into literary practice – as the previous quotations from Krauss and Derrida clearly suggest. Not only does theory feature in fictocritical texts, though, but fictocritical writing also puts these thoughts to practice, letting them in/form the writing on several levels. With regards to the self-reflexive disposition of fictocritical writing, therefore, special attention is commanded where its more theoretical passages relate to linguistic and textual practices. Ultimately, I want to suggest that these moments provoke a curious scenario of short-circuitry that is still under-theorised as a central fictocritical characteristic.

What is more, fictocriticism frequently deploys post/modern literary means in a manner that endows their supposedly aimless playfulness with practical direction and ethical import. The result is not a post/modern playfulness that would spiral out of control into irrelevant realms, but one that serves a self-reflexive movement which is ultimately grounded in our textual practices. At this crucial point, I want to suggest, fictocriticism's theoretical interest, performative experience, and ethical motivation culminate in a fictocritical trope that is yet to be assessed and theorised properly. And to provide just this theorisation is the main goal of the present thesis. One central challenge will thus be to think together the surprising fictocritical short-circuitry between post/modern literary theory and practice with its resulting performatively self-reflexive awareness, on the one hand, and a fictocritical ethical import, on the other.

Some Previous Theorisations

Additionally, it is worth noting that fictocriticism has previously been theorised either according to its respective underlying ethical motivations or with regards to its more formal features. Several possible strands of conceptualising the fictocritical have thus emerged. Yet none of them can claim to fully accommodate the other perspectives in a transcending model because either they have been formulated position-strategically, which makes them tendentiously exclusive, or they neglect central fictocritical elements that other strands have prioritised. Subsequently, another challenge for this thesis will be to retain the possibility of all these salient features in an embracing model that still remains open to potential new forms not yet in evidence. As yet another introductory exercise it will be helpful to consider a few of these previous strands. In so doing, it will be furthermore productive to point out both their virtues and shortcomings in preparation of a new model of the fictocritical.

Firstly, fictocriticism has often been theorised in terms of its marginal/ised provenances. The single most significant strand in this respect has conceived of it as a special form in the tradition of experimental feminist writing. In opposition to male-connoted and -dominated academic discourse, fictocriticism has been cast figuratively as the female form. Perhaps the best-known example in this vein is the aforementioned collection *The Space Between*, but a more recent volume of the online journal *Outskirts* (Bartlett 2009) has been dedicated to fictocriticism from a feminist perspective, too. Notably, in both of these concentrated publications an element of strategic essentialism is well-balanced by the texts' circumspect and self-aware positioning, which underscores the motivational aspect of writing female speaking positions differently, with fictocritical means, while simultaneously critiquing the marginal/ising discursive powers and male-writerly principles that be.

Similarly, it is possible to conceive of fictocriticism in terms of queer theory as a form of queering genre. In this sense, fictocriticism presents a specific form of genre-crossing textual practices that not only align figuratively with but also contribute practically to wider discursive gender- and boundary-crossing interests. Again, the motivational aspect here derives from specific speaking positions that aim to critique dominant discursive structures with a view to deconstructing the hierarchical dichotomy that keeps them marginal/ised (e.g. Probyn 1996). Such a queer strand of understanding fictocriticism may be less in evidence than its prominent feminist counterpart, but the motivational parallels between them are striking. Of the primary texts in this study, for example, Katrina Schlunke carefully considers the connection between a queer identity and her fictocritical output in *Bluff Rock: Autobiography of a Massacre* (2005: esp. 199-208). However, while Schlunke clearly perceives the logic behind queer speaking positions opting for writing fictocritically, she does not claim such practices as a predominantly queer form. Instead, other aspects of fictocritical writing, such as its text-cultural and text-ideological implications with regards to history prove more centrally important to her project.

More frequently in evidence, again, is a post/colonial studies approach to conceiving of fictocriticism. This strand theorises ficto-critical writing – usually in its hyphenated variant – as the figuratively predisposed textual form to deal with cross- or inter-cultural hybridity. Again the motivational impetus here derives partly from marginal/ised speaking positions that demand a textual form suitable to convey their hybrid identity defining experiences, and partly from the urge to mount a post/colonially inflected critique of continuing – even systemic – (text)discursive praxes of domination. This perspective is especially pertinent in the work of Fred Wah, for example, whose book *Faking It: Poetics & Hybridity – Critical Writing 1984-1999* (2000) presents what amounts to a theory of the ficto-critical along these lines in ficto-critical form. From the many texts that lend themselves to such a post/colonial reading of ficto-criticism, perhaps George Alexander's *Mortal Divide: The Autobiography of Yiorgos Alexandroglou / Γιώργος Αλεξανδρόγλου* (1997) should also be mentioned here.

These respective motivational backgrounds that have engendered fictocritical writing, although genetically significant, are yet insufficient to conceptualise it as a quasi-genre. While each of them marks an occasion to which fictocritical writing can contribute considerable momentum, none of them can lay exclusive claim to providing the terms in and on which to understand the fictocritical. Hence, the challenge in re/conceiving of the fictocritical is to bundle its strands and weave a mutually incorporating threat from them, a model that can accommodate both the motivational logic behind the marginal/ised speaking positions that have turned fictocritical and the powerful figurations that have enabled the respective strands to lay claim to fictocriticism as a form. A new theory thus needs to capture the common motivational pattern behind writers from marginal/ised speaking positions to engage their issues and concerns fictocritically. It also needs to maintain and enhance the figurative potential that these different strands have mobilised for their models. Plus, such a theory also needs to account for the textual levers that fictocritical writers avail themselves of *differently* to advance their specific cases and causes.

Secondly, there are also more formally oriented ways of conceptualising fictocriticism that have pursued different routes. On the one hand, it is indeed plausible to think of academic textual genres that have turned fictocritical at a moment of great, mostly poststructuralist, theoretical influence. There is no shortage of examples to back this claim. Greg Dening has endowed the history essay with his own fictocritical flavour that can be sampled, for example, in the collection *Performances* (1996). Michael Taussig has pioneered unheard-of, fictocritical ways of writing that deviate from generic ethnographic treatises in books such as *The Magic of the State* (1997) or *What Color is the Sacred?* (2009) and other anthropologists, like Kathleen Stewart with her *Ordinary Affects* (2007), have followed this general direction in their own idiosyncratic ways. Alphonso Lingis is one philosopher who has taken his subject on a fictocritical itinerary in publications such as *Trust* (2004) or *The First Person Singular* (2007), to name but two. Likewise, Meaghan Morris or Katrina Schlunke have turned their cultural studies writing fictocritical, as is evident in texts such as *Identity Anecdotes: Translation and Media Culture* (Morris 2006) or "Ethnografts" (Schlunke 2008). Earlier, Ann Game and Andrew Metcalfe's book *What is Passionate Sociology?* (1996), arguably, made the case for their discipline to do likewise. On the other hand, the reverse theorisation, which conceives of fictocriticism as a form of theory-driven literature, is equally legitimate. While certain works in the predominantly literary output of Aritha van Herk, J.M. Coetzee and Gail Jones, for example, would convincingly make this case – such as *Places Far From Ellesmere: a Geografictione – Excavations on Site* (Van Herk 1990), *Elizabeth Costello* (Coetzee 2003), and *Fetish Lives* (Jones 1997) – it should still be noted that their entire oeuvre hardly fits the description. In any case, an encompassing theorisation of the fictocritical needs to find a model spacious enough to accommodate both of these possible perspectives.

Furthermore, the fact that in most fictocritical writing the speaking position is not disinterested but personally situated, located and involved – while often also cultivating a jocular attitude – has provoked comparisons to the tradition of New Journalism. However, while it may seem intuitively right to group *some* fictocritical writers – Michael Taussig comes to mind – and their output together with Tom Wolfe, Hunter S. Thompson or Joan Didion, the same cannot be maintained throughout (neither, of course, would it be helpful to reduce the tradition of New Journalism to such stellar names alone); not least, because there is usually a much greater degree of theoretical knowledgeability and self-reflexive writerly awareness at play in ambitious fictocritical writing. While there may be proximity and certain similarities between Fictocriticism and New Journalism, it should be clear that the defining moments of the fictocritical lie elsewhere – as has been the recurring point for all the self-perceptions and theorisations considered thus far.

The last strand that I would like to mention here in any detail takes its cue from much earlier than New Journalism. Fictocriticism, which has predominantly favoured essay length texts, has also been conceived of in terms of the French *essai*, meaning attempt, trial, or test. Whereas the essay form used to be precisely an *unfinished* attempt on a subject, in academia it has long since coagulated into fixed manners of dealing with certain subjects in certain ways. Aspiring academics are groomed to write a pre/scribed kind of essay, which is prerequisite to establishing themselves in their fields. In other words, to master a discipline one has to become the disciple of its textual form. By contrast, the fictocritical essay is still claimed as a consciously experimental and provisional writerly attempt as opposed to a finished treatise by an academic author/ity. This, of course, is the tradition of Michel de Montaigne's essays (2012), but perhaps also the experimental Gertrude Stein evident in *Look at Me Now and Here I Am* (2004) as well as the perceptive Joan Didion of *The White Album* (1990) – both of whom have their own distinct credentials as fictocritical forerunners – could be cited as later proponents in this vein.

If taken seriously, however, a problem arises for this perspective. Treating the essay as *essai* basically claims a fluidity and transience for the textual content that is performatively contradicted by its medial form. Just as the textual medium is in and of itself a territorial structure, so its inscriptions are, paradigmatically, neither fluid nor transcendental. This, of course, changes as soon as interactive and hypertextual means enter the equation with digital media, whose implications and possibilities Kathrine N. Hayles has examined in her *Writing Machines* (2002). Simon Robb, for example, has argued for (1996) and engaged in (2001a, 2001b) fictocritical hypertext – or: "electric fictocriticism" (1996: 100), as he calls it – for his fictocritical doctoral thesis. In the last instance, however, I would maintain that digital text provides such a wealth of means to create fictocritical effects precisely because *paradigmatically* a textual structure, which we can meaningfully read or write, is a rigid and territorial affair. While fictocritical means often aim to partly disrupt the mechanics of our ingrained textual practices, I want to suggest, their critique usually relates very much to our paradigmatic understanding of these textual practices and their wider discursive and cultural implications.

In the same manner, the experimentally provisional and transitive attitude of much fictocriticism needs to be taken in conjunction with the critique of our textual practices it mounts. For example, the performative contradiction of writerly ideal and medial parameters sometimes creates a relief that actually propels the fictocritical theory and critique of our textual practices onto the meta-level. What is required in this light is a reassessment of the conditions of the possibility of our textual practices and the ways in which fictocritical writing conducts them differently. A new theory of the fictocritical, I want to argue, needs to focalise this self-reflexive turn onto the meta-level. Thus, instead of following the above strands in burdening ever more contextual baggage onto the notion of the fictocritical – knowledge that these texts do not always contain or convey, but which they yet require the reader to bring to the encounter – the present approach shall closely examine how exactly fictocritical texts play off their understanding of the *constitutive* medial and contextual parameters against our ingrained generic approaches to text.

Ultimately, with regards to these different perspectives on fictocriticism the challenge for a non-reductive and productive approach is thus to take the central aspects of all the above strands into account for a model that can also avoid their respective shortcomings. With this aim in sight, I am now going to outline a number of consequential shifts in perspective.

The Objects of Study

As indicated, there is now a slight preference to refer to fictocritical writing rather than fictocriticism. This manner of speaking is, firstly, indicative of the non-generic credentials of the fictocritical, which would sit rather uneasily labelled as an 'ism'. Secondly, the term "writing" acknowledges a shift in textual ideology: from the author of singular, monolithic works towards the writer of productive text. Thirdly, it implies a move away from textual form towards textual practice – emphasising writing as processual and performative: writ*ing*, rather than the written. Having said that, for the present thesis the objects – quite literally – of study remain very much texts: fictocritical writing, precisely in the sense of the written. Yet, my approach takes the emphasis on textual practices seriously indeed. Hence, the subject of study will be writ*ing* – just as much as read*ing*. In this manner, the erstwhile author/itative textual work shall re/emerge, in a thoroughly de/centred model, as comprised of writerly and readerly textual acts. While the textual medium thus remains central to the equation, it presents simply the anchor around which the textual work is paradigmatically de/centred – split between the two linguistic-discursive agents at work.

Additionally, the focus on the textual objects is divided by the twofold nature of this matter between, firstly, the manifestly inscribed textual structures on the page and, secondly, the discursive structures enshrined therein, which we access in read*ing* but may perceive and interpret differently in our reading*s*. In this sense, the following study examines the relationship between, firstly, the manifest medial substrate of our writing and reading and, secondly, the mediations, or readings, pre/structured thereby. Anticipating even further, we could formulate that the objects of study are manifestly inscribed ficto/critical textual constellations that, *qua media*, p/re/structure the realm of possible re/configurations for their enshrined discursive constellations in our readings and (re)writings. As a result, the text-cultural practices of reading and writing in a certain way – generic or deviant – enter the picture, turning formerly static textual analysis into a more performance oriented text-*cultural* analysis. As generic and fictocritical read*ing* enter the picture – already cast as opposites – this study remains textually based, but its primary interest shifts towards our textual practices; especially towards our wider textual relations as practices of relat*ing* textually.

The main question shall no longer be what characterises fictocritical texts, but rather what effect fictocritical texts have on our textual acts – or better: what fictocritical effect some texts have on the linguistic-discursive agent. Hence, the point is not to collect the definitional textual characteristics of fictocriticism but to ask, firstly, how fictocritical texts deploy their means within the text-medial parameters differently and, secondly, what is so distinctly fictocritical about the effect this creates. Thus departing from the textual objects of study towards our text-cultural relations and mediations of read*ing* and writ*ing* as the subject of study effectively de/centres the literary work from a fixed textual notion – epitomised by the finished book – into the literary work that is comprised of the different textual acts that paradigmatically relate (to) the text: writerly production and readerly reception. For the thesis approach, proceeding in this manner implies, firstly, a distinct *textual theory* that accounts for the complex encapsulated and translational structures of textual inscription and discursive understanding in terms of the fictocritical as well as, secondly, a broader *text-cultural analysis* – rather than just textual analyses – that allows for the wider discursive significance of our ingrained textual practices as well as for fictocritical ways of resisting them.

A Possible List of Fictocritical Textual Features

Although this study has good reason to emphasise fictocritical strategies and effects at the expense of (whichever) fixed textual features, it is, of course, still possible, legitimate, and even helpful to list some conspicuous textual features that are frequently evidenced across fictocriticism. We only need to keep in mind that there is little definitional value in such a list. While a set of quasi-generic textual markers can provide a good retrospective introduction to the existing field, it cannot serve as a guide to what makes texts fictocritical – and this point relates back to the above distinction between the objects of study and the subject of this study. Because fictocritical effects are produced *between* text and linguistic-discursive agent, different textual features will be more or less effective to fictocritically address different linguistic-discursive contexts, textual cultures, and idiosyncratic backgrounds. Important is thus not which textual features there are but what they can do *strategically* in conjunction with given textual agents and their respective contexts. At least this level of abstraction from textual features is required, I want to argue, if we want to capture but not arrest the subversive potential of the ficto-critical, which unfolds only in the interplay between these ultimately variable parameters.

On the back of these cautionary remarks, however, I still want to offer one possible list of fictocritical textual features below – firstly, because at this introductory stage it will help to further fine-grain the picture of fictocriticism and, secondly, because it will serve as a good basis from which then to research the patterns according to which such textual means are deployed strategically to trigger fictocritical effects in the specific contexts of our textual practices. What follows are thus just some possible entries in such a list.

For example, fictocritical writing frequently opts for the subjective perspective of the first person singular, often paired with an invested personal interest in the subject matter of the text, yet circumspect in attitude. The reason behind this choice usually lies in a motivated critique of the allegedly withdrawn, depersonalised and objective voice of the academic essay. For instance, most of the essays in *The Space Between* (Kerr/Nettelbeck 1998) are prime examples of this. Thus, far from being a mere formal preference this feature is, in fact, deployed against a certain generic textual conduct of which the texts are critical. Note, however, that some fictocritical texts also emphasise their subjective first person singular perspective literarily in order to play with the fictionalising distance between narrator and author, rather than implying an almost journalistic intersection of the two. Michael Taussig, for example, fictionalises his non-fictional research and speaking position in *The Magic of the State* (1997). The result is often a degree of uncertainty regarding the epistemological status of the writing. Other fictocritical texts create similar effects by opting for the second or third person singular to present their involved perspective. For example, Aritha van Herk deploys the shifter "you" to this fictocritical effect in *Places Far From Ellesmere* (1990), while Kathleen Stewart uses "she" to re/lay her experiences and the affects they trigger to the same effect in *Ordinary Affects* (2007). As the latter explains:

> "I write not as a trusted guide carefully laying out the links between theoretical categories and the real world, but as a point of impact, curiosity and encounter. I call myself 'she' to mark the difference between this writerly identity and the kind of subject that arises as a daydream of simple presence." (2007: 5)

Others, again, shift freely between all three options, as does Lesley Stern in *The Smoking Book* (1999), for example. In other words, there is just no formal unity on the textual level. Discernible are only different strategies, which could also take different routes, to create certain effects. As before, the point here is that suggesting a fixed fictocritical form in this respect would defy the fictocritical point of critiquing established textual forms and their concomitant discursive formations via form.

Another point is that fictocritical writing often features only minimal characterisation and dialogue because its narrative or fiction is not an end in itself but supports the theoretical argument. In this respect, fictocriticism has greater proximity to philosophical thought experiments than to the fully-fledged fictional worlds of literature. Perhaps Stephen Muecke's essays in the collection *Joe in the Andamans* (2008) exemplify this characteristic best. At the same time, formal experimentation is a regular feature. Some fictocritical texts incorporate challenging neologisms and curious typographical contrivances. In this respect, Aritha van Herk's use of the slash and curious word formations in *Places Far From Ellesmere* (1990) immediately come to mind. Others let content determine form, as opposed to academic genres that dictate *one* proper form for all possible cases. For example, when Stephen Muecke in his famous fictocritical travelogue *No Road (Bitumen All The Way)* informs us at the beginning of a fragment, which would indeed fit on a postcard, that this is where he begins "the necessary digression which the fragmentary narrative of tourism demands, texts no bigger than postcards" (1997: 33).

Implicitly at stake here is also the difference between learning how to write a proper ethnography that can be applied to each and every culture you may encounter and letting the practices of the culture you study in/form your writing. This is frequently the case in Michael Taussig's work, for example in *My Cocaine Museum* (2004), where he models the structure of his text on a gold museum whose counter-discourse he writes. Elsewhere, in his preface to *Walter Benjamin's Grave*, Taussig inimitably airs his guiding sentiment thus: "It is more like having the reality depicted turn back on the writing, rather than on the writer, and ask for a fair shake. 'What have you learned?' the reality asks of the writing." (2006a: viii) Note, in any case, that while philosophical thought experiments describe a scenario to ponder, the formal experimentation in fictocritical writing makes just such pre/scription central to the scenario. Thus, where these two connotations of experimentation meet, writing becomes the subject matter of the fictocritical in a twofold sense.

Furthermore, fictocritical texts tend towards the fragmentary. Examples abound, but Anna Gibbs's "The Gift" (1998) is one striking example of this characteristic. The essayistic – read: *essai*-istic – style and format of much fictocritical writing certainly contributes to this impression. I would supplement the following qualification, though: fictocritical texts are often fragmentary, albeit meticulously structured. For instance, the seemingly random fragments in Kathleen Stewart's *Ordinary Affects* still neatly link up to form a framework of theoretical considerations that keep approaching the same issue from different angles in order to illuminate their object more adequately. On the one hand there is a general fictocritical tendency against closure and whole-ness. Thus, Stewart writes "still lives" (2007: 18-9) as momentous snapshots of her experiences, rather than a definite memoir. On the other hand, text is favoured as discontinued and open for the interpretive work of the reader, which the writing is nevertheless at pains to p/re/structure fictocritically.

In this sense, the unfinished state of such texts in itself is a neatly rendered statement, which leads from the level of textual form not only onto the level of propositional content, but furthermore towards a meta-perspective on our textual practices of making sense of textual structures. Our readerly work is, after all, not fundamentally different between a flowing and a fragmentary text – only the latter makes our workings perceptible while in progress. Figuratively, the fragmentary composition of a text thus illustrates the proposition that any textually enshrined discursive constellation always already puts to the reader. But then, far from every fictocritical text is fragmented, and hence there is again no formal unity here, only patterns of textual strategies that aim at fictocritical effects.

Also, intertextual means – such as not only referencing a text but suggestively evoking its context – are frequently put to good use in fictocriticism. On the one hand, there is a lot of textual grafting and quoting to be found, for instance to implicitly invoke other texts without a dominant interpretive gesture. In this manner, David Shield's *Reality Hunger: A Manifesto* (2010) is a collage of quotes. But there is also the technique to montage, onto the same page, a juxtaposition of two texts, in order to visualise the space between them as well as making perceptible the readerly act of setting them in relation to each other. In such cases, the intertextual space between becomes visible as the con/textual realm of the white page. A good fictocritical example of this can be found in Stephen Muecke's *Textual Spaces: Aboriginality and Cultural Studies* (1992: 101-18), but an earlier influential text in this respect is Julia Kristeva's "Stabat Mater" (1986).

Bricolage, which is both performed and conceptualised in the seminal collective effort *Reading the Country: An Introduction to Nomadology* (esp. Muecke 1996), presents a further means of this kind. Krim Benterrak's paintings in this publication are also a prime example of how intermediality features in some fictocritical texts – most frequently, however, in the form of photography. In this latter respect, it is worth considering the different effects to which photography is used in texts such as W.G. Sebald's *Die Ringe des Saturn: Eine Englische Wallfahrt* (2007), Ross Gibson's *The Summer Exercises* (2008), Michael Taussig's "Walter Benjamin's Grave: A Profane Illumination" (2006b), Margaret Somerville's *Body/Landscape Journals* (1999), or George Alexander's *Mortal Divide* (1997).

On the other hand, fictocritical texts are often protocols of reading, which conduct experimental re/readings and re/writings of other texts. Exemplary cases are Aritha van Herk's *Places Far from Ellesmere* (1990) and John Hughes's *Someone Else: Fictional Essays* (2007); more radical examples, overall, can be found in Kathy Acker's *Great Expectations* (1982) or her *Don Quixote: Which Was a Dream* (1986). Notably, while in the former two examples the interpretive gesture is certainly part of the project, it is yet only applied in a manner already in/formed by the critique which is produced at the same time. Curiously, fictocritical writing thus comes to function as mediation *inter textus*: reading a protocol of reading adds a sense of sequence to our own textual encounter. Altogether, there is again no fixed formal pattern here, because different strategies can achieve these desired effects.

Furthermore, textual ambiguities are a means favoured in much fictocritical writing. For example, consciously wrought interpretive ambiguities sometimes create indeterminate referential status and at times epistemic uncertainties about the text's fictional or non-fictional relation to the world, as is epitomised by Guy Maddin's somnambulistic film MY WINNIPEG (2007) and seconded by the accompanying script book *My Winnipeg* (2009). Likewise, the clever use of shifters can create a slippery subjectivity or even extradiegetic referential potential to address the reader im/mediately and draw them into the intended scope of the text. A prime example of this feature will be the subject of analysis in my close reading of Muecke's "The Fall" (2008b) in the second chapter. An uncertain subjectivity of the text can also be evoked by ambiguous speaking positions, for example when Sally and Richard Price in *Enigma Variations* (1995) co-author a subjective text that features both of them in the third person perspective. The sounding out of multiple speaking positions, by contrast, can be a fictocritical means that follows the literary exploration of different forms of subjectivity as an ethical virtue. For example, Steven Shaviro's *Doom Patrols: A Theoretical Fiction about Postmodernism* (2007) boasts such shifting perspectival exercises. Another textual feature of this kind are strange juxtapositions, sometimes of textual types, sometimes of paradoxical statements that challenge the text-interpretive work. The effect of such juxtapositions is that they increase the amount of conceptual work required to accommodate these seeming contradictions, to understand the text and make sense of it. Textual ambiguities, too, aim to create fictocritical effects. They are not to be confused with fixed generic markers but need to be recognised as text-strategic means to an end.

Two more textual features, of which we will hear much more below, are the self-reflexive turns and textual performativity of fictocriticism. Firstly, in addition to a self-reflexively circumspect awareness of one's own speaking position, ficto-critical texts often contain self-reflexive, at times meta-fictional, passages that have something to say about the textuality of the text and about our reading and writing – in particular as well as in general. In addition to Muecke's "The Fall", two other essay length texts of central importance for this study provide exemplary cases of this aspect – they are Michael Taussig's "The Corn-Wolf: Writing Apotropaic Texts" (2010b) and Gail Jones's "Thaumatropes" (1998). Echoing the short-circuitous trope mentioned earlier, such meta-fictional fictocritical means sometimes raise the non-fictional question of fiction from within fiction. Apart from the more common content-related self-reflexivity, special attention is due to passages in which a textual self-reflexivity gains meta-significance for our textual practices.

Secondly, in passages of performative textuality fictocritical writing often aims to make the text exemplary of its own contention, to make it perform what it constates, not unlike the performative compound. In this sense, fictocriticism avails itself of the means under critique – most broadly: our textual practices – in a manner that already implements insights of that critique. Again, Michael Taussig's "The Corn-Wolf" is exemplary in this respect as his text on counter-magic practices itself becomes an exercise of the apotropaic. Two other novel length texts of central importance for the present study exemplify this aspect brilliantly – they are Katrina Schlunke's *Bluff Rock* (2005) and Aritha van Herk's *Places Far From Ellesmere* (1990). Endowed with a different kind of performativity fictocritical texts are also often composed to narrate the process of acquiring knowledge, rather than just presenting their gained knowledge as a given. Such a structuring works against the passive consumption of meaning – ultimately, these texts work by making the reader work. Apart from a plain textual performativity, then, special attention is due to passages in which the subject of the text and the readerly performance coincide and in which our relat*ing* textually thus enters the textually related scenario. At this stage, however, it suffices to realise that ficto-criticism avails itself of different kinds of self-reflexivity and performativity to achieve different fictocritical effects.

Just to summarise then, none of these frequently instantiated textual characteristics are in evidence across the spectrum of fictocritical texts, which take a diverse range of experimental forms. While I hope that the preceding list has served an introductory function, it is important to stress, again, that its entries are by no means to be mistaken as generic or definitional textual markers of the fictocritical. Instead they are indicative of textual strategies to create fictocritical effects. As a consequence, such lists can serve our definitional ambitions only indirectly if we are to avoid re/territorialising the fictocritical potential. In other words, advocating a certain fictocritical form is the opposite of advocating the fictocritical because generic textual forms and practices are the constitutive target of the fictocritical. Instead, I want to suggest, the fictocritical can offer a twofold directed line of flight that leads, firstly, towards a meta-awareness of our textual conduct and, secondly, indicates its implicit practical significance. What is fictocritical, thus, is the formally generated self-reflexive effect, not just the reflexive form. Likewise, what is fictocritical is the performative insight into formal pre/structuring, not just the performative form. Such impetus, however, can only be achieved textually by continuously breaking with established forms, not by fixedly establishing other forms in their stead.

An Underdetermined Definition *Ex Negativo*

Acknowledging that lists of textual markers are insufficient to capture the defining fictocritical characteristics forces the question of how best to venture on defining the fictocritical instead. Working towards an answer, it will be advisable to re/consider exactly why a list that determines fictocritical form simply will not do. There is an important claim that the fictocritical aim of exploding the tools of dominating academic theory can only be advanced outside precisely this realm of academic discourse, of which definitions are an essential part. A good argument is thus required to justify the definition and theorisation of a non-genre whose power has been argued to reside in its resistance to precisely such theorisation. Once its shifts in perspective have been allowed to emerge fully, I want to suggest, the following approach can deliver just such an argument.

Notably, just when Amanda Nettelbeck reiterates that "[i]t is here at the intersection of literature and postmodernism, that fictocriticism appears as an increasingly familiar form", she also warns us that "[t]o call it a 'form' is necessarily simplistic, since its interest lies in its capacity to adapt various literary forms" (1998: 4). Accordingly, exploiting the interstitial generic spaces between, fictocriticism thus comprises genre-subverting and genre-defying writing practices, yet remains itself non-generic. Therefore, if we – somewhat paradoxically – consider this to be fictocriticism's quasi-generic marker it still presents some kind of anti-genre.

Likewise, with reference to the genre evoking label, Anne Brewster has alerted us to a similar point by saying that "[t]he nomination 'fictocriticism' […] necessarily represents a provisional naming; its narrowness and genre-specificity belie the dispersed emergence of the practice of fictocriticism and its generic diffuseness and indistinctiveness" (1996b: 29). In fact, precisely because the common denominator of fictocritical practices is their resistance to genre-specificities, the formally unpredictable aspect of these writing practices should be their one unifying virtue. As a consequence, definitional lists of positively identifiable textual features always run the risk of arresting the resistant dynamics and subversive potential of the fictocritical. If we treat such a list as definitional, fictocritical generic resistance goes belly up, its textual practices cease to be genre-defying and instead turn into a generic form themselves.

And yet, surely, if we can identify texts as fictocritical, then it must also be possible to define what exactly makes the specific ways in which they deploy fiction and mount a critique fictocritical. So, again, how *can* we define it? Trying to answer this question I think it is necessary to introduce the notion of strategy into the equation. Fictocriticism is a critique via form, but its defining marker is generic resistance rather than a predictable textual form. It is thus defined by a strategic pattern of breaking with generic form to fictocritical effect. In other words, fictocriticism is a strategic form of generic resistance. The fictocritical can be directed against diverse sets of generic conventions and their functions. The target genre could be different, yet the strategic pattern would still be instantiated accordingly. All the particulars on the textual level could be different, but the same schematic pattern would still emerge. What we should be looking for is not a generic pattern but a strategic pattern of generic resistance.

Therefore, I want to argue, the fictocritical should, firstly, be defined formally indirect – *ex negativo* that is – since it strategically forms against certain dominant textual genres (which it critiques as genres of textual domination). Secondly, it should be defined variably, so that both its target genres and textual form are left underdetermined definitionally. Only at this level of abstraction can the fictocritical be defined as a strategic pattern of (quasi) generic resistance. In this manner, the aim should be to formulate a pattern whose internal relations adequately reflect the constitutive fictocritical mechanisms at play while yet leaving the particular variables underdetermined so as not to prematurely delimit the field of possible fictocritical textual forms. Ultimately, this will yield a formula with variables on the strategic level that, in turn, determine textual form.

Such an indirect formulaic definitional approach to understanding fictocriticism, I want to argue, firstly, no longer re/territorialises the fictocritical while, secondly, still allowing us to subsume the very different fictocritical strands mentioned above. The virtue of this perspective is that it can indeed accommodate something so diffuse and unpredictable in a meaningful manner because it allows for different textual means to be deployed strategically, fictocritically, against different generic target conventions and their respective mechanisms of domination. Furthermore, such an understanding shall eventually enhance, rather than limit, the fictocritical impact of texts by sensitising *us*, their otherwise generically expectant readers.

Aiming for such an understanding of fictocritical strategies, whose means would then be in evidence as stylistic textual features, we are no longer concerned with positive regulatory rules of specific genres (which fictocriticism claims to subvert anyway). Rather, the focus of this approach shifts attention towards the more abstract constitutive rules and mechanisms within which such rules of genre can occur in the first place: the laws of the laws of genre (Derrida 1992b). The concern is really directed at the conditions of the possibility (and impossibility) of textual communication and representation.

Thus framed, fictocriticism is concerned with our linguistic-discursive and especially textual practices of being in the world. Fictocriticism is critical of the current forms our textual practices take because of the practical effects they create and the functions they serve in our wider discursive practices of being in the world. Although the fictocritical scope is very much directed at the relation between self and world, its self-reflexive point of departure is the relation between self and text. Thus conceived, the possible forms fictocritical writing can take are only determined in relation to actual fields of writerly and readerly practices. The strategies enacted by fictocritical texts do not follow a rigidly pre/scribed generic order, but rather they circumscribe a fluid non-generic pattern when they flow experimentally in antagonistic relation to certain target-genres. Fictocritical strategies thus result from within the prescriptive generic patterns under critique, but they are designed to betray these genres by liquidising their "fictional institution" (Derrida 1992a: 37-40) in subversive textual acts.

Usually the underlying motivation for fictocritical writing derives from a dissatisfaction with our generic text-discursive practices – mostly academic – in wider discursive contexts of both relating (to) and treating the world and an/other. Fictocritical strategies, by contrast, lead elsewhere generically as traitorous cases of fictive abduction. Yet their functional role is very much concerned with the contexts from within which they derive as well as with the contingent moments that give rise to them. In this way, the subversive fictocritical attitude towards the hermeneutical gesture and the moral high ground of traditional theory or criticism is bound up with its critique of the functional role that our linguistic-discursive practices of textual communication fulfil as a cultural technique that effects various perceived gaps, divides and the policies they enable. Fictocriticism opposes this generic form of *divide et empera*. Fictocritical strategies turn towards the generic divide between aesthetic and scientific, literary and philosophical, truth-constituting and truth-representing discourses because they have a different textual and text-practical ideology to offer when it comes to conceiving of our text-cultural techniques and the ways in which they in/form and p/re/structure our relations to the world.

The Subject of this Study

After these preliminary thoughts on how best to define fictocriticism without stifling its subversive potential in the process, I am now going to outline the subject of this study in some more detail. A good way to announce the particular focus of my approach might be to unpack the thesis title because it already reflects several underlying premises and anticipates central theoretical shifts while also indicating how the formulaically variable definitional approach characterises the project throughout. Ultimately, the title's phrasing shall thus emerge as displaying the structure of both the trope of and my thesis on the (slashed) ficto/critical.

Main Title (I): Strategies

As a first statement of intent, the main thesis title focuses on the strategic side of generic resistance:

> Ficto/critical **Strategies**
> Subverting Textual Practices of Meaning, Other, and Self-Formation

Fictocriticism, fictocritical texts, fictocritical writing are now under examination from the angle of strategic generic resistance, strategic deployment of textual means, and the strategic aims they pursue in so doing. In this manner the title signals that this study does not focus on anti-generic textual markers so much as on textual strategies that are directed against generic textual forms as well as our generic textual practices. The aim is to isolate a strategic pattern of breaking with both genre and generic practices to fictocritical effect. As a result, my examination shall depart from a notion of the fictocritical effect and then work its way backwards from the readerly position that realises this effect to the writerly practice that pre/scribed it – ultimately to the wider discursive concerns that have led to this textual intervention.

Because there is a difference between textual performativity and the readerly performance of a textual pre/scription, the textual focus of the present approach is required to do justice to the performance and performativity of textual representation and communication that lies at the heart of fictocritical writing and reading. It is not the text itself, but its recalcitrance in relation to our generic expectations, conventions and laws (which a reader experiences in the textual performance of reading) that is fictocritical. What can be fictocritical about a text is the encounter with it – the textual performance that unfolds between the text and the individual self that encounters it. It is the textual relation performed by the self that renders a textual experience fictocritical. This textual relation can thus be twofold: the writer can produce text fictocritically and the reader can receive text fictocritically. This shift in perspective regarding fictocritical effects needs to be grounded in a theory of our textual practices in general that allows for specific fictocritical strategies.

Accordingly, my use of the term "strategy" furthermore implies an underlying (fictocritical) background understanding of our textual practices against which certain textual means can then emerge as strategically deployed with the aim of resisting the textual practices of given target genres. Theorising the fictocritical as strategy allows us to leave its target genres underdetermined while yet accounting for the different levers it sets to work. The aim is to account for the mechanisms involved in fictocritical writing and reading – ultimately, to deliver a strategic contraption that, depending on which actual (con)textual circumstances it is applied to, takes a different textual form, each time. Therefore, the goal is to formulate a strategic trope whose internal relations adequately reflect the constitutive mechanisms at play in the fictocritical, while yet leaving the particular variables un(der)determined in order not to pre/structure the textual field of fictocritical possibilities.

Positives of a Negative Definition: Some Strategically Fictocritical Features

Accepting the route of a negative definition to appropriately theorise fictocriticism, we can now ask slightly more positively: What are these particular strategies? Which patterns do they instantiate, and what tropical figure do they cut in the process? Furthermore, what are their specifically fictocritical effects and merits? On the back of this new perspective, our earlier list of textual features in evidence can be transformed into more positive formulations for a strategic definition *ex negativo*.

For example, some means such as fragmentary structuring or otherwise experimental form, intertextual references, and interpretive ambiguities of all kinds serve to foreground the textual acts we are engaged in with the text. In this sense, fictocritical texts create interpretively ambiguous situations in order to foreground their self-consciously performative aspects – as texts, certainly, but also with regards to writ*ing* and read*ing*. Other means, such as subjective perspective and personal involvement as well as minimal characterisation and dialogue, serve to sharpen a text's critical aspect. These seem to be two main axes along which fictocritical writing deploys its generically deviant textual means strategically: firstly, there are theoretical and, secondly, critical implications directed at our textual practices. Notably, fictocritical texts link these axes in a crucial manner: the fictocritical is marked by a clear strategic tendency towards a meta-generic perspective onto our textual practices from which both its theoretical and critical concerns take their cue. Significantly, the resulting fictocritical pattern thus amounts to more than the sum of its two constituent parts.

By the same token, I want to argue, fictocriticism generally engages genre-blurring in order to highlight, firstly, the conditions of the possibility of our generic textual practices and, secondly, their wider discursive functions. The various textual features it deploys strategically serve either one of these fictocritical aims. In sum, this marks a shift towards the meta-level of our generic textual practices, towards their constitutive frame/work. By conflating truth-representing and truth-constituting discourses, fictocriticism problematises the regulatory rules of the academic genres and diverts attention to the constitutive rules of textual practices *per se*. Through this meta-perspective, I want to argue, the self-reflexive and performative aspects of the fictocritical gain new dimensions. Ultimately, at the centre of the strategic fictocritical pattern, there is a self-reflexive and performative focus on the very textual practices through which we are engaging with the text's further critical propositions. What is at stake on the meta-level is precisely our understanding of the paradigmatic situation of textual representation and communication in its significance for wider discursive formations.

Fictocritical texts usually contain (at least fragments of) a theory of reading and writing, often at the same time as they themselves are already protocols of that kind of reading or display it in some form. Yet when they offer us, from within, a theory of the kind of activity we are simultaneously performing in accessing them – suggesting a back-feeding movement in the reading performance that is simultaneously under scrutiny, under way and thus at stake – the performativity of this scenario extends to, always, *this* side of the page, namely to the reader. Paired with a meta-perspective, this awareness leads the reader to a vantage point from which to realise an important fact: unlike other explanations, our understanding of what it is to read – and moreover what it involves to read correctly – directly affects the practice of reading because the same entity that conceives of the practice is also guiding the practice on the basis of this conception. Here the textual subjects at work and at stake intersect to congruence. It is precisely this potential for a short-circuitous power cut within the linguistic-discursive agency at work that fictocritical texts aim to tap. Paradigmatically, this happens when fictocritical writing intersects a poetics of textual practice with a textual aesthetic at the same time as it makes that same aesthetic relevant for practically directed concerns, thereby ultimately endowing the text's formal aspects with an ethics.

The first part of this claim is that fictocritical texts break with genre on the textual level in order to highlight the ingrained genres of our writ*ing* and read*ing* practices. When they are intersecting a textual aesthetic (i.e. the literary) with a poetics of textual discourse (i.e. literary theory), they are aiming to highlight the conditions of the possibility of genre, firstly, by way of the self-reflexive direction of their theoretical insights and, secondly, by way of a performative awareness of reading and writing. Later in the thesis we shall come to understand this poetico-aesthetic aspect as a simultaneously twofold highlighting of the proposed theoretical subject in the performance – as making perceptible (*aisthesis*) the text-discursive workings (*poiesis*). This first understanding, which recognises the fictocritical as aiming at its own conditions of im/possibility, effectively puts the fictocritical on track as an *aesthetic of deconstruction*.

The second part of the claim is that fictocritical texts consciously deploy their features strategically against a theoretical background understanding in order to indicate how our textual performance is implicated in generic textual practices and their wider discursive effects. Thus, when they are intersecting a textual aesthetic (i.e. the literary) with an ethics of textual discourse (i.e. literary criticism) they aim to endow their critical agenda with a peculiarly striking significance by way of an im/mediate interpellation of the reader as textual agent. We shall later in the thesis come to understand this ethico-aesthetic aspect as the edge with which both textual form and our textual practices emerge as ethically meaningful. This second understanding additionally puts the fictocritical on track as an (im/mediately striking) *interventionist aesthetic*.

Across the range of fictocritical texts in evidence is thus discernible a theory of our textual practices, against the background of which fictocritical strategies instantiate a distinct constellation of self-reflexive theory, experiential awareness, and critical positions. Between these heavily interrelated elements the fictocritical works its effects in a manner that, firstly, highlights performatively what it re/theorises constatively and, secondly, links this theoretical insight to the critical concerns it also raises in the text. In this fashion, I would like to suggest, the fictocritical departs from the vantage point of an exceptionally induced, meta-generic perspective on our textual practices simultaneously under way and under scrutiny. The hinge between these theoretical and critical aspects emerges as the crucial fictocritical trope. This twofold fictocritical direction and impulse shall henceforth in/form the present research project and re/conceptualisation of the (unmarked) fictocritical or (hyphenated) ficto-critical as (slashed) ficto/critical. In fact, the rest of the thesis will now be an exercise in examining, defining, and refining this figure as well as spelling out some of its far-reaching implications.

Main Title (II): Ficto/criticism
The Performative Compound Revisited

Analogously, my use of the slash in the thesis title – which illustrates both the separation and conjoining of the constituent parts and perspectives of ficto/criticism – already reflects the twofold strategic direction indicated in the previous section:

Ficto/critical Strategies
Subverting Textual Practices of Meaning, Other, and Self-Formation

Re/conceiving of the performative compound "fictocriticism" or "ficto-criticism" in terms of strategy, the slash in "ficto/criticism" shall henceforth mark the combined perspectival emphases of the *ficto*-critical and the ficto-*critical*.

Firstly, the *ficto*-critical – with an italicised emphasis on the initial part – marks the perspective that aims to self-reflexively, performatively, and im/mediately highlight our textual acts while theorising them differently. For example, the second chapter of this thesis is dedicated to defining, refining and elaborating this aspect in great detail from a close reading of Muecke's "The Fall". To anticipate the gist of this reading here only briefly, the *ficto*-critical creates an im/mediate and theoretical awareness of one's own textual practices under way. The first syllables "ficto-" are not emphasised on account of the means of fiction on the textual level, but rather because eventually the fictional mode shall emerge as primary to non-fiction in a systematic re/assessment of our textual practices. This insight, however, stands only at the end of a thorough deconstruction, along *ficto*-critical lines, of the generic hierarchy which all too readily assumes fictional language use to feed on its allegedly primordially non-fictional capabilities.

A first glimpse of the combined self-reflexive, performative, and im/mediate *ficto*-critical trope can be found in a witticism by Alice Kaplan that she formulates in *French Lessons: A Memoir* somewhere between the influence of Stéphane Mallarmé and her French teacher Ann Smock: "Literature lies and tells the truth about lying." (1993: 75) In other words, where literature 'lies' by virtue of the fictional mode, it may yet convey both experiential truths and theoretical insights into the nature and poetics of that mode which constitutes its fictional 'lying'. The crucial point is that with their special brand of self-reflexivity and performativity *ficto*-critical texts generate both constative theoretical insights into our textual practices and im/mediately highlight experientially our textual practices under way. In combination with their at times uncertain epistemological status, their *ficto*-critical aesthetics subtly suggests a deconstructed understanding of the triad fiction, theory, and criticism, with fiction emerging as the primary term on the systemic level – whence the emphasis.

Secondly, the ficto-*critical* – with an italicised emphasis on the rear part – marks the perspective that aims to connect the *ficto*-critical awareness and understanding just outlined with the issues and concerns that are also being raised constatively in the text. Rather than taking their marginal provenance or textual features as indicators, this shall eventually produce a more insightful approach to differently structured ficto/critical clusters (re)grouped according to the respective constitutive mechanisms of our textual practices that they problematise and re/conceive of differently.

On the one hand, the stress on the rear syllables "-critical" thus resonates Muecke's prompt answer to the self-posed question: "And what of the 'criticism' in fictocriticism? This is not about moral agendas, like, 'I can do a *critique* of this or that because I am equipped with some kind of incisive intellectual tool'. Far from it, that kind of critic is *always right*, and we should steer clear of them for that reason." (2008a: 14-5, original emphasis) With regards to this post-critical sentiment, the twofold ficto/critical perspective always already contains a self-reflexive gesture by rooting its wider discursive critique in our textual practices and simultaneously routing it through each linguistic-discursive agent's co-present performance thereof. This self-reflexive turn in the critical gesture thus has the virtue of turning in on its own practices before turning them on others.

On the other hand, the stress on the ficto-*critical* also emphasises the fact that any such critique of our wider discursive practices is mounted first and foremost by way of a critique of our core text-discursive practices – thus following the by-way of the text's *ficto*-critical aspects. In this manner, the ethical dimension of criticism is here coupled to the poetics of praxes that we are of necessity engaging when we encounter it in writing, in read*ing*. Such, at least, is the dimension of meaning that I would like to invest in Muecke's words which immediately follow the above quote, namely that "when we couple criticism to fiction, to the imaginative, we seek rather to perform a kind of ethics" (ibid: 14-5). Precisely through an unheard-of pairing of self-reflexive, performative, and im/mediate *ficto*-critical aspects can ficto-*critical* texts develop surprising interpellatory forces that provide an equally unheard-of edge to their respective critiques.

Thus framed, the ficto/critical is concerned with our linguistic-discursive and, especially, textual practices of being in the world. It is critical of the current forms our text-cultural practices take because of the practical effects they create and the functions they serve in our wider discursive practices of relating to the world. Although a text's ficto-*critical* scope is thus very much directed at the relation between a linguistic-discursive self and the world, its *ficto*-critical point of departure is yet, reflexively, the relation between self and text.

Subtitle: Meaning, Other, and Self-Formation

Accruing a first refining layer, the twofold ficto/critical perspective is then unpacked in the subtitle:

> Ficto/critical Strategies
> Subverting Textual Practices of **Meaning, Other, and Self-Formation**

In fact, the twofold ficto/critical perspective examines precisely how our textual formations of meaning – this is the *ficto*-critical focus – are implicated in the wider discursive formations of self, other, and world – which is the ficto-*critical* focus.

With regards to the *ficto*-critical aspect Heather Kerr, having first noticed that "[c]ross cultural work will frequently be at pains *not* to position the other as 'text' for commentary", then establishes that "[l]aying bare the devices of its own production and reflecting on its deployment of disciplinary knowledges, the fictocritical effect in cultural studies writing practices is to aestheticize ethics as a self-conscious (formal) gesture" (2001: 114, original emphasis). In this observation, Kerr recognises that what I have termed the ficto-*critical* kind of aestheticised ethical writing departs from the self-reflexive meta-turn of what I have called the *ficto*-critical kind of an aesthetic grounded in a poetics of writing. She lucidly envisages the complex interrelatedness of poetics, aesthetics, and ethics in the ficto/critical, which, I want to argue, is most productively phrased in terms of the formations of meaning, other and self.

Approaching the same complex from the ficto-*critical* side, Muecke then makes the following case:

"One might urge the interested writer not to feel that their practice has to conform to one of another model, but to have the confidence that the problem characterizing the situation before them will surprise them into *changing* their practices. Like all literature, fictocriticism experiments with ways of being in the world, with forms of subjectivity if you like." (2008a: 15, original emphasis)

Although Muecke characteristically focuses on the writerly side of things here, his assessment is much to the point of the ficto-*critical*: the aim of the interpellatory aspects of the ficto/critical is to address – both constatively and performatively – our textual practices in their wider discursive function of in/forming the subjectivity of the textual agent in relation to the world by way of her relation to the text. In this sense, the self-reflexive *ficto*-critical stance towards our textual practices finds its ficto-*critical* end in the textually effected and affected formations of the self in relation to the other as well as in relation to the world.

In both these senses, the phrasing of the subtitle addresses the epistemological implications of meaning formation from the *ficto*-critical perspective as well as the ethical implications this might have for other and self-formation from the ficto-*critical* perspective. The subtitle thus addresses the processes of text-discursive meaning formation in their relevance for the wider discursive processes of other and self-formation as well as re/formation. Using only the elements foregrounded by the subtitle, there is also a formulaic way of spelling out the twofold ficto/critical directedness, which might help to distil the trope further. On the one hand, the text-epistemological and text-theoretical implications of meaning formation are concerned with the relation between the reading self and the text:

(self – text)

Using the hyphen here as a symbol for relation, or rather for the process of relat*ing*, this is what I call the *ficto*-critical relation, the gist of which is that the text works *ficto*-critically by making the reader work, self-reflexively. That is with its self-reflexive, performative and im/mediate direction the text works *ficto*-critically by making the reader experience and re/conceive of their work of relat*ing* to the text and making sense of its mediations.

On the other hand, the text-ethical implications of other and self-formation are concerned with the relation between the (reading) self and the world or the other:

(self – other/world)

This is what I call the ficto-*critical* relation, which concerns the practical relevance of the insights that the *ficto*-critical relation can provide for certain issues and concerns. To re/phrase the foregone formulation accordingly, the text works ficto-*critically* by getting the reader to work on themselves in terms of their relation to the other and the world. That is with its interpellatory force the ficto-*critical* text aims to rouse the reading textual agent into changing their ways of going about their textual activities, because they are implied in the wider subjects under critique. This is how the ficto/critical removes both the academic and medial distance of criticism and makes the issue under discussion personal for each and every receptive recipient.

Taken together, the twofold ficto/critical trope now takes the following combined formula:

([self – text] – other/world)

Although the focus of the ficto-*critical* relation is very much directed at the identity defining relation between self and world/other, the self-reflexive, performative, and im/mediate point of departure is of necessity the *ficto*-critical relation between self and text. The ficto/critical, firstly, theoretically re/assesses the fundamental conditions of the possibility of our (generic) textual practices and, secondly, points out how these constitutive mechanisms have been deployed generically to detrimental effect. This pattern is potentially valid for all the differently motivated ficto/critical concerns with certain discursive implications that our textual practices may have in processes of wider discursive formations.

At the same time, however, it should already be noted in these introductory remarks that not every ficto/critical text instantiates both of these aspects in equal measure. Most of the texts in evidence – even the primary texts of this thesis – exemplify perhaps one aspect to a greater extent than the other or instantiate maybe just a fragmentary picture of the ficto/critical pattern. Nevertheless, I am going to formulate this ficto/critical ideal rather strongly in what follows because I am convinced that it can propel our understanding of ficto/critical texts and inject new significance into our practices of writing and reading ficto/critically. Therefore, I would like to take this pattern and its implications seriously even though not every worthwhile ficto/critical text instantiates it in full. If they have a fragment to contribute to the bigger picture of the twofold ficto/critical understanding or the concomitant ficto/critical background understanding of our textual practices in general, all ficto/critical texts and their concerns, I hope, will only profit from this kind of theorisation.

Asymmetrically, then, the *ficto*-critical first brings to awareness the relation between self and text, which is the constitutive frame for any reading experience. As the reading process is thus frictioned by the textual structure, the frame/work of this mediating relation is performatively foregrounded from within. At the same time, however, this framing relation is also the subject of the relational mediation that constitutes the reading process – it is thus made the constative subject of the text. In this manner, a meta-commentary is provided constatively on the same kind of textual relation that is self-reflexively brought to experience from within the performance. Secondly, this constatively and performatively raised awareness of the relation and relat*ing* between self and text is often given practical ficto-*critical* direction by the text's other content and the issues it raises.

As textual work, ficto/critical reading and writing practices aim at creating an experience that simultaneously comprises an awareness and understanding of one's own performative relation to the text and of the practical significance and function that this performative relation has within the wider discursive formations of meaning, self, and other or world. In this manner, ficto/critical texts make perceptible the crucial twofold relation that always already constitutes our textual practices. *In reading*, the gap between self and text is constitutively bridged, the relation established in relat*ing*. At the same time, this constitutive bridging always already relates the textual formation to the world through the reader and their idiocultural background. The text – whether fictional or non-fictional – is given worldly relevance only through the reader. While the reader works on the text, the text actually works on the reader. The ficto/critical point is, firstly, that these constitutive relations are usually being abstracted from in the way we are conditioned to read. And, secondly, that a self-reflexive awareness of these relations, as relat*ing*, would suggest a different picture of how our textual formations and practices in/form and affect our wider discursive formations and practices.

1.2 THE PROJECT

Some central ingredients of what I am going to present as a re/conceptualisation of (unmarked) fictocriticism, or (hyphenated) ficto-criticism, in terms of (slashed) ficto/criticism have been around for some time. I would argue, however, that neither has yet enough effort been made to thoroughly follow through their implications nor to think them together. Pursuing both these aims might just open up new and perhaps surprising perspectives, which, after all, has always been an important goal of ficto/critical practice.

For example, with regards to the ficto/critical trope Nettelbeck has clearly identified the self-reflexive direction of what I have now termed the *ficto*-critically theoretical aspect, especially in its relevance for meaning formation, when she notes that "the stress in fictocritical texts on the fragment or on the representational image or on the arbitrary connection might be read as signalling not so much a disappearance of value into a long, flat plain of relativity but rather a coming-to-grips with the contexts in which value is produced" (1998: 8). For Nettelbeck the ficto/critical goes beyond the notion of competing values, whether on the textual or generic levels, when it turns towards the constitutive level of value production via text, which the ficto/critical investigates and criticises at the same time as it practices it. Firstly, there is the constitutive con/text, which presents the conditions of the possibility of textual value production. Secondly there is the wider discursive con/text, within which certain values are produced and maintained for certain reasons. To convey an awareness and understanding of the former is the focus of the *ficto*-critical, while the latter is the concern of the ficto-*critical*.

In a similar vein, when Kerr notes that in fictocriticism "'[t]heory' is the 'sign' for 'reflexivity'" and that, as a result, "[t]he fictocritical story knows that what it is doing is suspect, but continues to do it anyway" (2001: 113), she lucidly captures the special performative twist that ficto/critical self-reflexivity entails because it is paired with constative theoretical import. In her terminology she concludes that "[f]ictocriticism is perverse" because "[i]n fictocriticism the project itself must be scrutinized at the same time as it is performed" (ibid: 113). Kerr has thus earlier laid her finger precisely on the crucial under-scrutiny-while-underway aspect, which I am later going to qualify figuratively as the *ficto*-critical vector and twist. Although the new kinds of textually induced self-reflexivity and performativity at work in the *ficto*-critical are already implied here, they have not hitherto taken centre stage. They are yet to enter our thinking of the ficto/critical to an extent that can do justice to their systemic importance. Precisely this potential I now want to tap for the purposes of this thesis.

The ficto-*critical* counterpart to these early *ficto*-critical observations has also been in evidence before. For example, Flavell has identified precisely the connection between fictocritical form and wider discursive formations when she writes that "[f]icto-critical forms make a connection between the style of writing and the content, asking both writers and readers to examine at the level of form what structures of domination are in place in our own writing and reading practices" (2004: 295-6). A concomitant point is then to identify how dominant textual structures play a part in wider discursive structures of domination. Instead of simply acknowledging the fact that these structures are in place, the virtue of ficto/critical writing has always been to bend its own practices in a manner that both makes perceptible the textual mechanisms in question and indicates the wider realms of critical concern. Thus, a certain symmetry between ficto/critical concerns and textual mechanisms is likely to emerge which could provide a catalogue of systematic ficto/critical clusters rather than – ultimately contiguous – strands of marginal/ised provenance as well as textual features to explain the emergence, motivation, and patterns of ficto/critical writing.

In what follows, I would like to think these preliminary insights regarding the ficto/critical together with other key perspectival shifts in my approach. The aim is to assemble a systemic understanding of ficto/critical writing both as an interventionist practice and as an aesthetic of deconstruction within the paradigmatic parameters of our textual practices that ficto/critical writing makes perceptible. Pursuing this, one specific challenge will be to maintain the attention on structures of discursive domination while yet shifting perspective from the textual level towards our textual practices.

Ficto/critical Shifts in Perspective

Some major shifts in perspective are already implicit in what I have outlined so far, the most important of which I would like to recapitulate more detailed in this section.

Firstly, I have anticipated a significant shift from the generic between towards the meta-generic. As a result of prioritising the prominent self-reflexive theoretical turns in ficto/critical writing, focus shifts from the interstitial realms between genres onto the meta-level of our textual practices. This perspectival shift happens somewhat, but by no means entirely, at the expense of the suggestive analogy between marginal/ised speaking positions and the generically marginal. Taking the text-theoretical and text-epistemological aspects of ficto/critical writing seriously simply shifts attention from the level of our generic textual practices onto the level of the conditions of the im/possibility of our generic practices of textual representation and communication. In even more Derridean terms, focus shifts from the level of the laws of genre onto the level of the laws of the laws of genre (Derrida 1992b). In this sense, the *ficto*-critical relation aims to re/assess the field of our textual practices, not to entrench itself in its already pre/structured marginal interstices. The second chapter, in particular, shall re/trace how *ficto*-critical texts guide their readers towards this self-reflexive meta-perspective.

Secondly, and this coincides with the meta-generic shift, I have promised to take seriously the implications of the ficto/critical shift from texts towards our textual practices. Note that this is closely connected to the *ficto*-critical aspect of the twofold ficto/critical trope. Primary attention has moved from *the* textual work towards *our* textual acts in an attempt to come to terms with the non-generic patterns of the ficto/critical. It has departed from the one written textual work towards the combined writerly and readerly textual acts of read*ing* and writ*ing* of which textual work comprises. This shift in perspective has effectively changed understanding from an essential and fixed model of the textual work towards something much more de/centred and performative, from the parameters of textual form towards the parameters of the medially pre/structured communicative situation within which our textual acts combine to per/form the textual work.

A significant knock-on effect of this shift in perspective necessitates a third, almost methodological, shift from textual analysis to text-cultural analysis. Note that this practical dimension is closely connected to the ficto-*critical* aspect of the two-step ficto/critical trope. Connecting a *ficto*-critical theory of our textual formations with a ficto-*critical* assessment of their role in wider discursive formations, shifts focal attention towards our culture of textual practices. Arguably, there is an intermediary step to be acknowledged in the transition that actually moves along the scale from textual analysis towards critical discourse analysis and from cultural studies towards something like a ficto/critical discourse analysis, perhaps, which has the potential to develop some text-philosophical import with both a theoretical and a practical orientation. The overarching aim along this scale should be to comprehend the ideological function that our textual acts serve within wider discursive contexts. The third chapter, in particular, shall establish the polar distinction in textual cultures between academic and ficto/critical text-practical ideologies and their concomitant practices.

A fourth shift in perspective on the ficto/critical that I have only briefly outlined so far shall eventually flow from the previous shifts. Eventually it will entail (re)drawing the ficto/critical field no longer according to provenance in terms of the writer's personal background or the text's formal features, but according to the respective connections between a constitutive textual mechanism and the wider discursive practices that a text highlights ficto/critically. The future prospect is thus to replace the notion of different strands in fictocritical writing (that are supposedly maintained by certain writers) with the notion of individual texts that cluster around the constitutive mechanisms of our textual practices in order to ficto/critically highlight and critique their wider discursive function from a positioned and involved perspective.

Fifthly, the perhaps most consequential – as well as previously most underrated – shift moves from the dominant textual and writerly perspectives towards a readerly perspective, albeit without neglecting these other two aspects. It ultimately amounts to the deconstruction of another hierarchical dichotomy, this time between the writerly and readerly positions in relation to the text. Systemic primacy shall henceforth be emphasised in the erstwhile minor – because allegedly passive and hence negligible – position of the reader. Especially my formulation of a de/centred and processual understanding of our textual practices will thus shift focus towards the readerly side of the equation. Ultimately, I want to suggest that the readerly act paradigmatically performs the necessary de/territorialising movement that is so highly valued in ficto/criticism, whereas writing necessarily enacts its re/territorialising counterpart, leaving only the manifest territorial structure of the written.

In line with this point, it is of particular importance, firstly, that the kind of self-reflexivity at work in ficto/criticism expands from the textual and writerly levels to include the readerly act and, secondly, that the kind of performativity at work in ficto/critical texts expands from the textual and writerly levels to include the readerly performance. Thus, ficto/critical self-reflexivity shifts from the constative towards the performative at the same time as ficto/critical performativity shifts from the conceptual towards the experiential side of reading. It is particularly important for the ficto/critical to think both of these shifts together. Implicit here are these further changes in perspective: from a writerly self-reflexivity, via a textual self-reflexivity, towards a readerly self-reflexivity; from the transparent text, via the opaque text, towards always *this* (i.e. *your*) im/mediate and readerly side of the textual work; from a one-way instrumental understanding of language, via a notion of linguistic or textual self-centredness, towards the ficto/critical textual relation which is rooted in and routed through the reader. All these facets have their respective insights that need to be taken into account.

Note, furthermore, that the im/mediate effect of *ficto*-critical writing highlights these kinds of self-reflexivity and performativity experientially while under way, not constatively at a remove. In other words, the *ficto*-critical comprises texts that experientially highlight the im/mediacy of reading. In this manner, (slashed) ficto/criticism makes its issues and concerns personal for the reader, too, by im/mediately implying their practices in the subject of critique. This latter shift from textual mediation to textual im/mediacy also provides the theoretical hinge of the *ficto*-critical vector, which roots the constative and performative in the im/mediate readerly present in order to highlight how the wider issues under critique are routed through the very practices under way *in reading*.

Attuned to this, I would now also like to recapitulate very briefly the shift in approach towards the (slashed) ficto/critical against the background of probably the best theorisation of the matter so far. When the opposition between non-fiction, as truth-representing discourse, and fiction, as truth-constituting discourse in its own right, is targeted in its function for institutionalised genres of knowledge production, two crucial questions need to be asked. First, at which level is genre at stake here? And second, how does the ficto/critical intend to effect re/medial change to generically instituted praxes of linguistic-discursive domination? The following excerpt provides Flavell's answers to these questions:

"[B]ringing into play the other of academic discourse while combining it with a critical/theoretical position, ficto-criticism problematises the concepts of judgement, interpretation and representation. In addition, it mixes fact and fiction, self-reflexively entertaining its own fictionality as a means to situate itself socially and historically. [...] It also reveals the fiction of genre. Ficto-critical forms make a connection between the style of writing and the content, asking both writers and readers to examine at the level of form what structures of domination are in place in our own writing and reading practices. Many ficto-critical works thus function as models for a mode of critical writing that does not colonise the object of its analysis, but attempts a reading of and with the text/subject; an empathetic engagement that understands subjectivity as informed by and changing with context and event." (2004: 295-6)

Flavell here lucidly identifies the crucial features of ficto-critical practice. Yet, although she puts Deleuzian thought to good use in describing ficto-criticism as writing-between in its essential resistance to being generically conceptualised, I want to suggest that she nonetheless remains on the level of the laws of genre in her overall description. Departing from this notion, I propose that the step towards the framing laws of the laws of genre has to be undertaken if ficto/criticism is to be adequately conceived of as a self-reflexive meta-commentary that addresses the movements, mechanisms, and functions of our linguistic-discursive modes of constructing meaning, the other, the world, and a self. Thus, differently from Flavell's approach, I want to argue that ficto/criticism demands to be read as a writing practice that steers attention towards the constitutive structures of the intentional structures at work in textual encounters as well as towards systemic the role of the former in the perpetually re/producing the latter. In this regard, I am going to diagnose a different kind of reflexivity as in/forming these texts – one that is concerned with the laws of the laws of genre rather than the spaces between genres.

I want to propose a reading of ficto/criticism that takes the framing laws of the laws of genre into account as our fundamental practical modes with which we constitutively set ourselves in relation to the world, the text, and the other. Again, I believe that Flavell is lucidly pointing in exactly the right direction when she identifies ficto-criticism's concern with "the concepts of judgement, interpretation and representation" (ibid: 295). Yet, departing from her approach, I want to suggest that the ficto/critical post-generically addresses these concepts as the constitutive tropical movements of our linguistic-discursive interaction with the world, the text, and the other that have hitherto been conceptualised for textual practices as the basic genres of criticism, theory, and fiction.

'Subjecting' Ficto/criticism: The Methods of Approach

Asserting a theory of the ficto/critical over the course of this thesis I am going to make recourse to a number of primary ficto/critical sources. It is important to note, however, that I will not only use these ficto/critical texts as examples to prove my point, but also as primary sources for their background theory of our textual practices, against which their textual conduct can then emerge as strategically deployed. Note that there is no flawed circularity in doing so. Even outside of theoretical passages that are explicitly dealing our textual practices, ficto/critical texts are usually saturated with ideologically differing perceptions of the constitutive mechanisms and generic forces of our reading and writing practices. After all, these perceptions strategically bring them in formation to begin with. On these grounds, I want to take directions for a theoretical re/assessment of our textual practices directly from those ficto/critical texts whose resistance to generic textual practices it already in/forms.

The point is to theorise ficto/criticism on its own terms. With regards to the ingrained hesitance among many primary writers towards theorising the ficto/critical, I would like to offer the following angle. Because it is in any case possible to theorise ficto/criticism, I think it were better for it to be done from a benevolent stance that is in/formed by primary ficto/critical texts, rather than with a theory that is plucked from somewhere else and then thrown at the ficto/critical. Rather than subjecting ficto/criticism to a theoretical regime that is alien to its own, I want to 'subject' it to only the combined theoretical implications that emerge from the primary ficto/critical texts in this study. Hence, the task is to induce a theory on the basis of the texts already in evidence, albeit in a non-reductive manner, which leaves unpredictable the realm of ficto/critical forms to come while still providing a firm grasp of the concept of ficto/critical strategies. In this manner, readers and writers can be sensitised towards the ficto/critical, which, I believe, will enhance it as a broader project. To achieve this goal, and in pursuit of the steps outlined below, I am going to conduct the following primary readings towards a systemic re/conceptualisation of the ficto/critical.

Firstly, in the second chapter "Realising the *Ficto*-critical Vector and Twist" I shall examine, define and refine the primordial *ficto*-critical turn of the ficto/critical trope. Special attention needs to be paid to its peculiar composition of both an experiential awareness of the textual performance under way in reading – which I refer to as realising the *ficto*-critical vector – and a simultaneous self-reflexive theoretical account of our textual practices that we thus find in writing. This *ficto*-critical relation, that short-circuits the performative side of read*ing* and the constative side of the written, produces a *ficto*-critical twist that I am going to re/trace in Stephen Muecke's essay "The Fall". At times, I may have to read Muecke's text against the explicit authorial voice in order to realise its full textual potential. In other words, almost despite himself, while yet adhering to a different concept of the (unmarked) fictocritical, which the text aims to define, Muecke has here wrought a textual structure that epitomises what I call the *ficto*-critical turn of the (slashed) ficto/critical trope. In a pre/post/erous way, I would thus like to read Muecke's splendid text into its (slashed) ficto/critical self, thereby leading this study into the primary turn of the twofold ficto/critical trope.

Secondly, in the third chapter "A Theory of the Ficto/critical" I shall re/deploy the terminology of previous theorisations of the ficto/critical in order, firstly, to characterise the trope of ficto/critical strategies, secondly, to ideologically refine the spatio-temporal background understanding of reading and writing and, thirdly, to formulate a theory of the ficto/critical. In particular, I hope to sharpen my ficto/critical perspective in terms of previous theorisations with a view to supplementing and infusing their often witty and ingenious terminology with the insights of my study. In this respect, Michael Taussig's "The Corn-Wolf: Writing Apotropaic Texts" (2010b) and Heather Kerr's "Perverse Writing – Maternity and Monarchy: Fictocriticism and Exorbitant, Plural Bodies" (2002) provide exceptionally fertile grounds. At the same time, revisiting previous conceptualisations of (unmarked) fictocriticism, or (hyphenated) ficto-criticism, is going to provide an opportunity to further refine the text-practical background theory and re/configure our understanding of the constellations that mark the ficto/critical accordingly. Both Aritha van Herk's *Places Far From Ellesmere* (1990) and John Hughes's *Someone Else* (2007) are particularly rewarding texts for these purposes, which will help to refine both the encapsulated spatial and translational temporal logic of our textual practices. One aim is to refine a theory of ficto/critical strategies in light of these readings, simply because the theoretical background understanding of our textual practices plays such an in/formative role for them. To conclude the third chapter, my readings of Guy Maddin's film MY WINNIPEG (2007) and Kathleen Stewart's text *Ordinary Affects* (2007) will both re/trace their respective strategies and tap their particular figurative potential in order to substantiate the envisaged re/theorisation of the ficto/critical in terms of both artistic and artful thought-experimental writing.

Thirdly, in the fourth chapter "Developing Ficto-*critical* Edge" I shall examine the secondary aspect of the ficto-*critical* turn in the ficto/critical trope on the back of a primary reading. The exemplary text to help define the notion of ficto-*critical* edge will be Gail Jones's essay "Thaumatropes" (1998) which makes this tropical turn perceptible in admirable fashion. Following on this, a reading of Katrina Schlunke's *Bluff Rock* (2005) will qualify her novel-length book as another complete ficto/critical text in the sense of my theory.

Just to briefly recapitulate the methods of this study then, the second and fourth chapters shall engage in detailed close readings to establish the twofold turns of the ficto/critical trope. In both cases the point in focussing on ficto/critical strategies lies in relating a more general ficto/critique to the individual text's functioning, its locatedness, and its depictions. In between, the third chapter shall then formulate a new theory of the ficto/critical by way of re/deploying the formulations of previous theorisations on the meta-level. Ideally, this approach would allow for bi/directional in/formation between formulating the background theory of our constitutive textual frame/work and the central theory of ficto/critical strategies as they are grounded in the textual evidence. As my readings are going to move from one primary text to the next, my theorising would thus ideally move back and forth between these three interrelated levels that, between them, in/form the subsequent theses and thesis.

All in all, my selection of central primary texts tries to establish a representative ficto/critical field. The idea is to reflect the different parameters in evidence across ficto/critical writing, yet without prioritising or excluding any one of them disproportionally. For this reason, my selection of central primary texts includes a roughly equal number of essay-length and novel-length texts. More importantly, perhaps, both genders are just about equally represented. Time-wise, all primary texts have been published from 1990 onwards. Notably, an emphasis on Australian writing results from the productive place that ficto/critical writing has been accorded at universities there since the mid-90s.

Carving out a field like this is necessarily arbitrary, but with regards to the ficto/critical this is perhaps the point. Texts that have been published as minor essays, such as Muecke's "The Fall" and Jones's "Thaumatropes" are on the same textual footing as publications of more decidedly academic or literary aspiration, such as Schlunke's *Bluff Rock* and van Herk's *Places Far From Ellesmere* respectively, while texts such as Kerr's "Perverse Writing", Taussig's "The Corn-Wolf" and Hughes's *Someone Else* make the distinction between secondary and primary texts untenable. My selection thus hopes to strike the right balance to accord a theory of the ficto/critical with general intent that is yet rooted in these rather particular texts with all their different formal and positional idiosyncrasies.

Location, Scope, & Limits of the Study

Ahead of engaging in these analyses, a few more introductory words are in order with regards to the general situation of the present PhD project. Institutionally, this thesis is the result of a joint award PhD program between FUB and UWA, where it is located in the *Institut für Englische Philologie* and the English and Cultural Studies department respectively. The project is therefore located firmly in the realm of literary studies, as an exercise of literary theory. As such, the study follows its subject matter, the ficto/critical, in factoring in the overlap between the literary and the academic, the theoretical, the critical, and, sometimes, even the experimental.

Academically, however, the present thesis is situated somewhere in-between literary studies, philosophy, textual analysis, critical discourse analysis, and cultural studies. It incorporates elements from all of these disciplines, but sometimes interprets them differently, with an inflection that is, again, in/formed by the subject of study. The ostensible aim of this study is to theorise and critique fictocriticism from a literary studies perspective. In order to do so in terms of its subject matter, however, the study also develops a theory of our textual practices from a more philosophical perspective that is yet in/formed by ficto/critical texts. Furthermore, on account of the tropical hinge that is the (slashed) ficto/critical, this study examines generic as well as ficto/critical texts and textual practices *and* their wider discursive or cultural implications. The goal is to show how the primary texts contain, firstly, *ficto*-critically deployed textual means, secondly, (at least) fragments of a ficto/critical theory of our textual practices, and, thirdly, a strategic ficto-*critical* pattern that connects the mechanisms of textual representation and communication to such wider discursive practices as worlding or othering. Accordingly, the methodology of this thesis veers between close readings, philosophical theorising, and assessing our text-discursive formations in their relevance for our cultural formations.

While partially engaging in all these disciplines, it is vital to recognise them as also the primary subject of the broader ficto/critique thus taking shape. While I believe that a general theory of our textual practices is possible, if only we took their medial conditions of (im)possibility as our starting point, the virtue of any specific kind of critique that emerges from such a re/assessment ought to be to turn in on itself, on our own textual practices of literary theory and criticism or philosophy, before turning elsewhere, against other practices from which it is allegedly removed. The primary subject of critique thus lies not elsewhere but is precisely the entire realm of our text-cultural practices – especially where they are of systemic relevance for wider discursive formations simultaneously under critique. The idea, ultimately, is precisely to re/theorise our textual practices of theorising the world, and critique our textual practices of critiquing other practices; furthermore, to do so in the uneasy knowledge that *qua textual practices* such theorisations and critiques participate in the text-cultural formations that really ought to be under critique. It is very much to the problematic point of the ficto/critical that all this must be achieved in yet an/other text. Ficto/critical strategies, I believe, are most productively understood along these lines. Consequentially, reading and writing practices that do live up to these aims will indeed qualify as *textual activism* proper, because they effectively remove the gap between explanatory critique and interventionist performance for both writer and reader.

Objectives of the Study

Appropriately, the literary studies perspective in the present thesis will be most prevalent in the primary close readings. Note, however, that many of these are predominantly concerned with the relations between fiction, criticism, and theory and the respective texts' re/assessment thereof. Hence, while this thesis employs a literary studies methodology its outcomes are likely to affect our notions of literary theory and literary criticism in their relation to literature. At the same time, the study further politicises the textual culture of literary studies through a perspective that recognises not only literary criticism as (ethico-)political but also the very textual practices which constitute the entire discipline just as much as its objects of study. The aim in this respect is to raise awareness among literary scholars of the systemic implications that their practices share with their objects of study – not only in the theoretical sense that deconstructing the perceived hierarchy between theory, criticism, and fiction would yield an *aporia* which must challenge the discipline, but also in the practical sense that participating in the established generic order systemically perpetuates the very discursive formations that ought to be under critique together with the respective subject matter.

The philosophical aspects of this study are concentrated in two perspectives, both of which concern the philosophy of language. Firstly, the self-reflexive, performative, and im/mediate mode of the *ficto*-critical addresses a deficiency of the allegedly objective, uninvolved, and removed perspective of philosophy and philosophical language use. In this regard, the *ficto*-critical experience actually contradicts the alleged passivity of our textual practices that much philosophy of language simply assumes. This is the perspective on the *ficto*-critical as an aesthetic of deconstruction that has, above all, something to say about our guiding notions of reading and writing. Secondly, the interventionist, activist aesthetic of the ficto-*critical* addresses an ethico-political dimension that is still rarely at the centre of attention in much philosophy of language, simply because the distanced and objective model would suggest otherwise. In this combined sense, the (slashed) ficto/critical avails itself of the practical relevance of the core theoretical philosophy discipline that is the philosophy of language. For the present thesis, the goal in this respect is to capture the different philosophical assessments of our textual work that frame the emergence of ficto/critical strategies.

There is an important element of critical discourse analysis at work in this study – albeit without the associated clear-cut method (Fairclough 1995: 23-83) – that re/traces how exactly ficto/critical texts examine and critique the ways in which generic text-discursive formations serve to effect and affect wider discursive formations. Note that the core ficto/critical relation

([self – text] – other/world)

also captures the main interests of critical discourse analysis. In any case, given the peculiar nature of ficto/critical textual form/ations and their modes of conduct, we should perhaps distinguish this characteristically experimental approach as one of ficto/critical discourse analysis. This, at least, is what the following study hopes to bring into relief when it defines the characteristic performative, self-reflexive, and im/mediate turns of the ficto/critical, all of which set it apart from more traditional critical discourse analyses that remain academically aloof from their subject matter through an objective form of writing even where their critical motivation is personal.

Finally, to complete the picture, the cultural studies aspect of this study is directed firmly both at the text-cultural practices that ficto/critical strategies resist as well as at those they develop to this end. Textual practices are here treated precisely as cultural practices. Paradigmatic in this respect is anthropological writing, which purports to study cultures, yet in so doing produces a distinct kind of textual culture itself, which always already ties into broader cultural practices. Notably, the practical dimension of this interest relates not only to these text-cultural formations but also to the ways in which such text-cultural practices are of almost foundational importance for some of our cultures in a more general sense. Our textual practices thus command the cultural studies attention of the present thesis in this twofold and interrelated sense. Firstly, there are particular textual practices that have been cultivated to the point at which they have become text-cultural practices. Secondly, textual practices *per se* often play an almost constitutive role for certain aspects of our cultures more generally. Hence, genres of textual form and practice are of ficto/critical interest precisely in their function for wider cultural practices that are facilitated or advanced through these textual practices. Such, at least, is the cultural studies insight that my thesis aims to highlight. Herein all of the aspects mentioned above come together.

Axiomatically, the ficto/critical trope also splits the scope of this study into two major directions. Firstly, there are text-epistemological consequences, which, if thoroughly followed through, could unfold considerable potential for our textual practices. Although this study aims to re/conceptualise ficto/criticism, which understands itself as only a marginal writing practice, it yet lets these ficto/critical texts in/form a theory of our textual practices that carries general significance. Underlying here is the thesis that this marginal textual phenomenon makes perceptible mechanisms that are always already at work in all our textual acts and yet never appear in the process as such because we constitutively abstract from them. Textually wrought ficto/critical frictions, however, make these mechanisms perceptible again. Ficto/critical writing and readings can thus ultimately provide text-theoretical insights which are not only of particular relevance for the kind of academic writing against which the ficto/critical has predominantly been motivated, but which furthermore imply all our textual practices on the constitutive level. Ultimately, in its most aspiring philosophical proportions, my study thus envisages a small metaphysics of our practices of textual representation and communication.

Secondly, the text-ethical consequences of this study are potentially uncomfortable, because ficto/criticism foregrounds the ethical dimension of our textual actions in such a way that its own textual practices of reading and writing, as well as our ingrained textual practices of reception are implied as the target of the critique it mounts. Such a ficto/critical perspective thus turns in on and against especially the supposedly objective academic perspective and its textual practices, which implies a re/conceptualisation of our academic speaking positions and textual practices. From this ethical perspective, too, the ficto/critical trope has wider discursive consequences for all our textual practices – but especially for generically academic ones. To put it pointedly, from a ficto/critical perspective there is nothing innocent about our allegedly disinterested and objective academic textual practices.

While the primary goal of this thesis project is to deliver a (slashed) ficto/critical trope, the scope of the project goes well beyond the interests in an allegedly marginal writing practice. In fact, the general text-epistemological and text-ethical scope of the ficto/critical aim to unhinge the erstwhile field within which ficto/criticism emerged as marginal. And precisely therein lies the ultimate virtue of the ficto/critical – as the opening Derridean quote would suggest.

Adjunct to this late introductory stage, I would now like to make an important point about the limits of the following study. Because I am going to define the ficto/critical as a post-critical and post-generic form of critique that is directed at wider discursive issues and concerns through a *ficto*-critical stance towards our textual practices and thus reflects its own textual acts in the ficto-*critique* it mounts, there arise two limiting consequences to my approach.

Firstly, texts that do not fully instantiate this rather sophisticated connection in a recognisable manner will, for now, fall outside of this particular definition of the ficto/critical. Certainly, not every text currently regarded as fictocritical is going to qualify according to this model. In fact, some texts that qualify as (unmarked) fictocritical or (hyphenated) ficto-critical may not qualify as (slashed) ficto/critical. Or, to turn this around, not every form of critique that mixes fiction and non-fiction is going to qualify as ficto/critical according to this model. Note, however, that I devise this theory of the ficto/critical in order to be productive for the philosophical implications of literary theory, not in order to dismiss certain texts that fall short of its necessarily ideal/ising definition. Much to the contrary, in keeping with the shift in perspective away from the essentialised textual work towards de/centring textual acts, ultimately, the ficto/critical must be understood to reside with the textual agent who brings it to the encounter and invests it in the text – any text, in the last instance. In this sense, the ficto/critical, ultimately, emerges as a stance. Thus, while my definition may appear to unnecessarily limit the field of ficto/critical texts in evidence, actually, its aim is to fertilise and extend this textual field by spreading the seed of ficto/critical text-ideology among potential recipients.

Secondly, even entirely within the textual realm, however, the present theory also makes no pretence to include texts that deploy ostensible fictocritical means and address purportedly fictocritical issues, yet fail to endow their respective critiques with the ficto-*critical* edge of a related *ficto*-critical vector and twist in the manner that my theory defines as ficto/critical.

The Subjectivity of this Study

At the end of the day, there is, of course, also a considerable personal factor at play in my work. Although much of this will probably remain hidden from me in the writerly blind spot of a vain subjectivity – and maybe so much for the better – I would still like to outline at least some personal aspects that have impacted upon the present thesis, for better or worse.

Most controversially, perhaps, I would suggest that my academic background probably in/forms this study more than a direct, personal, and positional involvement in the debates that have originally engendered ficto/critical writing. Whereas this could be construed as almost counter-revolutionary to a particular cause – depending on your point of view – I would maintain that it need not be counterproductive for the ficto/critical as such. In fact, I want to argue that quite the opposite is the case. My academic background is in philosophy and English literature, and more precisely in the philosophy of language and literary theory, where the focus of my *Magister Artium* studies has lain. At least theoretically, this should be a good position from which to re/conceptualise a kind of writing that wilfully exploits the grey area between the two. Via the FUB and UWA literature institutions I now bring all this to bear in the context of peculiar writing practices that originally emerged on the post/colonial academic margins in Canada and Australia. If anything, I want to argue that this grafted perspective gains the chance to approach the field from a different angle and hopefully circumvent some of the more entrenched positions that exist in ficto/criticism, too – even if that may risk alienating some proponents of fictocritical discourse whose work has greatly inspired me.

After all, I am not interested in theorising the ficto/critical in a reductive manner at the expense of its respective causes, but precisely on behalf of them, with a view to enhance the effectiveness of their ficto/critical strategies by sensitising their readership towards them. In this sense, this academic part of the study, which has been written for the further personal hope of earning a PhD, aims to advance the ficto/critical as a cause, which is not necessarily the same as partially advancing the respective causes that have engendered it, yet still entirely compatible with such a stance. In any case, my overriding aim is to improve our understanding of the ficto/critical so as to empower a greater number of textual agents to realise, engage, and develop ficto/critical practices, irrespective of whence and at which angle they are coming at it.

In this sense, too, my study hopes not to pose a threat to (unmarked) fictocriticism – or (hyphenated) ficto-criticism, for that matter – although it has sometimes found reasons to question these previous attempts at theorisation. In fact, my approach is partly motivated by the insight that (all) fictocriticism *qua* its territorialising textual medium is always already arrested and open to theorisation of any kind, and that it would hence be preferable for this to be done in a benevolent, even advancing, manner that serves and encourages its de/territorialising impetus and can legitimately hope to propel the ficto/critical forward into as yet unknown realms. Note that it is only in this vein that my approach is at times pre/post/erous enough to read its primary texts against their explicit self-perceptions. In those moments my textual conduct already avails itself of the insights its analyses yield, thus letting my own work be in/formed by the theory it proposes.

I guess my ultimate subjective objective here is not to re/territorialise the ficto/critical impetus, but rather to advance ficto/critical strategies as a general project – to write it on (not to write it up) while yet writing on it – simply because I enjoy reading and writing ficto/criticism and cherish its revolutionary potential. Now, *that* I would like to keep going – even if it were only by presenting a legitimate target for the ficto/critical to come should I fail.

Brief Recapitulation

After this comprehensive introductory advance on my theory, I would now like to briefly recapitulate the working definition of the ficto/critical that shall be developed, attested, and refined over the course of the following thesis.

According to what has been established so far, ficto/critical texts sometimes intersect a detached explanatory understanding (i.e. a poetics) of our textual practices with a subjective, captivating narrative or an enticing literary description (i.e. with an aesthetic). In terms of a strict academic division such practices hence intersect truth-representing discourses (e.g. philosophy) and truth-constituting discourses (e.g. literature), which may introduce some degree of epistemological uncertainty, prompting questions such as: What is the truth value of what I have just read? What is the exact epistemological status of this representation that has just been successfully communicated? How am I to relate to it? How am I to relate it to the world and my idiocultural reality? Is this reliable information, trustworthy outside its own immediate con/text, or is the reverse the case and it is 'only' a good read? Can this distinction even be sustained? And finally: What is the text's point of posing these questions, and – in the process – of exposing me to them?

For example, such performative experiences of epistemological uncertainty in the *ficto*-critical encounter, while textual communication, albeit frictioned, is yet left intact and fully functioning, aim to re/direct the individual reader's attention towards their own agency in the processes thus simultaneously under way (performatively) and under scrutiny (constatively). In a reflexive movement, this curious realisation makes perceptible to the reader their own performance as reading self, while still establishing the constative significance of the text. This trope – which I am later going to refer to as *ficto*-critical vector and twist – makes perceptible (*aisthesis*), from within, one's own agency in making a text work (*poiesis*) and endowing its meaning with sense. What becomes palpable, then, is how the truth-relation a reader assigns to a given text is dependent on the generic relation the reader establishes, or is allowed to establish, towards that text. *Ficto*-critical strategies indeed often friction this first sense of textual relating: to relate to a text meaningfully.

In this sense, the *ficto*-critical conflates the regulatory rules of academic disciplines and fictional discourses on the textual level in order to pinpoint the epistemological uncertainties that constitutively underlie textual representation and communication *per se*. Attention is thereby placed on the constitutive rules of the more basic generic distinction between truth-representing discourses (e.g. philosophy, the sciences) and truth-constituting discourses (e.g. literature) and their mutually constitutive interdependence. In other words, the *ficto*-critical highlights how the constitutive level of our textual practices – which I am later going to re/formulate in terms of the post-generic tropes of fiction, theory, and criticism – harbours a fictional kernel at the heart of truthful representation just as much as fictional discourse of necessity carries real life representational relevance. Such perspectives render *ficto*-critical commentary on our textual practices meta.

Where texts intersect their aesthetic side with a poetics of reading to ficto-*critical* effect, they present the experience of a problematic and self-reflexive reading performance that furthermore ties into those concerns that are simultaneously being raised constatively. This may put at stake the reader's understanding of the construction of meaning from a text (epistemology) in its practical significance for the wider discursive constructions of self and other (ethics). Such ficto-*critical* texts present a problematic experience of the act of read*ing* whose practical significance for issues such as identity formation, worlding, and othering is given direction by their narrative concerns. In this way, textual strategies that are motivated by experiences in specific con/texts might engage post/modern formal means to serve a general ficto/critical agenda against particular forms of representational domination. The uniting ficto/critical aim would be to inscribe such textual structures that could lead the reader towards realising their own ficto/critical discourse analysis both from their respectively positioned point of view and from within the textual practices under critique. Thus, in conjunction with highlighting the readerly agency at work a sense of potential – perhaps even a moral responsibility – to transform existing practices is conveyed. Ficto-*critical* strategies thus in fact problematise this second sense of textual relating: to relate to something else textually.

In light of the above, the aim of the present study is to formulate a theoretical description of ficto/critical textual forms and practices that emphasises central elements of a pervasive understanding of textual representation and communication. This underlying understanding shall help to relate the texts' subversion of generic forms to the embedded functions that these linguistic-discursive practices serve within wider social and cultural practices of discursive identity formation, othering and worlding. In this sense, ficto/criticism not only describes the mechanisms or structural relations at work in our practices of meaning, other, and self-formation when encountering a text, but also engenders an experience of these mechanisms and thus indicates our complicit role in them when it disrupts our smooth agency in the reproduction of dominant generic modes. Because it addresses this connection constatively as well as performatively, reading ficto/critical texts can generate a more im/mediately unsettling impact than conceptual description alone could provide. Foregrounding the in/formation of our generic textual practices in their function as formal blueprints for meaning and self-formation as well as for worlding and othering in textual encounters, the ficto/critical intends to engender both a new understanding and an im/mediate awareness among its readers of their own reading performance – ultimately, however, to engender ficto/critical reading practices.

Against the background of this advance, I would thus like to propose the following working definition:

> The name "ficto/criticism" gathers genre-conflating, -eschewing, or -defying, withal themselves non-generic, reading and writing practices that are conducive to yielding a self-reflexive meta-commentary on our generic and constitutive acts of textual representation and communication.
>
> As textual work, these reading and writing practices aim at generating an awareness that simultaneously comprises, firstly, an im/mediate experience of the present linguistic-discursive agent's relat*ing* to text, secondly, a mediated theoretical understanding thereof, as well as, thirdly, an ethico-political sense of this performative relation's practical significance and ramifications for our wider discursive formations of meaning, other, and self.

Afterthought

Additionally, I would like to just briefly mention that ideally – and beyond the scope of this thesis – the ensuing model of the (slashed) ficto/critical should eventually be exported and re/traced in other texts and approaches that instantiate its characteristic patterns. For example, although only a hunch at this stage, it could be productive to re/think the relationship between the generally post/modern and certainly *ficto*-critical approach of the L=A=N=G=U=A=G=E poets (e.g. Andrews/Bernstein 1984) and their comparatively marginal, yet decidedly more ficto-*critically* conscious and aware, follow-up movement New Narrative; for example, in the form of contributions such as Dodie Bellamy's *Pink Steam* (2004) or *Academonia* (2006). It would seem quite possible that the shift in emphasis between the two groups instantiates precisely the motivated additional step from the core textual relation (self – text) of the *ficto*-critical to the wider discursive relation ([self – text] – world) of the ficto-*critical* (Glück 2004).

In any case, pursuing this thrust to locate the relevance of the (slashed) ficto/critical in texts and approaches not previously subsumed under this name would thus supplement my internally directed consideration of previous theorisations of the fictocritical with its outwardly directed counterpart. In so doing we would not only tap the realm of future potential that is opened by the (slashed) ficto/critical, but also begin to treat the concept as our readerly stance towards text – which would practically underwrite the theoretical ambitions of this thesis.

2. Realising the *Ficto*-critical Vector & Twist

Frictioning Conceptual Work & Its Im/mediate Significance

A *ficto*-critical close reading of an exemplary text, which can precipitate some of the shifts and re/conceptualisations anticipated in the first chapter, is now in order. In this respect, Stephen Muecke's seminal essay "The Fall" (2008b) presents an especially powerful textual structure. Reading "The Fall" can provide a prime example of how *ficto*-critical textual strategies aim to exceed the realm of the purely textual when they highlight our practice of relat*ing* that constitutes an act of textual representation and communication. Firstly, between the text's explicit self-perception and my deviating reading the focal shifts prefigured in the first chapter shall be re/traced as much as followed through. Secondly, my reading shall extract central theoretical tropes for the wider theory of ficto/critical strategies to be developed over the course of the thesis. In any case, it should be noted that my approach to "The Fall" is in many respects already in/formed by the theory it will advance.

The goal of the following reading is to re/trace the combined tropes of the *ficto*-critical vector and twist. However, their performatively experiential nature must remain elusive to reproduction on the page, as their point emerges only in the act of reading. The initial task is to capture and explain in writing an experience that even though induced by its space of representation yet exceeds the written page from which it departs in reading. For the experiential remainder of such description there is no substitute but to read a text of this kind. The following close reading shall thus establish new concepts and re/deploy familiar ones in order to provide a frame of awareness that will let the tropes of the *ficto*-critical vector and twist emerge to better performative effect in future readings. More specifically, I am going to consider the text's own question "what has the reader felt, and then also, what has the reader learned" (Muecke 2008b: 23) from a somewhat unexpected angle. Controversially, perhaps, my reading thus proposes a different understanding of "The Fall" as ficto/critical than the text itself would suggest. Above all, my aim in so doing is to enhance the practice of *ficto*-critical *reading*.

2.1 PERFORMING "THE FALL" IN READING

"The Fall" consists of six fragments. Between them these well-wrought and skilfully interwoven – fragmented, yet neatly structured – sections present the simple overarching narrative of the narrator, Monsieur Mouche,[1] falling in love while comparing the experience, amongst other things, to reading. Importantly, as is signalled by the earlier title "The Fall: Fictocritical Writing" (Muecke 2002), the text simultaneously presents a definitional attempt of its own kind of writing practice. An enticing bit of self-reflexive textual theory is thus engaged by way of the narrative of falling in love. The text already performs its understanding of the (unmarked) fictocritical as an inextricable mixture of fiction and theory or criticism, as literarily argumentative.

At this point, it is worthwhile to briefly remember the textual structure of "The Fall". After the first very short fragment sets the minimal stage for the framing narrative of falling in love (Muecke 2008b: 18), the second section wastes no time to introduce fictocriticism as the leading topic of the text (ibid: 18-19). After this, the third fragment then establishes, through conversation, the newfound lovers' link to writing (ibid: 20-1), and the fourth passage contributes the further perspective of falling for deception (ibid: 21-2). Next in line, the fifth section draws attention back to texts and textual encounters (ibid: 22-3), before the whole textual structure then culminates in the multilayered analogy of the pitcher plant in the sixth and final section (ibid: 23-5) which carries the complex explanatory burden of its preceding subsections lightly, in a literarily aesthetic manner. To the reader, this dazzling as well as puzzling finale poses the question whether it all adds up on the narrative as well as theoretical levels – and, eventually, whether there is not perhaps a subtle point that exceeds the text's constative definition of (unmarked) fictocritical writing.

While the minimal narrative thread of falling in love is not the main point of "The Fall", the text's first accumulative, then culminating explanatory structure still rests on this storyline. Throughout, the narrative strikes the right balance between the description of subjective experiential occasions and the more theoretical branches of thought into which these lead. The essay's fictocritical point is provided at last by the imagery of the pitcher plant, which densely painted literary analogy ventures to explain the different theoretical threads that have wrought the structural build-up of "The Fall" as well as of its main *topos* of falling.

1 To avoid naïve identification with the author Stephen Muecke, I shall refer to the narrator as "Monsieur Mouche", as is humorously suggested in the text (2008b: 18).

The final passage of "The Fall" skilfully re/lays a picture of falling that pertains to the following layers: falling in love (ibid: 18, 20-1), falling for deception (ibid: 21-2, 23-5), falling into the loss of representation (ibid: 22), falling for an explanatory account (ibid: 24), falling into the immersing drum of a pitcher plant (ibid: 24), falling into the immersion of narrative (ibid: 24-5), and the impact of the experience, the memory, as well as the representation and communication of falling from a horse (ibid: 24). These widely varying layers all come to bear on the condensed metaphoric imagery that is at once an integral part of the narrative and an explanatory account of reading.

As a result, the textual structure of "The Fall" could also be described as constellational in the sense that a number of theoretical scenarios are shooting off from the narrative thread, around which they then revolve as interrelated elements. Their complex interrelatedness is then presented in the explanatory metaphor of the pitcher plant in the final passage. Thus, the narrative elements charge the imagery of the pitcher plant theoretically, but the big picture at the end does not fall into place smoothly. Neither is it elaborated in the text, nor can it easily be followed through consistently – both of which only enhances the text's enigmatic aura. And yet, I want to argue, the greatest merit of "The Fall" may in fact be the potential it creates as a skilfully 'broken' text, which goes well beyond its mere fragmentary form. In this sense, its *ficto*-critical potential derives precisely from a textual structure that does not add up without remainder in the textual equation it proposes.

While the preceding fragments thus contribute perspectives on the poetics of reading in terms of immersion, corporeality, and epistemology, the final metaphor of the pitcher plant becomes a most challenging and complex phenomenon in its own right, despite its deceptively simple textual appearance. Despite its perhaps ultimately incongruous analogy, it is precisely this textual strategy of a simultaneously narrative aesthetic and explanatory poetic account *thereof* that emerges as the text's great achievement of *ficto*-critical quality – albeit from a slightly different perspective than the text itself would have us believe.

"The Fall", I want to argue, paradigmatically exemplifies a textual structure that steers its reader towards realising a *ficto*-critical relation to the text. My suggestion is that there is a productive focus on the recipient's side to the essay that aims to highlight experientially, for each reader, their readerly performance that re/constitutes the textual relation as a singular relat*ing* between self and text in Derek Attridge's sense (2004: 63-4). Yet, while "The Fall" rightly demands the question of what a text does and can do *qua* text (2008b: 23), it remains mired in an earlier understanding of what makes writing (unmarked) fictocritical, despite the fact that its textual structure carries the potential to momentarily surpass this notion experientially (perception) and eventually overcome it theoretically (conception). Contrary to my readerly focussed approach, however, the text's self-perception as (unmarked) fictocritical remains centred around the writing agency. And yet, almost despite itself, the formidable textual structure of "The Fall" can be used to precipitate the perspectival shift of the initial *ficto*-critical part of the (slashed) ficto/critical.

On the one hand, there are the text's constative propositions for (unmarked) fictocritical texts that it meets *performatively*. On the other hand, there is its readerly potential for (slashed) ficto/critical textual *performances*. In a way, the task is to liberate the text's implicit potential from its explicit definition – to salvage its subtle, *ficto*-critical experiential potential from the text's outgoing attempt to explicitly contain the (unmarked) fictocritical form it displays. While the text's structure thus intimates a *ficto*-critical potential in the sense of this study, its attempt at performing, on the textual level, its more explicit definition yet remains behind this structural awareness. Hence, two conceptions of textual performativity shall frame my reading of "The Fall". Firstly, the performative text which already enacts what it proposes and, secondly, the textual performance by a reader who enacts the text's pre/scription. It is crucial to acknowledge that while "The Fall" constatively presents itself as a performative text, its potential for a specific kind of experientially self-reflexive performativity, which exceeds the purely textual realm, needs to be realised in read*ing*.

Note how the thin overarching narrative thread of Monsieur Mouche's experience of falling in love is paralleled by the text's striking final imagery and account of the fly that falls for, falls into, and finally gets fatally immersed in the pitcher plant. This is the text's central literary imagery that is furthermore presented in such a way that it simultaneously delivers a poetics of reading. Significantly, the metaphor of the pitcher plant thus yields a structural understanding of the epistemological mode in which it presents this understanding.

In deploying, firstly, explanatory considerations on reading with, secondly, a narrative of falling in love and, thirdly, a structural metaphor that lets these explanatory and narrative strands intersect in the same imagery, "The Fall" provides at the same time, firstly, a distanced account, secondly, an immersing narrative and, thirdly, a simultaneously beautiful as well as explanatory description. All of which opens up a significantly new perspective on a text's otherwise generic referential status as either fiction or non-fiction. As poetics and aesthetics are thus brought to coincide, the generic conflation referenced in the beginning of "The Fall" as characteristic of (unmarked) fictocritical texts (ibid: 18) is inextricably exemplified by the text itself. However, if the deeper tropical implications of the deployed structural metaphor are sounded out, there will emerge a degree of self-contradiction in the understanding *of* (unmarked) fictocritical texts *by* the particular fictocritical text that is "The Fall". At that point, the current approach shall aim at bringing the implicit textual potential of Muecke's piece into its own by revising some of its more explicit understandings in terms of the (slashed) ficto/critical.

In order to achieve this pre/post/erous aim, I shall first follow the text into the explicitly suggested conception of its (unmarked) fictocritical self before then casting a different light onto the same scene from the blind spot of its performative textual potential that would beg to differ. Just to be clear, there are two central explanatory accounts in "The Fall". On the one hand, the text accounts for (unmarked) fictocritical writing practices, which it predominantly addresses as a matter of speaking positions, generic conflation, and the performative text. But, on the other hand, it also delivers an im/mediately striking account of our reading practices in general. This is the point of the structural metaphor of the pitcher plant which, in due time, will lead us to the central tropes of the (slashed) ficto/critical vector and twist.

Now, the following reading of "The Fall" seeks to bridge the gap between these two accounts. The perhaps counter-intuitive move of my approach will be to give primacy to the far-reaching implications that flow from the *readerly* account of our (ficto/critical) textual practices. Yet the task is also to avoid a mere privileging of the 'new' readerly over the 'old' writerly focus. This shall be achieved by re/conceiving of the apparent dichotomy on the level of the conditions of the im/possibility of the textual work – conditions, as we shall see shortly, that do not usually emerge as such from the all too familiar writerly perspective that is mediated via a text. Firstly, however, the self-perception and definition of the text shall be extrapolated. Secondly, the shift in perspective, which this study suggests, needs to be introduced and corroborated by a close reading. Thirdly, the implications of this paradigm shift shall then be elaborated and the central ficto/critical tropes of the vector and twist refined further.

"The Fall" as Textually Performative

"The Fall" is definitely a performative text in the traditional sense that it already conforms to its propositions in proposing them. In other words, it already enacts (performative) what it describes (constative). After the minimal stage setting of the first section (ibid: 18), the second fragment provides a definitional introduction to (unmarked) fictocritical writing practices (ibid: 18-9). These definitional characteristics are clearly met by the essay itself, whose textual form thus performatively displays what its propositional content constates. This first kind of performativity at work in "The Fall" presents a *static* kind of textual performativity.

As captured by these qualifications, however, there is something inherently paradoxical about such a performative text, because the processual notion of performance is evoked for something as static, even rigid, as an inscribed text – which, on its own, does very little. From an unproblematic angle, of course, this is the same kind of performativity displayed by the word "**green**", which lets its announcement of the colour coincide with the display of said colour in its textual form; or the performativity constituted by the sentence "This sentence consists of six words." While these examples can be said to display or constitute a static kind of performativity, it seems slightly more problematic to say that they enact or perform something in the *processual* sense of performance.

From this latter angle – which is to the point of this chapter – the first kind of static textual performativity misses, even obstructs, the second kind of processual readerly performativity in the textual relation which is thus really a textual relat*ing*. To further anticipate this second sense of performativity at the heart of "The Fall" we could say that processual readerly performativity consists in the recipient's enacting of the textual pre/scription. This understanding would thus restore the temporal performance aspect to our considerations of textual performativity. And precisely this kind of processual readerly performativity is epitomised by "The Fall", whose central trope of falling is, after all, a figurative approach to the readerly act.

For the purposes of this chapter, however, it will still be advisable to start with the static textual performativity of "The Fall", which is expressed in its self-reflexively definitional second section (ibid: 18-9). After carefully examining the text's perception of itself as a performative fictocritical text in this sense, we shall then have to return to the above distinction of textual performativities in order to follow this less explicit textual potential. Because "The Fall" actually engages both kinds of performativity, this enigmatic text, like no other, can bring into contrastive relief the perspectival shift this thesis aims for. Hence, against the text's explicit conception of itself as (unmarked) fictocritical, its more figuratively achieved *ficto*-critical potential shall come into focus in the subsequent reading.

What then, in more detail, is the understanding of (unmarked) fictocritical writing proposed in the second fragment? In order to illustrate the skilfully wrought textual performativity of "The Fall" we shall, firstly, consider its proposed quest for non-universalising speaking positions that, on the one hand, allow for the particular writerly position to emerge in the text and, on the other hand, allow the reader to re/trace the way that leads up to these propositions. Secondly, we shall turn towards the more dominant self-reflexively definitional focus of "The Fall" that lies on the generic conflation of fiction with criticism and theory, of literature with philosophy, of truth-constituting with truth-referencing discourses. Thirdly, we shall have to examine, in particular, how Muecke here formulates this conflation of generic principles in the Deleuzian terms of concept and percept.

Speaking Positions

First of all, "The Fall" not only proposes to collapse the detached subject into the text but has already accomplished this feat. Where story and argument become indistinguishable a new kind of generic ground *between* is opened. The intersection of literary and philosophical discourses, for example, allows for such otherwise generically precluded textual practices as the experimentation with textual speaking positions. Such explorations have, traditionally, been especially dear to fictocritical writing of feminist provenance. But more generally, the appearance of literary subjectivity in the generic (con)text of critically distanced arguments can be produced purposively to sometimes unsettling effect.

As the second fragment of "The Fall" maintains, fictocriticism takes issue with presenting a certain view from a withdrawn speaking position that assumes the authority of a generic form to vouch for its content (ibid: 18-9). By contrast, the fictocritical text also contains the positioning and experiences on which the presented view rests. Muecke reflects this as follows: "One common effect of [the fictocritical] was the collapsing of the 'detached' and all-knowing subject *into* the text, so that his (or your) performance as a writer includes dealing with a problem all contemporary writers must face: *how the hell did I get here?*" (ibid: 18, original emphases) What distinguishes (unmarked) fictocritical writing, thus understood, is the writerly subjectivity that enters the text and eschews a generically assumed, distanced – almost withdrawing – speaking position.

Relating to the same point, Muecke also makes the following further suggestion:

> "Faced with masses of ways of knowing things coming from all points of the compass, the contemporary writer asks what now can legitimate his or her point of view, and then tends not to just *add to* existing views of the world, but traces a path (which the reader will follow, avidly of course) showing how we got to this position, and what is at stake." (ibid: 19, original emphasis)

Including a subjective narrative of attaining the knowledge presented in the fictocritical text not only allows to circumspectly mark the author's own positioning, which is preferable over a distanced and – allegedly – objective critical stance, but also requires the reader to follow and judge the textual lead. With regards to speaking positions a twofold (fictocritical) strategy thus emerges: firstly, to circumspectly mark the speaking position from which the text is composed; secondly, to create a composition, a benevolent pre/scription, that invites the reader round to attain the insights of this point of view herself in reading.

Firstly, on one level this collapsing of the critical subject into the text is wrought from the appearance of Monsieur Mouche as the narrator, whose name is a mildly ridiculing cognate of the writer's name (ibid: 18). Yet, paradoxically, this also serves as a distancing strategy. At the same time as subjective experience and positioning are admitted into the text, this admission yet allows for a subtle break between writer and narrator. Above all, marking the subjective speaking position in the text has the post-critical impetus to remove the writerly positionality from its unassailable high ground of claiming general pro/positions. To collapse the subject into the text, and thereby admit subjectivity into the equation, may leave the account more vulnerable and less author/itative, but in turn it becomes more engaging and co/operative as well. The project of justifying a certain position is thus enlarged from the aspiration of an unassailable account to a subjectively appealing and circumspectly exposed positioning of the presentation. The fictocritical writer hopes to invite her reader along a continuing path, rather than summoning her from a final state of insight.

Thus, part of the idea to conflate the generic division between the critical or theoretical treatise and a more literarily inspired, fictionalised account is to bring subjectivity into play, not only as a subjective account but as a circumspectly marked and acknowledged subjectivity that comes from a certain perspective, positioning, and outlook, all of which are grounded in experience. In this sense, a fictocritical text would aim to also deliver a narrative of how the narrator got round to the knowledge that is the subject of the text.

Secondly, however, the problem is as much of a readerly as it is of a writerly nature. To be able to re/trace the path to knowledge, to follow the path of a laid out thought experiment to attain a certain understanding, not only gives the text a less dominating attitude, but opens the subjectivity of the experience in the recipient's direction. It thus shifts emphasis from the presentation of a theoretical construction to its engagement and exercise on the reader's side. The fictocritical writer thus pre/scribes a subjective reading experience to the reader, who is encouraged to take the argument, which she also receives in the process, on that basis. Once the desire for an omniscient critical subject withdrawing in the textual account is removed, the motivation for a certain perspective or subjective examples of experience can be admitted into the picture, whose textual frame can now present its motivational objective together with its propositional subject matter.

While this kind of strategy collapses the critical distance of the speaking position, it opens to adjudication not only whether one accepts the knowledge presented but also how that view was obtained.

Such strategies ensure that a fictocritical textual rendition becomes less of a manifesto that hits its reader over the head with general pro/positions – much like the General of which Deleuze and Guattari warn (1978: 17-8, 25). Instead, ficto-critical writing invites the reader to critically assess what she encounters in light of the particular positioning from within which it was motivated. The readerly faculty of positional empathy is thus exercised while a particular – subjective and narrative – as well as a general – objective and argumentative – statement is considered. New entry points for the revision of ingrained views may thus be engaged by a fictocritical text's narrative lure as well as by its critical reasoning. Precisely such a path, I want to suggest, is laid out for the reader of "The Fall" by its fragmentary textual structure which is winding its entertaining way between the minimal but universally accessible narrative of falling in love and the various theoretical considerations into which it branches off, accumulating considerable explanatory burden along the way that is yet playfully met by the cumulative final passage and the readerly experience it pre/scribes.

Thus conforming to the framework established in the text's second fragment, "The Fall" indeed presents a speaking position that avoids the generality of the detached, all-knowing subject and marks its own speaking position as the subject of as much as subject to certain experiences that have led to the insights presented in the text. Furthermore, these experiences and musings are now laid out in the textual composition for the reader to re/trace. In this sense, "The Fall" both makes its speaking positioning visible and pre/scribes a performative read*ing* experience that pertains to its self-reflexive propositional insights.

Generic Conflation

Importantly, "The Fall" is also textually performative with regards to generic conflation. The text itself qualifies as one of "those 'critical' inventions which belong to literature while deforming its limits", as Muecke cites Derrida (2008b: 18). Its combined framing narrative – fictionalised, yet rich in subjective affective passages – branches off left and right into theoretical musings, all of which culminates in the final, figuratively expository image of the pitcher plant. Already instantiating its own understanding of the (unmarked) fictocritical, the generic ingredients of "The Fall" thus mutually undercut each other. The text's fictional aspects are endowed with counter-intuitive relevance for its theoretical argument, while its philosophical dimensions are rendered in a surprisingly literary manner.

The theme of generic distance and its collapse in fictocriticism thus not only pertains to speaking positions, as the following passage concisely establishes:

> "When criticism is well-written, and fiction has more ideas than usual, the distinction between the two starts to break down. It is a little crisis because criticism can't be relied upon 'to keep its distance', and fiction can't be relied upon to stay in its imaginary and sometimes politically irrelevant worlds." (ibid: 19)

While in this bi/directional process of generic pollution both genres take on the characteristic traits of the other, their generic function becomes less clear even though the texts remain fully functional as texts – only not in a generically predictable way. This unruly effect of the fictocritical leads into the much-heralded grey area of the generic in-between, a realm where unforeseen lines of flight can emerge in writing experiments. Hence, just as the distanced critical subject and the insulation of fictional worlds serve certain functions, so too are their deliberate erosion and collapse motivated practices.

Closer to home for this current exercise in literary criticism, "The Fall" further specifies the generic divide that fictocritical practices purposively disregard as follows: "The whole artifice of literary criticism was built up to do one thing really: to unmask the secrets of art. And the fiction was always there re-enchanting the world by putting on the beautiful masks again and again." (ibid: 19) *In other words*, literary criticism doubles the point of the literary text when it accounts for the actual significance of experienced immersion and encountered fictional worlds. Paradoxically, literary criticism thus writes non-fiction on fiction, while literary fictions have non-fictional effects in our actual world.

While the truth-referencing faculty of criticism thus invades the realm of fiction and the truth-constituting faculty of fiction invades the realm of the real world by re/presenting its concepts and facticity fictitiously, fictocriticism aims to do both at the same time: to render a fictionalised account in such a way that its conceptual structure regains real life relevance. "The Fall" achieves this when the narrative and aesthetic metaphor of the pitcher plant is harnessed to both exercise and explain the kind of attraction and immersion texts can provide in reading. And thus – just like his approving assessment of Derrida has it – Muecke himself is "telling stories while making his philosophical arguments" (ibid: 18). It is what they both do best in their respective inimitable ways. "The Fall" epitomises this by making its literary and explanatory sides indistinguishable when it presents, in writing, an aesthetically pleasing description of the pitcher plant that serves the narrative thread of falling in love as much as it functions as an explanatory account of, simultaneously, the pitcher plant, falling in love, and reading.

This formal intersection in the final passage of "The Fall", which exemplifies its earlier definition of (unmarked) fictocriticism, thus powerfully displays a static textual performativity. This initial claim to textual performativity consists in the manner in which "The Fall" illustrates the trope of falling, because it conforms to the text's explicit understanding of (unmarked) fictocritical writing. Yet this static account leaves a considerable remainder in the experience that reading "The Fall" furthermore has in store for the perceptive recipient. As we shall see shortly, the text not only illustrates but operates the trope of falling so that its readers enact a kind of fall*ing* in read*ing* – wherein lies another claim to textual performativity, because the constative textual object here is the readerly performance under way.

Percept & Concept

In the following passage, "The Fall" moves from generic conflation in terms of referential status into a slightly trickier philosophical distinction that it yet aligns to the broader fault lines of the generic divide:

> "Criticism uses concepts and fiction percepts. Philosophy, according to Deleuze, is about the invention of new concepts which have the abstraction and flexibility to be taken up and used by others. Art, on the other hand, invents percepts, monumental perceptions if you like, which are just *there*, either they work or they don't. They can stand alone. You can use someone else's percept, but it will be an imitation. And percepts and concepts chase each other around successively masking and unmasking." (ibid: 19, original emphasis)

Not only are concepts and percepts here introduced as generic markers, but as such they furthermore enact the equally generic principles of masking and unmasking. With regards to the generic conflation at the heart of fictocritical writing "The Fall" thus, firstly, suggests conceptual insights by way of generating percepts as well as, secondly, simultaneously unmasking and masking textual movements with regards to its subject matter. In terms of textual performativity, of course, this appears to be precisely what "The Fall" ultimately attempts in the structural metaphor – or (post/modern) allegory – of the pitcher plant, which intersects a *conceptual* understanding of the reading process with the aesthetically capturing trope of a fly falling into a pitcher plant as its *percept*. The text's – if not monumental then certainly perceptive and momentous – percept thus carries the conceptual power to explain readerly attraction to text. While the aesthetic description of the pitcher plant (re)enchants the textual object, it yet unmasks the reading process under way, which it makes its textual object.

Before we reach the final stage of the structural metaphor, however, the text rides the dichotomy between percept and concept some more – to sometimes puzzling effect. Going by the above quote, the percept is, on the one hand, characterised as independent from almost all substrate including the writer, text, and reader, but on the other hand it does seem to have its roots in *someone's* "monumental perceptions". Furthermore, a percept is somehow retained independently from the original perception on which it is based. Yet while it thus gains an autonomous life of its own, it still remains endlessly fascinating *for* individuals.

Was the focus so far geared towards the relation between percepts and concepts in different kinds of texts, their role in direct real life encounters is then also referenced – making the equation of the analogy confusingly complex:

> "The smile is a percept, it is not *in* you or *at* me. Nobody invented the smile, we are the bodies in whose relationship the smile, as an idea and affect, can manifest itself. Can I leave it at that? No, […] I want to know what your smile meant, by which I mean, what concept can I attach to it?" (ibid: 20, original emphases)

As before, the independence and im/mediacy of the percept in perception is emphasised, yet its conceptualisation is not as im/mediately available in the real life encounter. Thus, an experiential quality, an affective impact here precedes the desire for conceptual recognition of the percept's instantiation. But this is very different from textual encounters, where precisely the reverse is the case. In textual encounters the affective impact is triggered through a conceptual understanding of the text.

The magic of "The Fall" is thus grounded in the fact that texts necessarily deal in concepts *before* they can deal in percepts, that any percept they carry is already presented via concepts. Its sleight of hand is to pass over the different order of succession of concept and percepts in im/mediate real life encounters and mediating textual encounters. While Monsieur Mouche tells his attractive student that "[y]our succession of masks outstrips my unmasking, so that by the next day I have understood nothing and you have become a fantasy" (ibid: 20), the same order can indeed be outstripped, in turn, by a kind of writing that lets the same concepts that constitute a percept explain the operation of that percept.

Breaking with a Broken Text

The affective attraction of falling in love at first sight in a real life encounter thus presents a very different epistemological and communicative situation from the textual encounter and its potential for affective attraction. While textual affect is conceptually mediated experience, the attraction of a flirting lover is experientially im/mediate. The primary experience of the flirtatiously immersing real life encounter needs to be conceptualised after the event, but the textual experience thereof may already be delivered in the very concepts that comprise its immersing percept/ions. While it does present a real task to conceptualise the love at first sight encounter after the event, the textual encounter always already consists in accessing concepts that (in)form its mediated experience. Textual perception always already comes in the epistemological mode of "knowing that". Hence, the same situation does not emerge for both kinds of encounter and, as a result, the analogy of "The Fall" is slightly incongruous.

When Muecke returns to the question of concept and percept in the post/modern allegory of the pitcher plant, he suggests that both Monsieur Mouche's falling in love and the fly's falling for the plant is different from reading a text "[b]ecause [in writing] we can attach a concept to a percept" (ibid: 24). But this implies that we could in principle write or read a percept without attaching it to concepts, when the conceptual side of writing is, in fact, the condition of the possibility of its affective impact. Hence, this kind of intersection can hardly serve as a distinguishing feature of fictocritical texts. At this point, I want to suggest, the text breaks because the logic of its argument is no longer in tune with the logic of its structural metaphor, whose distinctively striking quality is not wrought from this static kind of textual performativity.

Also, Muecke's understanding of the interplay between percept and concept commits him to an unnecessarily strong theory of textual affect, which his ingenious textual architecture does not require to perform its magic. Any affective impact conveyed *in writing* will necessarily be triggered by the concepts thus encountered. When Muecke asks, "So what kind of capture does the literary text perform, when it is nothing much more than black tracks?" (ibid: 22), he lays his finger on the issue precisely. It is *not* the im/mediate perception of the text as a structure of black marks that causes its main affective impact but the conceptual structure that the text mediates. A text's affective side is conveyed through the needle's eye of its presentation of concepts. Writing creates affect through the presentation of concepts, not im/mediately.

As a result of this misrecognition of two kinds of affective encounter the text breaks. Firstly, in the negative sense, the text *breaks down*, or falls apart, because its conceptual side is theoretically flawed. On the one hand, its conceptual side does not add up with regards to a theory of textual affect that it presupposes without mention. On the other hand, and as a consequence of this, the idea of "The Fall" as a performative text with regards to its theory of concept and percept does not take off either. The analogy between falling in love, the pitcher plant, and reading fails to identify the specific kind of intersection that makes itself fictocritical because the analogy draws on situations that are different in precisely the respect that is at stake, namely the im/mediacy of their affective impact.

At the same time as the grand finale presents the textual form that would conform to the text's own ideas of the (unmarked) fictocritical – the intersection of fiction and non-fiction, of aesthetics and poetics, of the concept/ual and percept/ive – the central significance of the medium in the act of mediation emerges. In the event of encountering a percept different communicative parameters apply for textual and vis-à-vis encounters. Especially that we can repeatedly fall for percept/ive immersion, that "in writing [...] we can do it over and over" (ibid: 24), is indebted to the constitutively distancing medium. In fact, the medial condition of the possibility of our textual practices pre/structures the reading situation in a way that constitutes the experiential difference between immersed perception and textual percept.

The medial parameters underwrite the communicative situation of textual representation in such a way that, firstly, a percept emerges here only ever in conceptual terms to begin with and that, secondly, repetition (in [experiential] difference) is a constitutive possibility. Note, however, that within these parameters "The Fall" still manages to liberate the textual potential for intersections of concept and percept from further generic pre/scriptions. Its only mistake is to conceive of this achievement as specifically fictocritically wrought when, really, it cleverly exploits a constitutive medial characteristic of textual representation and communication.

Having phrased this criticism in perhaps unjustly stark terms, it is now time to retract a bit and re/member the text's considerable remaining potential. What makes Muecke's "The Fall" so special as a *ficto*-critical text, I want to argue, is something else. In a static performative sense, the imagery of the pitcher plant attaches conceptual significance to the percept of its aesthetic description. In fact, however, it achieves this with the notable extra twist that in textually accessing the conceptual explanatory side by way of accessing its aesthetic textual rendition the reader simultaneously performs the subject of the account. And this presents another kind of textual performativity in the sense that the text pre/scribes both a reading performance and experience.

Therefore, we shall have to re/trace the reading experience, as it is pre/scribed by this text, very carefully in order to re/formulate the explicit definitions in "The Fall" from a slightly shifted angle. Muecke rightly claims special status for his essay because he manages to intersect a certain conceptualisation with the main percept of the text. Yet, what I believe to be so special about this aspect of his text may be better expressed in terms of the unusual self-reflexivity of this intersection:

"The Fall" renders a conceptualisation of the readerly act in terms of the concepts by which it simultaneously presents its percept. It conveys a poetics of the immersion of reading by means of the same terms that immerse its reader. In making the performance of the individual subject accessing text its textual object, "The Fall" attaches self-reflexive conceptual significance to the rendition of its percept. All of which also enhances its performativity from a static textual kind to the processual and experiential textual performance of the reader.

Secondly, then, there is also a much more positive sense in which the misrecognition of two kinds of affective encounters *breaks open* a different perspective onto the text's striking performativity. While all the fragments of this purposively broken text are still up in the air and may just fall into place, I shall therefore attempt to re/configure the elements of Muecke's textual constellation anew. As the textual structure itself seems to imply, I would like to re/conceive of "The Fall" and its *ficto*-critical practice with a stronger medial focus. This understanding shall exceed the text's (unmarked) fictocritical self-perception in terms of speaking positions, generic conflation, and the intersection of concept and percept, and re/locate these key ideas in terms of a readerly emphasis, a meta-generic perspective, and the im/mediacy of textual immersion. The aim in what follows, will thus be to account for the text's im/mediately striking side while re/deploying its own terminology with a perspectival shift towards the significance of the textual medium at the heart of (slashed) ficto/critical practices.

The Fragmentary Spin of a Parable Flight

Now that the text is revealed as broken, its elements are up in the air. They are fragments that drift like so many things on a parable flight just before the controlled fall. At this point, my current reading has reached the crucial phase in-between gravitational fields during which the text's discursive constellation may find itself re/configured. While the elements of "The Fall" are suspended in mid-air, midway on the parable flight of my reading, chances are they will gravitate in new directions by themselves and start to spin. In the following, I am going to try to pick up some of these directions and follow their drift in order to precipitate, perhaps, a perspectival shift that can not only account for this textually structured fall but reasonably hope to propel its idiosyncratic momentum forwards.

The text itself steers its reader onto this path by attaching the percept of the pitcher plant to the concept of falling into the immersion of textual representation and communication. The conceptually unmasking aspect of the text is thus inextricably linked to the literarily masking percept of the fall, which finally carries the explanatory weight of all previous subsections. But reading "The Fall" we are rapidly taken to dizzying conceptual heights on the grounds of very enjoyable, yet also very little textual basis. Entering the final passage in free flight, this inert explanatory burden is playfully propelled into the image of the pitcher plant. In the final section the text changes gear while still carrying all the momentum of its earlier velocity. But although the incongruent analogy between an im/mediate and a textual encounter breaks the text's explicit self-conception, we need not feel left high and dry. As things begin to spin, the task lies with the reader, to pick up the pieces in mid-air and thus cushion the fall from the pre/scribed parable – to re/configure the constellation and change perspective. Yet before re/conceiving of the text's constellational arrangement anew, we first need to register the different directions in which the fragments themselves gravitate mid-flight.

Firstly, a potential shift towards a readerly focus lies dormant in the text's concern with writerly speaking positions. As the issue is introduced with only a bracketed wink to the readerly act, focal attention is clearly on the writer who "traces a path (which the reader will follow, avidly of course)" (ibid: 19). Likewise, the fictocritically collapsed speaking position is introduced first and foremost as a writerly concept (ibid: 18). However, the textual structure of "The Fall" also warrants a strong readerly focus with regards to the distancing devices that texts engage not only generically but constitutively – and that is especially: *medially*. In this respect, Muecke's writing pre/scribes an itinerary that leads elsewhere than the text openly suggests. This line of flight may take counter-intuitive turns and run against the official course, but it does carry some insights into collapsing the *readerly* distance of textual practices. Hence, in this respect, I shall propose a readerly as well as medial focus in my re/configuration of "The Fall" as *ficto*-critical.

Secondly, the text's concern with conflating textual practices between genres actually harbours the potential for a perspectival shift onto the meta-generic level – and, specifically, onto the medial conditions of the im/possibility of genres. "The Fall" bestows focal attention on our text-medial practices in order to explain our text-generic practices. In this sense, what is im/mediately striking about the imagery of the pitcher plant is not that it makes explanatory and aesthetic discourses indistinguishable but that it makes our textual practices under way the subject of this literary exposition. In terms of the generically aligned principles of masking and unmasking, the *ficto*-critically rendered form of the pitcher plant aims for a textual mask that effects an unmasking of its own masquerading. From the readerly point of view, this introduces an im/mediately self-reflexive aspect into the textual equation under way – the conception of which changes considerably as a consequence. "The Fall" intimates this shift when Monsieur Mouche asks, "what kind of capture does the literary text perform, when it is nothing much more than black tracks?" (ibid: 22) But unfortunately it does not pursue the crucial medial aspect, which can bring into relief the difference of im/mediate perceptional and mediated readerly immersion. Hence, my re/reading is going to suggest a text-medial meta-perspective onto our reading and writing practices, rather than a focus on the generic between on the textual level.

Thirdly, the idea of intersecting concept and percept harbours the potential to produce, in singular fashion, a shift towards the im/mediate aspects of textually mediated experience. Despite the breaking point of its static textual performativity mentioned above, the final passage of the pitcher plant still creates a special affect for its readers in the process of their textual performance. As we have seen, "The Fall" capitalises on mapping the foregrounded generic difference between percept and concept onto the difference between im/mediacy and mediation. *In writing*, the necessarily conceptual presentation of the percept "pitcher plant" can be composed in such a way that it simultaneously conceptualises the constitutive mode of accessing it *in reading*. The focus of the text's content thus shifts to the textual performance that brings it to life. In this manner, "The Fall" reverses direction and produces im/mediate referential awareness of the readerly act necessarily under way. It indicates to the linguistic-discursive agent at work the im/mediate side to textual mediation. Hence, my reading is going to re/trace how "The Fall" performatively illumines, from within, the im/mediate conditions of the possibility of textually mediated experience.

Taken together, these three structurally implicit aspects break open the textual level to include each particular readerly performance of "The Fall" in its textual object. They mark a shift from understanding a textual structure as inherently (unmarked) fictocritical, by virtue of its in-between form, to understanding a textual structure as strategically deployed to trigger *ficto*-critical effects. These effects would then suggest re/locating the crucial between-ness of the (slashed) ficto/critical on the constitutive level of performing the text-medial relation rather than essentially within the generically hybrid text. "The Fall" deploys its structural metaphor precisely to illumine and illuminate this shift. The passage of the pitcher plant is a textual structure that not only presents an understanding of the readerly act in the textual work under way, but one that can at the same time induce an experiential awareness of this readerly performance – to make its constative side hit home, as it were.

Along these textual lines of flight, "The Fall" lets its reader perform the trope of falling. The pre/scribed journey of this final textual passage manages to collapse the performative distance between reader and text (in addition to the critical distance between writer and text). In reading about the fly falling into the pitcher plant, the reader falls for the immersing aspects of a text that yet explains this very process. By self-reflexively short-circuiting the expository and enchanting aspects of the textual relation, "The Fall" thus activates an im/mediate experience of readerly performance. Such is the great *ficto*-critical potential of the essay's textual structure which my reading aims to bring into its own by activating its readerly experiential remainder in the text-interpretive equation.

Take-Off: A Readerly Line of Flight

Whereas "The Fall" draws explicit attention to how fictocriticism collapses the writerly speaking position into the text (ibid: 18), its textual structure is also designed to collapse the readerly distance in the act of textual mediation. This implicit readerly focus, I want to argue, endows the essay with the im/mediately striking characteristic that distinguishes it as an exemplary *ficto*-critical text. As the reader follows (avidly of course) the pre/scription of "The Fall", the self-reflexive experience of that reading performance identifies – even interpellates – her as textual agent in an un-mediated manner. The text's structural metaphor makes the process of readerly immersion its subject matter, which the reader thus cannot but encounter from within. The structural trick is that in accessing the text's constative account of readerly immersion, the reader is always already performatively undergoing this experience.

In this manner, "The Fall" both illuminates the readerly act by depicting it in terms of the fly and the pitcher plant and illumines it by performatively highlighting the im/mediate side of textual mediation under way. Firstly, the conceptual insights yielded by the reading process are here concerned with their own condition of possibility, namely the readerly act. Secondly, to realise this *in actu* performs a somewhat counter-intuitive trope, which I would like to introduce as the *ficto*-critical *vector*. To realise the relevance of what is textually mediated for the readerly act of mediation under way creates a kind of im/mediately striking short-circuitry that in fact reverses the direction of referentiality. Instead of leading into the conceptual realm of the text's proposition, the im/mediacy of such special reading occasions refers right back to the reader, and thus into the extra-textual present of the singular and processual read*ing* frame/work always currently under way.

This reversal of referential direction by the *ficto*-critical vector means that the text's unique potential for im/mediate affective impact is not grounded in readerly identification, empathy, or immersion in the intradiegetic goings-on. All of these may indeed occur, but its fragmentary nature and minimal characterisation do not especially favour Muecke's story in this respect – other texts are much more suitably composed to mediate these kinds of affect. Rather, what makes "The Fall" so special is not the way in which it describes its intradiegetic events, but the way in which it pre/scribes the event of reading to curl back in on itself. Its striking affective side is not grounded in the experience of mediated events so much as in the im/mediate experience of the act of textual mediat*ing*. This distinguishes "The Fall" as *ficto*-critical in the sense of the present study.

The intradiegetic theory of textual affect, which Muecke suggests by saying that "[a text's] mode of capture is multiple and sensational" (ibid: 23), thus falls back behind the crucial medial point implied by his earlier question "So what kind of capture does the literary text perform, when it is nothing much more than black tracks?" (ibid: 22) By the same token, Muecke formulates that "[t]he pitcher, like the line of text, is a one-way zone" (ibid: 24), which leads into the immersion of text and plant respectively. While Muecke identifies the medial condition of the im/possibility of immersing textual mediation, his explicit assertion of "multiple and sensational" textual capture yet prioritises what is mediated in the process. Note, however, that a text's capture is indeed "multiple" in the sense that performative immersion in the readerly act is the condition of the (im)possibility of "sensational" immersion in the text's affective propositional content. Ingenuously, the textual structure of "The Fall" steers its reader towards just this realisation.

There is a concomitant interpretation of the sentence "[w]e fall for the one who resembles a flower" (ibid: 25) that has no parallel scenarios for the fly and the lover. As we fall for the flowers of rhetoric and their metaphoric movements, we have always already fallen for the textual medium and the movements of its constitutive metaphoricity. In light of this, Muecke's conclusion that "to know the structure of the plant (or the text) as a concept, is to be able, incredibly, to climb out again" (ibid: 25) seems slightly misguided. The possibility "to climb out again" comes with the constitutive conceptual distance of mediation, rather than with the writerly ability to "attach a concept to a percept" (ibid: 24). Likewise, rather than the ability for their combination and conjunction, the different modes of access to the percepts and concepts involved create the difference between the existential immersion of fly and lover and the reader's immersion in mediation.

So when the text asks, "How are the insects snared by this carnivorous plant?" (ibid: 23), to which it provides the answer that "[t]hey are attracted, visually no doubt" (ibid: 23), then this creates a remarkable contrast with the earlier question "So what kind of capture does the literary text perform, when it is nothing much more than black tracks?" (ibid: 23) Almost against the highly curious importance of the visual in reading, this contradiction sets up the difference between experiential immersion and the immersion of mediation. Of course it is precisely not visually that we are attracted by texts. The deception of the plant is markedly different from that of the text, which does not even attempt to pass for the real thing – as perhaps a naïve view of painting could argue. At the same time, however, we are visually immersed in the act of reading. Any affection triggered by a text has to go through this needle's eye of the linguistic-discursive before it can rouse feelings in response, such as empathy, excitement, or attraction.

Thus highlighting the performative frame/work of textual immersion, a strong readerly and medial focus lies at the heart of what makes "The Fall" *ficto*-critical in the sense of an im/mediately striking read that collapses the distance of mediation in the textual act by bringing the mediated textual subject matter to coincide with the readerly act that is always already presently under way. This preposterous attempt at readerly short-circuitry skilfully creates the potential for realising an im/mediately striking *ficto*-critical vector in relation to "The Fall".

Dizzying Heights: A Meta-Generic Vista

Whereas "The Fall" proposes the grey area between genres as the productive space of fictocritical writing, its pre/scribed itinerary departs from this generic locus between towards a meta-perspective on our textual practices. In fact, generic conflation is specifically *ficto*-critical if it facilitates this perspectival shift onto the meta-level. The point of the intersected literary and theoretical directions in the imagery of the pitcher plant is not only its hybrid nature but the fact that this simultaneously masking and unmasking textual form is self-reflexively concerned with our textual practices. By way of the pitcher plant the final passage is an immersing read that conveys an understanding of textual immersion. Its textual percept carries conceptual significance for a structural understanding of how it works. This self-reflexive meta-commentary indeed turns the pitcher plant into a structural metaphor, whose aesthetic harbours a poetics of its aesthetics.

Thus intersecting literary and theoretical discourses in the same imagery the perspective does not remain between two generic textual spheres, but can elevate the reader onto the vantage point of a meta-generic perspective. The *ficto*-critical point is not to enliven a generically dry text with metaphoric language use or an enticing little anecdote. Much rather, the *ficto*-critical point is to performatively illumine and aesthetically as well as conceptually illuminate, at the same time, a poetics of our textual practices. The trope of structural metaphor, which engages its aesthetics to explain their poetics, presents one textual strategy to achieve this *ficto*-critical effect. Because the textual operations of "The Fall" constitute both the act of its masking as well as the object of its unmasking, the text manages to turn the alleged generic chasm between the two into a constitutive chiasm on the meta-level of our textual practices.

Consider at this point, again, the enigmatic definitional witticism which Alice Kaplan, in her book *French Lessons: A Memoir*, remembers from Ann Smock's teaching on Mallarmé: "Literature lies but tells the truth about lying." (1993: 75)

Initially, we are puzzled by the apparent paradox of simultaneously lying and telling the truth. Yet, what is even more remarkable, as we figure it out, is the way in which the reflexivity of the statement leads onto the meta-level. If we conceive of the fictitious aspects of literature as a generic kind of 'lying', it may still be the case that they convey the truth about this kind of 'lying'. We may not only learn about it by undergoing the experience of a fictitious text but we may also encounter a poetics of literature's 'lying' that is rendered in precisely this mode. The (fictional) world-constituting discourse of literature may engage a (real) world-referencing aspect when it exposes a poetics of itself in the form of whatever else it presents.

By the same token, an important non-fictional side to *ficto*-critical writing may be the meta-understanding of our textual practices it contains – rendered fictionally – within its textual structure. Figuratively, this trademark *ficto*-critical sleight of hand creates a picture puzzle in which one hand pulls up a screen while another hand projected onto the screen thus revealed underneath pulls down a third screen that is yet, paradoxically, exposed as the initial screen on which the first hand is located. In this dazzling manner "The Fall" not only puts the masquerading of art back into the "artifice of literary criticism", which "was built up to do one thing really: to unmask the secrets of art" (Muecke 2008b: 19), but also addresses the conditions of the possibility of both generic kinds of writing on the meta-level of all our textual practices. In this manner, the concepts of structural metaphor and the *ficto*-critical vector begin to make purposive sense of much – and regrettably much-maligned – post/modern playfulness in ficto/criticism.

An Elevated Fall: Immersion *En Abyme*

Whereas "The Fall" hails the attachment of a concept to a percept *in writing* (ibid: 24), on the constitutive level, a textually rendered percept is always already pervaded by concepts – we cannot not do it. What makes the essay a *ficto*-critical structure is the fact that it textually renders the percept of the pitcher plant in terms that conceptualise textual immersion. The *ficto*-critical point is that the conceptual insights of the pitcher plant pertain to the im/mediate act of textual mediation by which the reader accesses the imagery to begin with. When the passage of the pitcher plant draws the reader into a state of immersed reading, this textual act is simultaneously under way and scrutiny. Ultimately, what strikes us in reading "The Fall" is the self-reflexive disruption of immersion *from within*. The challenging conceptual work that the reader encounters at the same time as she is drawn into the text acquires im/mediate significance because it presently refers her back to her own processual frame/work under way, the immersing readerly act of textual mediat*ing*.

By subjecting the experience of textual immersion to the simultaneously immersed reader's scrutiny "The Fall" effects a *ficto*-critical intervention. It harnesses immersing textual mediations to create both an im/mediate experiential awareness and a conceptual understanding of the poetics of textual immersion. In fact, the im/mediacy that the text highlights goes against the grain of immersion even though premised on it. "The Fall" thus harnesses its textual magic to effect some counter-magic – what Michael Taussig calls "apotropaic magic" (2010b). The *ficto*-critical point of this textual strategy is to deploy the spell of readerly immersion to apotropaic effect. Im/mediately striking, its itinerary – from within onto the meta-level in a traitorous and self-reflexive spin – is just the kind of preposterous short-circuitry of the *ficto*-critical vector.

Yielding to the attraction of the flower, the fly is "suddenly transformed from free flight into a tumbling cadence" (Muecke 2008b: 24) and something similar could be said of Monsieur Mouche. While performing the pre/scribed itinerary, the reader, too, begins to fall – but she also begins to self-reflexively spin around her own axis as the text equips her, from within, with the means to re/conceive of the textual act she currently engages. The im/mediate relevance of the conceptual insight with which the post/modern allegory of the pitcher plant equips the reader, in fact, counters the immersion from within which it was wrought. Or, to turn it around: the im/mediate conceptual relevance of the pitcher plant turns the readerly agent on the very immersion from within which it was accessed.

As the short-circuitry of the *ficto*-critical vector hits home, the dazzled reader emerges at the end of the passage at which only knowledge that remains of the immersing performance:

> "But to know the structure of the plant (or the text) as a concept, is to be able, incredibly, to climb out again, wet, dripping, exhausted, on the lip of the world again. Now you *know*: that was *some* kind of trick." (ibid: 25, original emphases)

Only, the ability to "climb out again" is not connected to knowledge of the structure, but to the respectively different kinds of encounters that the fly, Monsieur Mouche and their reader are involved in. By the same logic it is also not true that "in writing […] we can do it over and over [… b]ecause we can attach a concept to a percept" (ibid: 24). In fact, the medial characteristics underlying all *textual* encounters constitute the possibility of this repetition (in difference).

Hence, a juxtaposition of im/mediate experience and mediated knowledge that, both of which are wrought from the skilfully pre/scribed immersion in "The Fall", might have been even more insightful. Let me suggestively re/emphasise the above statement in this respect:

"Now you *know*: that was *some* kind of trick. You look at the horizon, now, a little more shrewdly, more critically. But the *fall!* And you glance back with a delicious shudder." (ibid: 25, my additional emphasis)

While the im/mediacy of textual mediation is self-reflexively and performatively highlighted by an apotropaic engagement of the mechanisms of textual immersion, conceptual knowledge of how the text immerses us is gained at the expense of the percept's mediated experience. The performative perception of the percept ceases, yet conceptual knowledge that is retained from the experience. The self-reflexive experiential highlighting of the textual performance short-circuits the textual act it concerns, yet yields an understanding that may change future performances of the readerly act. Such is the future potential of the *ficto*-critical vector.

Performing "The Fall"

Its structural readerly focus in particular opens the possibility to re/conceive of "The Fall" as performative. Apart from static textual performativity the readerly performance of the textual work also plays a major role in ficto/criticism. What distinguishes "The Fall" as a *ficto*-critical in/scription is the way in which it pre/scribes the itinerary of the readerly work to turn in on itself. Engaging the essay, following its textual course, draws you in, like the pitcher does with the fly. The important kind of performativity is no longer contained by the text, but enacted in relation to it, by relat*ing* to it – while the textual content thus accessed yields an explanatory account of just that activity. Static writerly pre/scription here concerns the processual readerly act both constatively and performatively.

Furthermore, the textual structure of "The Fall" pre/scribes an *im/mediate* experience. This im/mediacy is indeed possible because the experience is of the act of textual relat*ing* in which the reader is necessarily engaged. Although the readerly performance of "The Fall" exceeds it as a text, it is yet induced by this textual basis. Because the readerly act of textual mediation is necessarily in progress in read*ing*, it becomes a sure-fire reference. Im/mediately, it is of a different order from any other reference that a text could make because it reverses the referential direction. Whatever con/textual knowledge a reader brings to the textual encounter, *in reading* there can be little doubt of the readerly act. Muecke's writing skilfully capitalises on this when it makes the readerly act its subject matter. It leads the reader to realise from within an immersing read the constitutive frame(ing)work that facilitates textual immersion. Despite luring the reader deeper into immersion, "The Fall" harbours the potential for an im/mediate reverse dive, a surprising *ficto*-critical pirouette out of immersion.

What makes "The Fall" such a striking read is the kind of textual performativity that self-reflexively identifies the readerly performance while it is under way and thus creates an im/mediate experiential awareness of the readerly act as part of the textual work. The textual structure of "The Fall" engages a processual kind of performativity that concerns the act of textual relat*ing* that we undergo in reading. Muecke figuratively conceives of this event as a twofold falling – firstly, *for* textual attraction and, secondly, *into* narrative immersion. In order to understand how exactly "The Fall" pre/scribes the realisation of the *ficto*-critical vector, the following close reading is going to re/trace the textual means that structure this readerly itinerary.

An Extradiegetic Turn of Events

The last fragment of "The Fall" ties a knot from the interrelated threads it has accumulated during the course of its earlier five sections. It presents the imagery of how a fly, firstly, falls for the deception of the pitcher plant by following its attractive lure until it, secondly, falls into the flower's drum where it is immersed by a dissolving liquid. The manner in which this imagery is presented endows it with analogical relevance for both the narrative of falling in love and the poetics of reading. The mechanisms and structures presented in the aesthetically appealing descriptive account have threefold relevance as, firstly, an aesthetic description, secondly, a capturing narrative and, thirdly, an explanatory account. While we may focus on only one of these aspects at a time, in their ficto/critical textual composition they cannot be disentangled.

The first fragment of "The Fall" sets the minimal stage for the fictional/ised narrative of Monsieur Mouche falling in love. Two words of utmost importance for my reading initialise the text: "you" and "immediately". To begin with, the text thus introduces both the shifter of direct address and the notion of im/mediacy: "*You* have invited me for lunch, because you want to pick my brains. [...] This is our first meeting and I *immediately* find you attractive." (ibid: 18, my emphases) Over the course of the essay, "you" is skilfully shifted. After initially addressing the student it later serves to address the reader. In this double function "you" marks the twofold perspective of the ficto/critical vector, which, while leading into the text's content and immersion, yet also interpellates the reader as the im/mediate subject of textual immersion – thereby short-circuiting the experience from within. By means of the deictic pronoun "you" the text creates the possibility for a perspectival change from within the intradiegetic, mediated events of the narrative to the im/mediate, extra-textual address of each reader as the (always) currently reading textual agent.

The referential use of "you" shifts from an intradiegetic address as the first word of the text (ibid: 18) and its use throughout the narrative (esp. ibid: 20-1), to a rapidly changing development in the final section (ibid: 23-4). There it functions no longer as Monsieur Mouche's means to address the student, but rather as a means to interpolate the reader. First, there is the inclusive, yet indeterminate, generality as well as consent seeking acknowledgement that "[y]ou fall into them" (ibid: 23) – which also riffs on the pun of Monsieur Mouche as a fly. But then it fully turns around in the im/mediate and extra-textual address of its reader as "[y]ou my critical friends" (ibid: 24). This direct interpellation sets the reader on course to realise the *ficto*-critical vector, which is the im/mediately experiential and self-reflexive realisation of the readerly performance *in actu*. Such is the first important aspect of Muecke's strategic deployment of deictic shifters to *ficto*-critical effect.

Im/mediately Twisted Awareness

A second important *ficto*-critical effect is also wrought from the same deictic shifter. After the initial "[y]ou fall into them" (ibid: 23) – which unites the analogical threads of, firstly, falling in love, secondly, falling into the pitcher and, thirdly, falling into textual immersion – the text veers between removing and implying the readerly perspective. "How are the insects snared by the carnivorous plant?" (ibid: 23) the text asks from a distance, before providing an answer that yet includes the extra-textual reader together with the intradiegetic narrator and fly as "[w]e the victims" and "us" (ibid: 24). The same multi-directionally inclusive "we" also re/unites the analogical threads in "[w]e fall for the one who resembles a flower" (ibid: 25). But then the direct readerly address introduces a significant difference into the analogy:

> "You, my critical friends, have now learned the difference between the true flower and the deceptive carnivorous trap. This is something which the insects [...] are destined, perhaps, never to learn. [...] For each insect victim it happens only once. But in writing [...] we can do it over and over again." (ibid: 24)

Here, the medially constituted critical distance of readerly immersion is put in relief against the existential immediacy of falling into the drum of the pitcher plant.

Against this background, the direct readerly address works its reversal of direction from intradiegetic reference to an extra-textual interpellation. The latter abounds at the end of the last paragraph in conjunction with the further deictic shifter "now". "Now you *know*" (ibid: 25, original emphasis), the text directly reaches out to its recipient, for example. At this point the significance of "you" has clearly moved from the intradiegetic present and addressee to the im/mediate present of always the current reception and recipient. In this manner, too, "The Fall" aims at an im/mediate affective registering of the mediat*ing* that is always currently under way rather than of anything it would mediate in the process. Such is the *ficto*-critically experiential awareness that the text's shifters spark for the reader, who they bring to self-reflexively and im/mediately realise their own textual performance under way. Muecke's deployment of shifters thus pre/figures the trope of the *ficto*-critical vector.

By itself, the reversed referential direction of a readerly address is perhaps remarkable, but not yet revolutionary. However, such a direct address rarely comes in the midst of an explanatory account of the very act that the reader is performing in accessing the address to begin with. As things begin to spin in "The Fall", the constitutive level of our textual practices becomes its subject matter from a readerly perspective that is characterised by a self-reflexively im/mediate experiential awareness. In light of these insights, the processual and performative melee between reading self and text emerges as the paramount *ficto*-critical locus. The *ficto*-critical vector thus directs our focus towards this constitutive realm of processual textual frame/work and thereby turns perspective from the generic in-between onto the meta-generic.

2.2 REFINING THE *FICTO*-CRITICAL TROPES

In order to get a more general grasp of the trope of the *ficto*-critical vector that I would like to retain from the foregoing reading of Stephen Muecke's "The Fall" and elaborate on, the following subsections shall in some more detail first consider aspects of the vector's tropical movement in isolation and then examine the additional turn of the *ficto*-critical *twist*.

The Striking Turns of the *Ficto*-critical Vector

It may be useful here to propose a compact working definition of the *ficto*-critical vector first, before then refining its characteristically interrelated elements in the subsections following below.

> From within the reading performance, ficto/critical texts make im/mediately perceptible a *ficto*-critical vector that self-reflexively turns in on aspects of the representational and communicative frame/work (always) currently under way. The trope thus interpellates the reader as textual agent by presently identifying the readerly act as a constitutive part of the de/centred textual work.

Figuratively the trope can be described as an intentional vector that departs from the reader's eye and, in excess of being productively met by the textual structure and its inscribed content, is also thrown back into the readers face. The reader's vector of focal attention turns *ficto*-critical in a self-reflexive move that bends back from the page, to poke her in the eye whence it originated. The *ficto*-critical vector describes a curious reading movement that, while facilitating access to something enshrined in the text, also performatively highlights the constitutively framing mechanisms set to work in so doing. In this sense, the *ficto*-critical vector illumines, from within, parameters of textual mediat*ing* that are conditions of the possibility of what is thus textually mediated.

For example, some *ficto*-critical textual strategies friction the conceptual work of reading. Such texts are wrought to rub against readerly habits and expectations that, ultimately, form a sort of generic approach. *Ficto*-critical writing of this kind aims to create internal friction in the reading process by disregarding generic regulatory rules and conventions that make both certain texts and their recipients work in a certain way. The goal is to interpellate the reader as the linguistic-discursive agent at work. Ultimately, the frictioning generic resistance of the textual structure highlights the equally generic readerly relat*ing* under way and thus suggests a shift to a meta-generic perspective with a distinct medial focus.

In the following subsections, the interrelated defining characteristics of the *ficto*-critical vector – its readerly focus, self-reflexivity, performativity, im/mediacy, and experiential character – shall be carefully de- and refined; where necessary in distinction from competing understandings of these terms.

A Readerly Focus

The self-reflexive trope of the *ficto*-critical vector is realised by the reader as the result of textually pre/scribed frictions that emerge from within the reading performance. Ficto/critical resistance on the textual level causes frictions in the reading process, which yet does not break down. The point is precisely that it does continue to make sense, only in an unusual direction. The textually pre/scribed structures cause internal frictions in reading that make perceptible the constitutive frame of mechanisms at work in our textual relat*ing*. Whereas the focus in reading is usually directed at the textual object it mediates, the structure of a *ficto*-critical text frictions the readerly performance of mediat*ing* this textual object, whereby such writing re(flexively)directs attention at the readerly act in the textual work.

The ficto/critical text that successfully brings its reader to realise the *ficto*-critical vector thus, firstly, taps into the im/mediate present of (always) the present reader's place within the textual relation and, secondly, highlights (always) the present reader's performative agency in the textual relat*ing* under way. By this surprising, im/mediate textual interpellation in the act of textual mediation, the *ficto*-critical vector makes perceptible for the reader the only concrete real life experiential level to our textual encounters, that is our always present encounter*ing* text. It highlights for the reader at work on the text, the readerly agency in the textual work. Ultimately, the referential direction of the *ficto*-critical vector reverses the anticipated referential direction of textual mediation. It does not point at a transcendental textual object enshrined in the concrete textual structure so much as it points back at the im/mediate agency and act of textual mediat*ing* under way between reader and text. In this manner the *ficto*-critical vector interpellates the reader *as* reader *in actu*.

If successfully realised, the trope of the *ficto*-critical vector performatively illumines the readerly act under way to the particular reader conducting the reading. This readerly turn of the trope thus already describes the particular kind of self-reflexivity that is characteristically activated by the *ficto*-critical vector.

Self-Reflexivity

The kind of self-reflexivity at work in the *ficto*-critical vector goes beyond both the self-reflexive act of inscription and a self-reflexive text. Just as a self-reflexive writerly speaking position is necessarily contained by the text, so too the self-reflexive text – wittily pointing at its own constructed nature *qua* text – remains self-contained. But the self-reflexivity of the readerly act, which is generated by a frictioning textual structure that highlights the textual relat*ing* under way, exceeds both the textually mediated as well as purely textual modes of self-reflexivity. This third kind of textual self-reflexivity is thus not concerned with the reflexivity of a narrator or text pointing back at themselves, but with the reflexivity of the readerly relat*ing* between text and self being brought to feed back in on itself, which creates the textual potential for im/mediate experiential interventions.

The kind of self-reflexivity experienced as the *ficto*-critical vector is triggered from within the textual structure but exceeds it because it pertains to the im/mediate readerly frame/work under way. This modal shift in textual self-reflexivity reverses the direction of readerly awareness from the mediated textual work to the im/mediate frame/work of mediat*ing*. The tropical turn of the *ficto*-critical vector changes the direction of reference. It no longer only leads into the representational realm but at the same time towards the agency conducting this pre/scribed passage. In this manner, the *ficto*-critical vector illumines a picture that contains its own frame, that im/mediately references its own condition of possibility, which is the frame(ing)work through which it is accessed to begin with.

Importantly, the particular reflexive bend of the *ficto*-critical vector experientially highlights to the reader precisely those aspects of their own textual work from which they usually – even constitutively – abstract in the act. Therefore, the self-reflexivity of the *ficto*-critical vector also has a fundamentally performative dimension to it.

Performativity

The particular kind of textual performativity that the *ficto*-critical vector highlights is distinct from that of a performative text. Its mode is not the static performativity of a textual structure that already conforms to what it constates, but the processual performativity of a textual act under way. The *ficto*-critical vector exceeds a textually contained performativity when it brings the readerly performance of the pre/scribed textual structure into the picture. Its tropical turn is thus characterised by a performative self-reflexivity because the readerly act is highlighted by and in as much as during the textual work.

In other words, the *ficto*-critical vector illumines the readerly textual frame/work *in actu*. It makes perceptible how the readerly act completes the textual work which a writerly act pre/scribed to begin with. In this sense, the specific kind of performativity that characterises the *ficto*-critical vector clearly re/emphasises the fundamental shift in perspective which lies at the heart of this study: focal attention is no longer exclusively directed at the textual level, with an eye to the between of generic hybridity, but simultaneously at the constitutive medial level of textual relat*ing*, where meta-generic insights may emerge from the vantage point of a text-practical perspective.

Significantly, the performative self-reflexivity of the *ficto*-critical vector also entails that it registers in an un-mediated manner. The impact of performatively realis*ing* the *ficto*-critical vector therefore experientially exceeds understanding the present constative expository account of it – because the *ficto*-critical vector im/mediately illumines what these present mediations can only hope to illuminate from a distance.

Im/mediacy

The un-mediated kind of recognition of the *ficto*-critical vector removes the distance of the textual mediation by presently foregrounding the always current act of mediating. Underlying here is the distinction between the im/mediate side of the textual relation, that is the act of mediat*ing*, and the mediated side of the textual relation, that is the content mediat*ed* in the process. While the reader constitutively remains at a distance from anything propositionally mediated in the textual relation, no such distance exists with regards to the readerly act of textual relat*ing* – except, perhaps, the gap between reader and text that is, however, always already bridged by the readerly act of textual mediat*ing*.

While much (unmarked) fictocritical and (hyphenated) ficto-critical debate centres around the question of how to break down the generic critical distance between an academic text and its object, or the affective distance between writer, reader, and what the text mediates, the ingenuity of (slashed) *ficto*-critical practices is to short-circuit the im/mediately underlying frame/work that is the condition of the possibility of such generic mediations. If you like, both generic scholarly and constitutive readerly distance evaporate in the heat generated by im/mediately engaging textual frictions that can spark the *ficto*-critical vector.

The im/mediacy of the *ficto*-critical vector collapses the distancing effects of the textual relation not only in terms of the circumspect writer who carefully relates her involved speaking position and affective motivation in the text, but it furthermore collapses even the constitutive perceptive distance of the textual relation. Such is the experiential significance of the im/mediately striking *ficto*-critical vector.

Experiential Knowledge

Another characteristic that distinguishes the event of realising the *ficto*-critical vector is the experiential character of the readerly awareness it generates. A *ficto*-critical text not only mediates conceptual knowledge that, but its textual structure works to create experiential knowledge of the im/mediate readerly frame/work under way. The *ficto*-critical vector thus constitutes a distinct *kind* of textual experience that is different, firstly, from propositionally mediated experiences in a text and, secondly, from immersed readerly affects triggered by such constatively mediated content. Two kinds of textual affect are thus put in relief: one is the affective readerly response to the mediated textual work, the other is the im/mediate experiential registering of the mediat*ing* readerly frame/work. This latter affective impact of the *ficto*-critical vector thus interpellates the reading individual as the textual agent at work, rather than facilitating an immersed kind of affective identification on the level of content.

Realising a *ficto*-critical vector can thus have a more im/mediately unsettling affective impact than a merely constative description could provide – albeit only ever in relation to constitutive aspects of the textual performance presently under way.

The Preposterous Short-Circuitry of the *Ficto*-critical Twist

As a consequence of the five aforementioned intricately interrelated aspects of the *ficto*-critical vector, *ficto*-critical texts reverse not only the direction of contribution to the 'debate' between fiction and criticism when they let the fictional, aesthetic and subjective side of literature actively contribute to theory, but they also change the kind of contribution to such debates from constative knowledge that to experiential knowledge of the reader's performative know-how. In so doing, *ficto*-critical writing goes against the grain of not only generic textual structures but of our equally generic textual practices. Against the ingrained generic order of discourses, according to which theory and criticism feed on literature and fictions can at best be illustrative or the object of philosophical arguments, *ficto*-critical writing sometimes brings literary discourse to mount theoretical or critical arguments, as well as fiction to enter the philosophical debate as an im/mediately striking means.

Ficto/critical texts are often saturated with – mostly poststructuralist – theory. But the way in which they are thus in/formed allows them to simultaneously contribute to theoretical debates in kind and to generate the counter-intuitive experiential dimension of the *ficto*-critical vector. By way of aesthetic means that are deployed to simultaneously illumine and illuminate a poetics of our textual practices, the *ficto*-critical revolutionises an otherwise one-directional debate that is generically keen to maintain a scholarly distance between the object of knowledge and the knowing subject's agency. The trope of the *ficto*-critical *twist*, which departs with as much as from the *ficto*-critical vector, intersects the propositional and experiential, the constative and performative, the expository and the im/mediate, as well as the referential and the self-reflexive sides of the textual relation to short-circuit this traditional scenario.

Structural Metaphor

The theoretical trope I have termed structural metaphor – but which is sometimes also referred to as "postmodern allegory" (Kerr 200: 156) – already encapsulates the basic elements that also define the *ficto*-critical twist. Throughout the thesis I take the term "structural metaphor" to imply an image that can explain the constitutive movements and workings of metaphoricity in language. Some paradigmatic structural metaphors can be found in Derrida's seminal text "White Mythology" (1982) as well as in its follow-up "The *Retrait* of Metaphor" (1998), both of which provide metaphors that not only explain the workings of metaphor, but ultimately also the metaphoricity of language in general – prime among them the coin (1982: 207-19), the sun (1982: 230-45), and the heliotrope (1982: 245-57). However, I would like to use the notion of structural metaphor here in a perhaps wider sense for metaphoric depictions that provide a poetics of their own mode of depiction in conjunction with whatever else they simultaneously depict thus.

For the purposes of this study I deploy the term "post/modern allegory" almost interchangeably to imply aesthetic imagery that has an expository function with regards to constitutive linguistic-discursive mechanisms on which it is premised. Hence, whenever a text beautifully renders its tropes at work, so that they both explain the underlying textual relation as well as serve the literary aesthetic or narrative logic of the text, we are dealing with post/modern allegory or structural metaphor. In this sense, I want to suggest, *ficto*-critical texts often centre around a carefully constructed node which condenses its aesthetic and theoretical – or even its (fictional) world-constituting and (real) world-referencing – aspects into the expository imagery of a structural metaphor or post/modern allegory.

For example, the structural metaphor of the pitcher plant effects the *ficto*-critical twist of "The Fall" because it serves up an explanatory poetics of narrative attraction and readerly immersion in the same stroke that it serves the text's narrative attraction and readerly immersion. In this manner, the *ficto*-critical twist short-circuits the structurally incompatible perspectives of a distancing theoretical overview and an internally involved outlook. The text thus restores to the textual relation a perceptible dimension that is usually abstracted from. Critical distance and literary immersion may be experienced simultaneously on both an im/mediately affective and mediated epistemological level. As it engages the reader in the subject under discussion, the pitcher plant is thus effective as both literary bait and its exposure. Departing from the structural metaphor of the pitcher plant in "The Fall", the *ficto*-critical vector performatively illumines (*aisthesis*) the readerly frame/work (*poiesis*) of textual immersion, while the simultaneous tropical turn of the *ficto*-critical twist constatively illuminates these textual poetics by way of a textual aesthetic.

The structural metaphor thus does not simply bridge the gap between the generically distanced overview of theory or criticism and the generically immersed outlook of literature and fiction. Instead, its tropical turn of the *ficto*-critical twist leads the reader to a meta-generic vantage point, whence the act of textual mediat*ing* emerges as the condition of the (im)possibility of either reservedly distanced or affectively immersing textual mediations.

The Tropical Intersection of the *Ficto*-critical Twist

Ficto-critical textual practices aim at creating an im/mediate textual experience for the reader in which they simultaneously realise, firstly, an experiential awareness by way of the *ficto*-critical vector and, secondly, an explanatory understanding of their own performative relation to the text – taking their textual relat*ing* under scrutiny (constatively) while it is under way (performatively). As textual object and performance are thus intersected, an explanatory textual relation is short-circuited with the im/mediate experience of its relat*ing*. What the *ficto*-critical vector illumines is furthermore illuminated in the texts. The performative self-reflexivity of im/mediately experiencing the *ficto*-critical vector is supplemented by a constatively self-reflexive, text-practical meta-commentary in the *ficto*-critical twist.

The combined trope of the *ficto*-critical vector and twist strikingly short-circuits the textual relation when it im/mediately highlights from within what it constatively examines from a distance. But its ambition does not stop there. The explanatory direction of the constative meta-commentary may even give further text-practical significance or spin to the self-reflexive bend of the *ficto*-critical vector. Ideally, the understanding thus communicated would aim to im/mediately back-feed into the same understanding that guides the agency currently at work. Momentum of the realisation could even hope to propel the explanatory direction of the meta-commentary into a performative direct*ing*. Theoretically this is indeed possible because we conduct our reading under way on the guiding authority of the same internalised "fictive institution" – to slightly abduct another Derridean term (1992a: 36) – that here comes under scrutiny and potentially revision. After all, our ideal of what it means 'to read the right way' guides our read*ing* performance. But if the ideal is transformed while in progress, that relation becomes theoretically short-circuitous.

Eventually, the combined tropical turns of the *ficto*-critical vector and twist effect a short-circuitry of the readerly textual work thus simultaneously, firstly, under scrutiny or even under critique, secondly, under way, and therefore, thirdly, at stake or potentially even under revision. In this manner, I want to suggest, *ficto*-critical texts aim to pull the plug on our ingrained textual practices for reasons that are provided by their respective ficto-*critical* aspects, which will be the subject matter of the fourth chapter. For now, though, such pre/post/erous short-circuitry epitomises the *ficto*-critical aspect of ficto/critical textual strategies.

A fully-fledged *ficto*-critical textual relation is realised where the self-reflexive, performative, and im/mediate *ficto*-critical vector is given further text-practical direction by the *ficto*-critical twist. Figuratively, perhaps, a moment of oscillating textual brilliance would turn the stunned reader's point of view – but then again, it might feel very different.

Concluding Notes

In drawing this chapter to a close, I shall now re/state the peculiar significance of the *ficto*-critical vector and twist by way of extracting and re/conceiving of an image from another early precursor to the fictocritical, Michel Leiris's *Manhood: A Journey from Childhood into the Fierce Order of Virility* (1992). In particular, the scenario evoked in the subsection "Infinity" (ibid: 11) will help me re(con)figure the *ficto*-critical significance of vector and twist as the reverse direction of a *mis en abyme* structure. For Leiris the significance of the following situation is his "first actual contact with infinity" (ibid: 11). At one point he was holding – let us assume in his left hand – a tin of Dutch cocoa which "was decorated with an image of a farm girl in a lace cap, holding in her left hand an identical tin, decorated with the same image of the smiling, pink girl" (ibid: 11), and so on to infinity. Leiris furthermore admits to still getting "dizzy imagining this infinite series of an identical image endlessly reproducing the same" (ibid: 11). This, of course, is the quintessential trope of representation *mis en abyme*.

Yet from a *ficto*-critical perspective, I want to suggest, the crucial point is not the endlessly fascinating vanishing point somewhere in the depth of this representational trick, but the easily neglected fact that the ultimate frame always includes the person currently holding the tin. The ultimate frame is not that of the first picture on the tin, but the additional circumstance that he himself is holding the tin in a similar pose to the Dutch girl. Realising this external frame, which is mirrored within, as the starting point of the abysmal representational chain, makes the viewer perceptible as its condition of possibility. The *mis en abyme* aesthetic of this representation makes perceptible (*aisthesis*) its frame/work of perception.

Likewise, where the reader realises the *ficto*-critical vector and twist, she re/focuses and reverses the direction whither the *mis en abyme* structure seems to be pointing – that is, the abysmal depth of the representational scenario leads her back to her/self as its recipient condition of possibility. The reflexive turn of readerly attention is thus not leading further into the maelstrom of representation, but out of it, towards its non-transcendental conditions of possibility, namely the communicative situation of textual representation and the readerly performance within its paradigmatic setting. In other words, the encountered fall into the loss of representation lets the recipient frame/work enter the picture – which is precisely what Muecke's exemplary pre/scription in "The Fall" epitomises.

From Leiris's admission that for him "the hallucinatory and actually ineffable character of the Dutch girl, infinitely repeated the way licentious poses can be indefinitely multiplied by means of the reflection in a cleverly manipulated boudoir mirror" (ibid: 11), let me here only elaborate its structural kernel. Consider the quintessential *mis en abyme* structure of two mirrors facing each other. Taking a glimpse from the side, all you can see is their endlessly multiplied frame bending along a line of flight into the bottomless abyss of their mutually self-reflexive re/presentation. Positioning yourself between these two mirrors, however, the abyss is equally obstructed by yourself. All you can now see is yourself purportedly staring into the loss of representation, yet curiously finding yourself endlessly framed. What you see, are two conditions of the possibility of mirror representation. The example thus figures how not only the frame but also the recipient enters the picture. Ultimately, the loss of representation does not lead into a bottomless abyss, but out of the representative realm and towards the recipient frame/work as its condition of possibility.

The same holds true for the combined tropes of *ficto*-critical vector and twist. They bring into the picture – both constatively and performatively as well as experientially im/mediate – their textual and recipient conditions of possibility. Their reversal of referential direction points not deeper into the transcendental realm of representation, but towards its non-transcendental frame/work of reception; towards the systemically determined, and yet still underdetermined, position from which alone one is able to contemplate this representational abyss. Similar to the mirror's invading external frame and the internally obstructing eye, what enters the picture of the *ficto*-critical text, therefore, is the reader's agency in reading as well as the frame that she brings to the textual encounter. In other words, by reversing the suggestive direction of the *mis en abyme* towards the recipient, the *ficto*-critical vector and twist extend the interpretive equation to the recipient's side. As a result, this text-interpretive equation needs to be re/conceived of as a formula with paradigmatically underdetermined variables. It is no longer an equation that lets either correct or wrong results (re)emerge.

Note, furthermore, that in both cases the set-up is guaranteed to fire, because before the representational structures can strike us in their respective ways, their conditions of possibility are always already in place. We can only see the encapsulated abysmal structure of textual acts *in reading*. Since reading is the only means of access, the textual activity that is the subject matter under scrutiny is necessarily in place on the reader's side, and the chain-like structure of representation can thus hit home as a *ficto*-critical vector. A *ficto*-critical strategy thus engages a counter-intuitive kind of real-life referentiality and significance when it im/mediately – that is, without representational deflection – addresses a state of affairs of which it can be absolutely certain, namely that the reader is currently reading this text and conforms to the constitutive requirements and mechanisms of the practice of reading. The special achievement of the *ficto*-critical text is thus not only to render the representational structure on display such that it contains a description of the necessary readerly position to access its representation, but also to point at always the present particular reader's occupy*ing* of the readerly position in the equation; thus filling its variable with her respective particularity. The im/mediate and singular interpellation of the *ficto*-critical textual strategy thus collapses the critical distance between recipient and subject in a move that threatens short-circuitry because what is at work is simultaneously under way and scrutiny.

Most importantly, the *ficto*-critical text thus manages to point out paradigmatic aspects of textual representation and communication as such by way of a particular kind of referentiality that, if realised, cannot be wrong because it im/mediately points to its own conditions of possibility while they are currently enacted by the reader. Ironically, it is thus where we suspect the most uncontrollably diverse side of the interpretive equation, namely in the outcome of readerly reception, that ficto/critical writing identifies the most important general parameters of said equation, the textual work. In this manner, the scope of *ficto*-critical insights into our textual practices is general, even where the writing is deliberately subjective and marginal, because the *ficto*-critical vector and twist in their inimitable ways address the conditions of the im/possibility of textual representation and communication.

Now, the *ficto*-critical vector and twist, as I have defined and refined them here on the back of Muecke's exemplary text, are somewhat idealised tropes. I have formulated them pointedly in order to render them productive for a literary theory of the ficto/critical. The claim is not that every ficto/critical text exemplifies them as brilliantly as "The Fall", but that often textual structures can be set to work in their direction – even where we least expect it – only we have to seek this potential and realise it in our *ficto*-critical readings. In this sense, these defining tropes of the *ficto*-critical are a readerly stance as much as a text-structural potential. And this readerly dimension is precisely the thrust that my theorising aims to propel forward when it formulates a rather complex and strong definition of what it takes to be the central aspects of a *ficto*-critical stance at its very best. The fragmentary nature of much ficto/critical writing as well as its predilection for essay length text means that often only aspects of these tropes are apparent from different pre/scriptions.

In any case, knowing about the counter-intuitive movements of the *ficto*-critical vector and twist can provide a more alert readerly frame of reference in our encounters with (not only ficto/critical) texts, because *ficto*-critical practices are just as much a readerly stance as they are based on a certain writerly and text-structural conduct. And in precisely this sense I hope that my protocol of reading "The Fall" can help to fertilise our future reception not only of ficto/critical writing as such, but also of other writing that we dare to engage in a *ficto*-critical manner. The claim is not that every fictocritical text exemplifies the same potential for the *ficto*-critical to the same degree, but that *we* ficto/critical recipients are required to produce it in relation to these texts.

Not to forget, the *ficto*-critical is also only the first part of the two-step trope of the ficto/critical. In light of this, too, it would be counter-productive to dismiss texts that do not exemplify all aspects in equal measure, when a benevolently applied readerly stance – akin to the principle of charity – can actually propel the ficto/critical stance forward. *You* can always take it from there.

At this stage it is reasonable to ask what the merits are of starting a poetics of our textual practices of representation and communication on the reader's side of the equation. Why structure such an explanatory account from the act of text reception rather than the act of text production or, even earlier, the ideas and perceptions that give rise to the act of inscription? In other words, what can justify the post/erior act of reading to be taken as the starting point when conceiving of the textual work, rather than the necessarily primary and pre/structuring act of writing? The answer is because the ficto/critical outlook onto the paradigmatic situation of reading and writing is in this sense pre/post/erous indeed.

As this chapter has argued, the *ficto*-critical readerly focus has the advantage that it can make perceptible a number of fundamental parameters at work, which are all too often effaced and abstracted from in our pre-theoretical conception of the interpretive equation of the textual work. As a consequence, our textual work may thus be ill-named as an equation because of its constitutive asymmetry that only the readerly focus can bring into sharp relief. Ultimately, I want to suggest, we may have to re/theorise the textual work as an interpretive equation which, firstly, is not one but two and, secondly, not equal. This as yet under-theorised perspective can contribute something new to the conception of our textual practices. Hitherto our understanding has been strongly in/formed from a writerly perspective and has all too often mistaken the question of the recipient's side for a matter of empirical research. The firm readerly focus of my study aims to redress both these points. Not least, because it is precisely on the recipient's side that certain paradigmatic mechanisms become perceptible that are always already at work in all our textual practices.

3. A Theory of the Ficto/critical

Experimenting Textual Strategies & Text-Practical Ideologies

3.1 Mischievous Ficto/critical Strategies

The goal of the next few sections is to qualify the strategic pattern instantiated by the ficto/critical. On the one hand, I shall indicate how much perceived playfulness in ficto/critical writing, while presenting its perhaps most appealing side, is also strategically purposive in a twofold and connected sense. On the other hand, I shall examine how the theoretical insights of the *ficto*-critical vector and twist are not only given practical direction but are furthermore endowed with ficto-*critical* edge by the concerns that these texts address.

Firstly, the ficto/critical strategy of generic resistance shall be addressed with regards to its inward-directed *ficto*-critical purposes. We have previously seen in the second chapter how the *ficto*-critical vector and twist, which are effects of artistic generic resistance, emerge for the recipient in reading from a specific kind of (post/modern) playfulness that causes *ficto*-critical frictioning. There is, however, also a strategic pattern to be identified whose purpose it is to defy generic order. So in a first step, this initial element of the strategically twofold ficto/critical pattern shall be qualified as a *traitorous* kind of unruly writing. Secondly, the strategy of textual intervention shall be addressed with regards to its outward-directed ficto-*critical* purposes. Ficto/critical textual practices do not only resist the traditional and academic generic order playfully, but they also do so for good reasons. Its specific kind of (post/modern) playfulness enables ficto/critical writing to develop a ficto-*critical* interventionist edge. It is thus not only to resist a generic style that ficto/critical texts turn playful, but also to intervene in the generic effects that other textual practices maintain, re/inscribe, and exacerbate.

On the one hand, there is an additional strategic element to be identified in ficto/critical textual practices whose purpose it is to address, counter, and remedy some wider discursive effects of our generic textual practices. In this sense, the theoretical *ficto*-critical twist is given a practical purpose and some ficto-*critical* edge when its im/mediate, self-reflexive, and performative insights are constatively connected to wider discursive issues, interests, and ethico-political motivations. So, in a second step, this additional element of the strategically twofold ficto/critical pattern shall then be qualified, in Taussig's terms, as an apotropaic kind of nervous system writing. On the other hand, such strategic textual interventions are based on ficto/critical theories that conceive of our textual practices – their parameters, mechanisms, and performances – differently from the traditional academic genres they target. Ficto/critical strategies are thus guided by a different text-practical ideology. At the centre of the present third chapter two interventionist paradigms of this theoretical understanding shall be re/traced in exemplary texts and then juxtaposed to the conservative models they counter.

Thirdly, the emergent theory of (slashed) ficto/critical strategies shall then be re/viewed from a different angle, namely in terms of the experimental qualities involved, which encompass the full constellational range between the scientific, the literary, and the philosophical, as well as the exploratory, the artistic, and the artfully thought-experimental. To begin with, however, I shall now focus on how ficto/critical textual practices resist our traditional and academic generic practices traitorously, and then compliment this by a focus on how they also aim to intervene in the wider discursive effects of certain traditional and academic generic orders apotropaically. Taken together, these two strategic elements form the characteristic two-step pattern of ficto/critical strategies.

3.1.1 Traitorous Writing – *Ficto*-critical Generic Resistance

The characteristic playfulness of *ficto*-critical writing is purposive because it serves a strategy of generic resistance. The artistically experimental nature of *ficto*-critical texts is directed against certain generic textual praxes. In the following, I shall examine the underlying strategic pattern of this playful, yet directed, generic resistance. In particular, I shall identify the simultaneous potential and danger of generic resistance in such a manner that the virtue of understanding ficto/critical writing as strategic textual practices, rather than as a non-generic form, emerges clearly. In so doing, I shall also re/conceive of the pervasive notions and terminology of the gap and the in-between space in terms of the core ambiguity of generic resistance.

As we have seen, it is possible to conceive of the ficto/critical between in terms of the compound "fictocriticism" which displays the generic hybridity that the writing practices it subsumes perform. Thus understood, (unmarked) fictocriticism aims for the hybrid space between genres, for the generic gap, as an experimentally productive grey area, in order to undermine an existing generic order and its function. The term thus highlights the essentially anti-essential hybridity of such writing. Yet, how to grasp fictocriticism in such paradoxical terms? Is its generic hybridity non-generic, anti-generic, or quasi-generic? Is there such a thing as a non-generic genre or an anti-generic quasi-genre? The underlying problem I am trying to pinpoint here is that if fictocriticism is by definition genre-defying, it is also already halfway towards a generic order itself. While fictocriticism is a self-stylised experimental non-genre whose defining feature is a resistance to traditional and academic generic patterns, it yet permanently runs the paradoxical risk of forming a genre in aiming to overcome genre.

This paradoxical complex thus poses the question of generic resistance precisely. The ambiguous expression "generic resistance" aptly encapsulates the problem because it can be taken to indicate both a resistance to genres and a genre of resistance. It spans the polar opposites of texts that aim to resist genre and texts that resist generically. In this ambiguous manner the term identifies the inherent danger for both fictocritical practices and attempts to define them. The danger is that resistance to generic patterns itself forms a generic pattern. In both our practical and theoretical attempts we thus have to tread carefully not to produce a genre of resistance to textual genres. The question is how to theorise the fictocritical while sidestepping the self-undermining danger of casting it as another genre.

In order to provide an answer, it will be productive to consider two previous suggestions that are already aware of the inherent danger of generic resistance. The first can be found in Anne Brewster's essay "Fictocriticism: Undisciplined Writing" (1996b) in which she maintains that "[t]he indeterminacy of the term [fictocriticism] is partly due to the fact that it precisely cannot be characterised by a particular set of stylistic features" (ibid: 29). Her conception ties in with my earlier concern that a list of characteristic textual features can never suffice to define fictocritical textual practices. Brewster's statement highlights that fictocritical textual practice goes against the grain of textual genres.

A little later in the same text Brewster adds that "in defamiliarising genre, fictocriticism interrogates the way in which academic knowledges are constructed. [...] It foregrounds and problematises in very productive ways the conventions – especially those relating to closure – of the genres it invokes." (ibid: 31) The second chapter has already examined in great detail how *ficto*-critical texts can performatively highlight these conventions, but Brewster here furthermore anticipates the wider practical, ficto-*critical* significance of these insights. In terms of the present study, she identifies the nexus between *ficto*-critical text-epistemological insights and ficto-*critical* text-practical significance. She thus effectively anticipates a definition in terms of fictocritical *strategies* – which is the eventual aim of the present section – as opposed to listing definitional textual features.

Before jumping too far ahead, however, I would like to dwell on the title of Brewster's essay for a moment. In order to re/phrase the paradox of generic resistance we could take "undisciplined writing" to mean that defying generic discipline can lead elsewhere than into another pre/scribed textual form. The generic gap, as the locus of undiscipline, would contain the fluid potential of experimental hybridity. Turning into disciples of undisciplined writing, however, would present the danger of coagulating this fluid realm of potential into a dry niche. Such is the core problematic of our paradox. To re/phrase the question of generic resistance in this light, we need to ask whether it is indeed meaningfully possible to be a disciple of undiscipline. And furthermore, should fictocritical texts be called generically undisciplined even though they are identifiable as *a certain kind* of undisciplined writing?

The crucial point here is that just what constitutes the generic gap as a place of anti-generic writing also constitutes the risk of re/turning it into generic boundaries. Figuratively speaking, the fluid potential of the generically hybrid gap is in constant danger of coagulating its formal resistance into a genre itself. The same marginal gap that has been identified as the de/territorialising, creative space between genres is constantly threatening to re/territorialise as the niche of a marginal generic centre. The same gap within which emerged the grey area of generic hybridity as a realm of experimental potential is constitutively in danger of being re/regimented into a new genre, a return to black and white. Just like generic resistance, Brewster's notion of undisciplined writing thus finely captures the potential and danger inherent to fictocritical practices.

Until recently, what was probably my favourite Kreuzberg graffito evidenced a somewhat less academic awareness of the same complex. On the back of a boarded up hut at the entrance of station Görlitzer Bahnhof, spray-painted in an odd light metallic blue, it said: "PUNK'S NOT ROCK!" This, of course, riffs on the old battle cry "Punks Not Dead" by The Exploited (1981) and in so doing wittily comments on the contradiction in terms of "punk rock". The question "What is punk?" has been discussed *ad nauseam* since its earliest beginnings sometime back in the late seventies, not least because the early anything goes was radical to the point of not going anywhere at all. Paradoxically, however, this idea has since 'found' its form and produced a surprisingly fixed pattern of music, look, and attitude – all of which certainly have their kicks on offer. And yet, punk was supposed to be *anti* rock, not an entrenched anti-*rock* genre. The sloganic graffito throws this self-contradiction in relief. Likewise, if not entirely congruent, consider the idea of Jazz as free form versus the many subgenres that have since been established as generic clusters within which you can again be central or marginal.

The second characterisation of the fictocritical that captures the problem of generic resistance in fictocriticism can be found in the following passage of Amanda Nettelbeck's introductory contribution to *The Space Between*:

> "These [foregoing] notes [by Juliet Mitchell] have gestured towards some notions of ficto-criticism as unruly writing. We [the editors] hope that, taken together, these writings [in *The Space Between*] will be read not so much as a boundary-setting collection but rather as a series of investigative writings connected by their agonistic relation to the interpretive gesture." (1998: 13)

As her cautionary remark against possible "boundary-setting" tendencies indicates, Nettelbeck is aware of the dilemma that a collection of fictocritical writing can be taken as not only exemplary but definitionally pre/scriptive of something unruly. Starting with this paradox potential, I would like to dwell on Nettelbeck's notion of unruly writing a little in order to introduce a useful distinction between two strategic patterns of generic resistance.

Once we conceive of fictocriticism as unruly writing, the question with regards to which rules such writing is unruly becomes highly significant on the back of the distinction between regulative and constitutive rules. On the one hand, if fictocritical writing were to primarily target the regulative rules of the genres it engages, then this regulative unruliness could become a factor to change the course of the particular genres in question. On the other hand, if fictocriticism were to primarily target the constitutive rules of the genres it engages, then this constitutive unruliness could become a factor to change the nature of the genre in question. Therefore, as far as the language games of genres (and their wider discursive implications) are concerned, the former strategy would aim to effect positional changes in the game, whereas the latter would aim to initiate a game change, that is a change of the game.

Before moving on we should note that both the regulatory and constitutive rules addressed at this stage are still on the level of the laws of genre. Different sets of regulatory rules make different fictional genres identifiable, but there is also a set of constitutive rules that makes their language use fictional – and *vice versa* for non-fiction. Both of these rules present the laws of genre. Breaking these sets of rules is indeed possible because they are not yet the constitutive rules of our textual practices which present the condition of the possibility of textual representation and communication. These constitutive rules of our textual practices present the laws of the laws of genre – and they are where my argument is ultimately headed.

It is in relating to the conditions of the possibility of genre, in re/conceiving of them differently, that (slashed) ficto/critical practices may change the genre game whose systemic order – as well as whose wider discursive order – they critique. In addressing the constitutive rules of our reading and writing practices ficto/critical writing may change the genre game and bring its recipients to realise the full scope of potential that our textual practices open up. For now, the point is to distinguish between the laws of genre, which comprise both the regulative and constitutive rules of – fictional and non-fictional – genres, and the laws of the laws of genre, which present the conditions of the possibility of our textual practices *per se*.

In light of the telling ambiguity of both Brewster's and Nettelbeck's terminology, two strategic patterns of un/discipline or un/ruliness emerge in relief – only one of which, however, captures the aim of ficto/critical resistance. In the context of border crossing and rule breaking, Manuel Ramos Martínez reminds us in his essay "Betrayed Borders: Double Agents and the Crisscrossing of Conflicts" that "Gilles Deleuze and Claire Parnet introduce in their *Dialogues* a significant distinction between two figures: the traitor and the trickster" (2007: 261). Deleuze and Parnet make a subtle, but significant, distinction between the rule bending or breaking patterns of the trickster and the traitor, which may seem deceptively close, yet have significantly different strategic implications.

> "A traitor to the world of dominant significations, and the established order. This is quite different from the trickster: for the trickster claims to take possession of fixed properties, or to conquer a territory, or even to introduce a new order. The trickster has plenty of future, but no becoming whatsoever. The priest, the soothsayer, is a trickster, but the experimenter is a traitor. The statesman or the courtier is a trickster, but the man of war (not a marshal or a general) is a traitor." (Deleuze/Parnet 1996: 40-1)

Clearly their distinction cuts along the line between the gap as a realm of fluid potential and the niche as a re/regimented space between. Trickster and traitor thus emerge as the agent figures strategically pursuing either of these possibilities respectively.

Building on this, Martínez sharpens the opposed patterns of the distinction further.

> "The schema of the traitor does not correspond to a plan defining an outcome in advance, but to an experimental plan that restlessly dismantles its interpretive bases. These traitors do not own the time to come. The trickster, however, is an 'orderly man ordering his future'.

Tricksters claim [...] 'to introduce a new order'. They adopt a course of action to reach a goal." (2007: 261)

On the one hand, the trickster aims to exempt himself from the rules and gain an advantage for his position. He tricks the traditional order in a certain context to improve his own position within a given system and hierarchy. In doing this, the trickster takes a calculable risk. The traitor, on the other hand, is traitorous to the very context from within which he departs. He betrays the systemic order, even though the new situation this entails may be to his own disadvantage. In so doing, the traitor takes unpredictable risks.

Schematically, the trickster wants to come out better positioned while yet perpetuating the system that he exempts himself from, whereas the traitor leads out of the system by propelling it elsewhere, potentially not even to his own greater advantage. And this, I want to suggest, is part of the crucial risk of ficto/critical strategies. In other words, the trickster bends the regulative rules with/in the system and thereby tricks the existing order – he follows a position changing strategy as he cheats with/in the system. By contrast, the traitor bends the rules constitutive of the system and thereby betrays the systemic order – he follows a game-changing strategy as he cheats the system. Along the lines of this distinction I would like to suggest conceiving of the generic recalcitrance of ficto/criticism – of its un/ruliness and un/discipline – in terms of *traitorous* strategies.

A good example of this opposition can be found in Mark Davis's *Gangland Cultural Elites and the New Generationalism* in which he juxtaposes two kinds of feminism: firstly, what he calls 'equity' feminism and, secondly, a more systemically directed feminism that some 'equity' feminists have derided as 'victim' feminism (1997: 91). As Davis defines it, 'equity' feminism "lacks a theoretical apparatus capable of analysing deeper sexisms. It seeks to make women equal, but only within the existing social system, which it seeks to validate." (ibid: 91) Its strategy is to distribute positions more justly within the same systemic order, but not to touch the unjust ordering system.

By contrast, a new generation of feminists have identified precisely systemic injustice as the root of female disadvantage and discrimination.

"They point out that 'equity' feminism not only aspires to a middle-class version of white masculine citizenship, but tends to be espoused by white middle-class feminists who can afford to take their 'individualist' privileges for granted. What 'equity' feminists tend to laud as the freedom of equality and freedom from ideology, more recent feminisms see as the logic of the status quo. They argue that to aspire to this kind of equity is to buy into a whole new set of (patriarchal) ideologies, even if no-one speaks of them as such." (ibid: 91)

Thus, while 'equity' feminists criticise a defeatist lack of individual initiative in what they polemically refer to as 'victim' feminism, proponents of this latter perspective in turn criticise that attitude and ideology of 'equity' feminism are a privilege of those already systemically advantaged. They are dissatisfied with the pyrrhic victory of having some women in some driving seats perpetuating a still patriarchal system.

With regards to a set of prominent Australian 'equity' feminists Davis analyses that "[h]aving championed at every turn a gender system that accepts them as 'equals', they are allowed popular forums in which to police its boundaries, gatekeeping [...] what henceforth is and isn't acceptable feminism" (ibid: 94). Their resistance to patriarchy has turned patriarchal itself. The initially emancipatory impetus of feminist resistance has turned its fluid potential into a regimented marginal centre, a niche with its own rules and borders. In other words, Davis criticises 'equity' feminism to follow a trickster strategy in re/structuring the order within the system, when a traitorous strategy could re/structure the systemic order. He thus addresses for feminist resistance in general the principles that are also relevant for strategies of – not only – feminist fictocritical writing. The question is what kind of (generic) resistance is fictocritical? Is the aim to occupy the marginal space of a generic between or is it to challenge the systemically marginalising centrality of generic practices? (Slashed) Ficto/criticism worthy of the name, I want to suggest, is systemically traitorous, strategic writing of the latter orientation.

Especially the traitorously ficto-*critical* direction in some strategies of *ficto*-critical generic resistance is an important element of ficto/critical textual practices. For example, instances of post/modern playfulness can either yield playfulness for its own sake or a purposive playfulness that serves a certain function. In fictocritical writing this marks the difference between a merely genre-conflating text and a text that conflates genres with a wider aim, an agenda even. In her PhD thesis, Helen Flavell has identified the stakes thus:

> "Since postmodernism and ficto-critical texts both question authority, value, representation and meaning they tend to be conflated. The application of postmodernism has, therefore, resulted in a diverse range of experimental ficto-critical forms being effectively lumped under one determinate label—or order-word—crushing other potential readings of this ficto-critical turn. Subsequently, given the debates and anxieties around postmodernism, ficto-criticism is often read as either all radical and challenging or dismissed as not rigorous, intellectual and disciplined." (2004: 135-6)

If post/modernist means in fictocritical texts are misrecognised either as aimless playfulness or as challenges against everything, this leaves no room to register the different ficto-*critical* purposes to which ficto/critical strategies employ post/modernist means *ficto*-critically.

There is, indeed, another way to understand post/modern playfulness which can accommodate the self-reflexive meta-perspective of the *ficto*-critical. As Niall Lucy insists in *PoMo Oz: Fear and Loathing Down Under*: "Postmodernism represents a continuation (by other means) of a critical project associated with the Enlightenment." (2010: 59) This project is "a critical scepticism towards received, official, orthodox, traditional, absolute or objective forms of truth and authority" (ibid: 59). In this sense, the post/modern means of the *ficto*-critical follow an enlightenment impetus because "it is 'postmodern' to ask after the conditions under which the meaning of a text might be said to occur" (ibid: 60). What enters the picture here is the idea of a self-reflexive meta-commentary to which we are guided by precisely the post/modern playfulness of such texts. It is often the purpose of post/modern playfulness in ficto/critical texts to drive our attention towards not only the limits but also the conditions of the im/possibility of our generic practices. This, after all, is the thrust of the *ficto*-critical vector and twist.

Additionally, however, we should productively read Flavell's reasoning that "ficto-criticism is a highly political discourse" (2004: 95) along the lines of this enlightenment understanding of post/modern textual means as well.

> "Ficto-criticism as a process that enables an autopoetic conceptualisation of the self destabilises the traditional subject of academic critical writing and dissolves the mastery of official discourses. It also reveals the fiction of genre. Ficto-critical forms make a connection between the style of writing and the content, asking both writers and readers to examine at the level of form what structures of domination are in place in our own writing and reading practices." (ibid: 295-6)

Thus, by im/mediately addressing the textual performance that we are involved in at the same time, the *ficto*-critical vector and twist make ficto/critical writing systemically emancipatory towards its reader even before it ficto-*critically* champions a particular cause of emancipation.

For example – and this shall return our focus to the distinction between gap and niche, between traitor and trickster – fictocriticism understood as positional feminist writing targets primarily the hierarchical male/female dichotomy, whereas ficto/criticism understood as emancipatory textual practice primarily targets the hierarchical perception of our textual relations and practices. In other words, emancipatory ficto/critical strategies go beyond positional feminist strategies because they target the hierarchical order of the male/female dichotomy in a manner that produces a self-reflexive meta-commentary not only on the hierarchy between writer, text, and reader but also on its role in maintaining the gendered hierarchy of speaking positions in academic writing.

We could thus apply the two earlier juxtapositions of trickster and traitor as well as gap and niche in order to separate the feminist impetus to claim a female form of writing from a more individual emancipatory impetus in ficto/critical writing. From this perspective, the primarily feminist principle prioritises targeting how generic academic writing re/inscribes the male/female dichotomy as significantly hierarchical. The strategy it adopts in its (hyphenated) ficto-critical practices aims to realign generic discipline so as to include a textual space for female speaking positions. By contrast, the primarily emancipatory principle prioritises targeting the hierarchical perceptions of our textual relations and practices. The strategy it adopts in its *ficto*-critical practices aims to realign the direction of textual disciplining on the level constitutive of genre. And it is precisely in this latter sense that the purposive post/modern playfulness in ficto/critical writing indicates how the hierarchical dichotomy between writer, text, and reader features heavily in perpetuating the hierarchical dichotomy between male and female speaking positions in academic writing.

On the one hand, a positional feminist focus follows the strategic impetus of the trickster in establishing a female textual form, even genre. Historically this is a highly significant factor in the genesis of fictocritical writing. On the other hand, however, the systemically emancipatory focus exemplifies a traitorous pattern by instigating idiosyncratic reading and writing that are motivated by unpredictable particulars. Therefore, I want to suggest that only a systematic analysis of this systemic enlightenment impetus in ficto/critical writing has the appropriate theoretical scope to unite all its different strands in evidence.

Brief Recapitulation

Ficto/criticism is an empty gap full of fluid potential. Its definitional outlines need to be theorised variably, so as not to ossify the space between into a niche. For the same reasons that punk is not rock, and jazz not always free form, ficto/critical textual practices are traitorous. Bridging the gap short-circuitously, the ficto/critical keeps its bridges gaping perceivably. Ficto/critical writing may be genetically feminist, but it is systemically emancipatory towards each individually engaged reading-writing agent. Tabling a just turn ficto/critically far exceeds just turning the tables.

3.1.2 Apotropaic Writing – Ficto-*critical* Textual Intervention

Having engaged a notion of ficto/criticism as experimental feminist writing to sharpen the profile of *ficto*-critical textual strategies in the previous section, I shall in the current section engage the notion that different academic genres can turn ficto/critical to sharpen the profile of ficto-*critical* textual strategies. Having detected the traitorous *ficto*-critical tendency to create a line of flight from a generic system by re/aligning its systemic lines, this shall now be supplemented with the ficto-*critical* tendency to counter the wider discursive effects of the generic textual practices on which such writing feeds. The most appropriate terminology for this strategic pattern can be found in Michael Taussig's "The Corn-Wolf: Writing Apotropaic Texts" (2010b), but the principle he so finely captures reverberates across the amorphous ficto/critical field: apotropaic writing as counter-generic textual intervention.

Writing in anthropology, Taussig has long gained a reputation, beyond his discipline, for his idiosyncratic style. Writing his studies on (other) human cultures, he is well aware that his discipline simultaneously produces its own culture in writing. This is a culture of writing in a generic academic manner that produces specific kinds of knowledge and effects. Reacting to this, Taussig has written ficto/critical ethnographies – such as *The Magic of The State* (1997) – with the aim to expose and counter, at least not be silently complicit with, some wider discursive effects of this generically disciplined writing. His short essay "The Corn-Wolf" presents an enigmatic theoretical reflection on the merits of writing ficto/critically in his field which, I want to argue, specifically captures the interventionist and text-practical dimension of ficto-*critical* writing.

To begin with, Taussig reminds us that anthropology cultivates a practice that converts a field under investigation into a piece of writing. This movement from "fieldwork to writingwork" (2010b: 26) involves at least a twofold translation: first from subjective experiences in the field into subjective notes on paper, then from the subjective fieldwork notebooks into an objective ethnographic treatise – that is, into a fixed textual genre. As he puts it, "fieldwork involves participant observation with people and events, being inside and outside, while writingwork involves magical projections through words into people and events" (ibid: 26). The transition goes from im/mediate experiences in the field to textually mediated experiences that are re/projected into the encounter via writing. This instituted practice of textual mediation can have real consequences because it can pre/structure future encounters with a culture thus written up.

Interestingly, a generic field of writingwork is thus being cultivated by anthropological fieldwork that investigates other cultures. On the back of this realisation,

Wittgenstein's idea that "[a] whole mythology is deposited in our language" (ibid: 28) becomes hugely inspirational for Taussig. In particular, it endows him with an "awareness about the magic in language, meaning the familiar moves it makes" (ibid: 27). Being thus sensitised towards mythological and magical patterns at work in the academic language which anthropology produces to demystify other culture's mythologies, Taussig turns his writingwork ficto/critical. Examining, in turn, how anthropology examines folk mythologies such as the corn-wolf, he suggests that generic ethnographic writingwork is the correlate of agribusiness practices in the field – it is a culture that displaces our cultural receptivity to mythologies such as the corn-wolf. He pursues the hidden mythology and magic at the heart of anthropology that enables *this one* cultural practice to dispel the mythologies and magic of other cultures.

Taussig thus detects a magic-defying counter-magic at work in anthropological writing. Because he is keenly aware of how anthropological textual culture implies one in its project, he begins to connive with the mythology in our language and the magic of our writing against their deployment to dispel other cultures' mythologies. In order not to be complicit with the wider generic effects of anthropological writing, in fact to expose and counter them, Taussig aims to replicate, to different effect, the magic *of* anthropology *on* anthropology. His writing follows an apotropaic strategy that works to counter the magic-defying magic of generic anthropological writingwork. His ficto/critical ethnographic writing thus hopes to re/enchant, not de/mystify, the object of his fieldwork.

The cultural practice of anthropological writing translates the magical practices of other cultures into the known order of Western culture. Just like magical healing in some non-Western cultures it is thus a practice that serves to re/establish the known cultural order. When ethnographic writing comes to terms with the mythologies and magic of other cultures by reducing the unknown and strange to the known and familiar, its promise is that "[a]s if by magic the disorder of the world will be straightened out" (ibid: 30). Anthropological writing itself thus serves a magical purpose, but this is rendered invisible by its culture's claim to generality. With regards to other cultures Taussig analyses that "[w]hat we have generally done in anthropology is [...] piggybacking on their magic and on their conjuring—their tricks—so as come up with explanations that seem nonmagical and free of trickery" (ibid: 30). A consequence of its "using magic to seem as if having none" (ibid: 30) is that anthropology "knows no wonder that [...] is really a wonder" (ibid: 29). By contrast, he implicitly outlines his apotropaic approach as writing that conveys "the sense of chaos moving not to order but to another form of chaos" (ibid: 30).

Taussig's anthropological writing turns this magic defying magic around by turning it on itself: such apotropaic writing estranges the purportedly known of anthropological culture. His point is that generic anthropological writingwork "assumes explanation when what is at issue is why is one required. What is an explanation and how do you do one, and how weird is that?" (ibid: 29) What needs explanation in Taussig's eyes is the all too familiar practice of explanatory writing. While generic ethnography re/establishes the order of Western culture and discourse in writing, Taussig's apotropaic writing subjects this anthropological ordering system to a dose of its own de/mystifying scrutiny – however, not without simultaneously re/mystifying his own ficto/critical writing and discourse. With regards to the mythologies deposited in our language Taussig's apotropaic project thus aims at "becoming aware of that presence in our lives, in our writing, and institutions, so as to neither expose nor erase but conspire with it, as does the wolf" (ibid: 28). Conniving with the mythology and magic of our language, Taussig thus works some counter magic himself to defy the magic defying magic of anthropological textual practices.

There are thus two kinds of counter-magic at work. Anthropological writing counters the magic of other cultures, but Taussig's apotropaic writing seeks to counter this magic-defying kind of writing. Turning ficto/critical, his writing furthermore re/enchants anthropology at the same time as it hopes to recant some of its wider discursive effects. The apotropaic magic of his ficto/critical writing aims both to counter the magic-defying magic of generic anthropological writing and to reveal it as only one (textual) culture among many – albeit a very powerful one. Taussig engages the mythology deposited in our language in order to cast a self-reflexive spell that can dispel the unmarked mythology of anthropological writing. His point is to work counter-magic in writing that paradoxically exposes the magic of writingwork by harnessing its magic. Such ficto/critical writing apotropaically re/directs received generic powers not without empowering its recipient with regards to the writingwork they encounter. In turn, it thus traitorously breaks the magic circle to let it unpredictably spiral – possibly out of control.

Rather than just being *ficto*-critically traitorous to the hierarchies and epistemologies of the genres from within which they depart, ficto-*critical* texts thus also re/direct the power that a given form can provide for a cause. In this regard it can be productive to consider Kwame Anthony Appiah's famous text "Is the Post- in Postmodernism the Post- in Postcolonial?" (1991), albeit strictly for the purposes of the present argument. In the following, I shall first re/trace the logic that Appiah sees in two successive phases of post/colonial African writing and then speculate on a logical next step in this development. The post/colonial potential of ficto-*critical* strategies shall be my main focus in all this.

In the first generation of post/colonial African novels Appiah finds a conservative strategy that pairs its realist (and/or modernist) form with a nationalist post/colonial agenda. Novels that Appiah has in mind are, for example, Chinua Achebe's *Things Fall Apart* and Camara Laye's *L'Enfant Noir* (Appiah 1991: 348) or Ahmadou Kourouma's *Suns of Independence* (ibid: 353). Typically, such texts would aim to provide the newly post/colonial nation with an epic narrative. In this sense, "these early novels seem to belong to the world of eighteenth- and nineteenth-century literary nationalism; they are theorized as the imaginative reaction of a common cultural past that is crafted into a shared tradition by the writer" (ibid: 349). They transplant the realist literary means and strategies of a European nationalist politics – which has contributed to colonialism – into their post/colonial context.

For Appiah, as for the second wave of African novels responding to these texts, however, the problem is that "[t]he novels of this first stage are thus realist legitimations of nationalism" (ibid: 349). Immediately after the revolutionary change, the strategy is again to preserve both the (new) politically and (old) generically dominant powers, as well as their orders. The critique of power in the first wave is thus not systemic, but distributive. It follows a clear trickster strategy. Not the marginalising logic is under critique but the fact that the newly stipulated post/colonial 'we' is located at those margins. Simply put, the aim is to cut the ties to the colonial centre in order to create a marginal centre, while yet perpetuating the same kind of nation and nationalism there.

In a second stage of African novels, as prime examples of which he names Chinua Achebe's *A Man of the People* and Yambo Ouologuem's *Le Devoir de violence* (ibid: 349), Appiah detects a more revolutionary approach. These texts present a kind of anti-epic narrative that problematises the concept of a post/colonial nation. Dwelling on Ouologuem's work, Appiah finds that in this text "he rejects, indeed assaults, the conventions of realism [...] because what it sought to naturalize was a nationalism that, by 1968, had plainly failed" (ibid: 249). The novels of the second stage thus mark the combined generic resistance to a certain textual form and to its associated post/colonial politics. They "reject not only the Western *imperium* but also the nationalist project of the postcolonial national bourgeoisie" (ibid: 353, original emphasis) and mount "a challenge to the novels of the first stage" because they have identified "the realist novel as part of the tactic of nationalist legitimation" (ibid: 349). The trickster strategy of the first stage is thus replaced with a more traitorous strategy. The second wave is both post-nativist and post-realist. It no longer aims to emancipate – or rather: to put in power – a native group within the existing nationalist order, but to mount a systemic emancipation from this ordering principle.

For *Le Devoir de violence* Appiah observes that it "is a novel that seeks to delegitimate not only the form of realism but the content of nationalism" (ibid: 352). But he cautions that this twofold delegitimation in novels of the second wave may "seem to us, misleadingly, postmodern: misleadingly, because what we have here is not postmodern*ism* but postmodern*isation*; not an aesthetic but a politics" (ibid: 352-3, original emphases). Akin to Flavell above, Appiah sees the need to defend a post/modern textual form as not aimlessly playful but purposively directed. Yet he maintains that "the basis for that project of delegitimation cannot be the postmodernist one: rather, it is grounded in an appeal to an ethical universal" (ibid: 353). Based on our findings so far, however, there is now reason to believe that a ficto/critical application of post/modernist means can indeed highlight the connection between the form of a text and the politics it espouses because it identifies the textual performance under way as the operative link between the two. The ficto/critical kind of purposive playfulness, I want to suggest, has thus found a way to make post/modernist textual means ethically significant, even (cultural) politically viable.

The systemically emancipatory aspect that ficto/criticism has brought to feminist writing it can also contribute to the line of post/colonial writing that Appiah so famously discusses. While *ficto*-critical strategies can highlight our generic textual practices to us, ficto-*critical* strategies can give ethically motivated, practical direction to our performances of these practices. In other words, post/colonial texts turn ficto/critical when they harness the critique of self-reflexive literary theory to their politically post/colonial agenda – one which is generically no longer neo- but finally non- if not anti-colonial. The underlying realisation is that the textual form does indeed matter, albeit only in its connection to our textual practices. The aim is to lead out of the dominating generic system just as much as out of the dominating political system; to lead, unpredictably, elsewhere. In this respect, the challenge of ficto/critical texts would thus be systemically post/colonial. Ultimately, they would highlight the potential inherent in our de/centred textual work to change direction on the practical level of meaning, other, and self-formation. They would tap the ficto/critical to work some traitorously apotropaic magic by deploying textual means in order to expose the power of such means while simultaneously harnessing this power in a new direction.

Notably, Taussig has an enigmatic term to capture the potential in our writing practices for both a generic regime with certain effects and its subversion. On the general level he calls such constitutively ambiguous complexes a "Nervous System" – to examples of which he dedicates an entire book by the same title (1992) – but he also specifically refers to our textual practices within them as "Nervous System writing" (2010b: 32). Taussig furthermore maintains that "[i]f it is true that there is a mythology deposited in our language, NS [i.e. Nervous System] writing aims not at exposing that mythology but at conniving with it" (ibid: 32). Importantly, there is good reason to distinguish between two fundamentally different thrusts, strategies, and principles of Nervous System writing.

On the one hand there is writing that sustains the order of a centralised nervous system. For example, Taussig characterises generic anthropological writing as "agribusiness" with regards to the field it investigates as much as with regards to the academic field it draws up, because it cultivates a magic-dispelling practice in writing that becomes culturally dominant, even hegemonic, and thus displaces the magic of other practices in both fields:

> "Agribusiness writing is a mode of production (see Marx) that conceals the means of production, assuming writing as information to be set aside from writing that has poetry, humor, luck, sarcasm, leg pulling, the art of the storyteller, and subject becoming object. It assumes writing to be a communicative means, not a source of experience for reader and writer alike." (ibid: 29)

With this concept, Taussig aligns the monocultures of the agrarian and academic sectors, both of which dominate at the expense of a multiplicity of other cultures and practices. Whereas the corn-wolf mythologises, the rational narrative of agribusiness cuts mythology out of the equation, reaping profits at the cost of a poorer fieldworking culture. Likewise, figuratively speaking, "[a]gribusiness writing wants to drain the wetlands. Swamps, they used to be called, dank places where bugs multiply" (ibid: 30).

On the other hand, there is apotropaic Nervous System writing, which re/injects the system with a dose of nervousness. For example, whereas the generic rules of literary criticism decree that "[y]ou can write about James Joyce, but not like James Joyce" (ibid: 29), this is precisely where Taussig's ficto/critical turn takes his writing. Equally, and this takes us back to the central paradox of generic resistance, whereas "[a]gribusiness writing wants mastery, not the mastery of non-mastery" (ibid: 29), precisely the latter becomes the unpredictable goal of the ficto/critical. Most importantly for the perspective of this current section, however, it becomes the ficto-*critical* task of Taussig's own anthropology to provide an antidote to the effects of agribusiness writing in order to pursue a re/medially apotropaic strategy.

Ultimately, Taussig's twofold terminology of Nervous System writing highlights that both agribusiness and apotropaic writing are strategies that depart from the same field whose means and mechanisms they apply to very different effect. Agribusiness writing presents a Nervous System in this twofold sense: firstly, it imposes an order, a system, onto the practices of fieldwork; secondly, it trembles with nervousness at the prospect of being thrown back into chaos by the preceding mythological spells it dispelled. To return these spells is the object of apotropaic writing which thus retrieves the nervousness in the nerve endings of the system. It is interventionist writing that targets the detrimental effects of a dominant monoculture from within and thus hopes to give its power not only a different but a re/medial direction. Yet, apotropaic writing is no less nervous (system) writing: firstly, it is jumpy writing that injects systemic nervousness into a generic order; secondly, it highlights and re/deploys the nervous system of our textual practices for its re/medial purposes.

For example, John Kinsella sometimes writes apotropaic pastorals. One of his poetry collections is called *Counter-Pastoral* (1999), but there is a whole range of publications such as *The Silo: A Pastoral Symphony* (1995), *The Hierarchy of Sheep* (2000), or *The New Arcadia* (2005) that testify to his sustained and apotropaic interest in the pastoral tradition. In his autobiographic text *Auto* Kinsella reflects on this writing strategy as follows: "I try to write a poetry that undoes the poetry I enjoy reading. To work an illusion is to tell alternative 'truths'." (2001: 61) His poetry not only counters a certain kind of poetry on which it feeds, but it is also concerned with the alternative 'truths' that it conjures up in the process. Perhaps it is thus closer to artful experimentation than the artistically experimental. His statement, in any case, comes in a chapter entitled "The Magic Circle" (ibid: 60-3). When his father initiates him to a circle of part-time magicians, the young Kinsella soon begins copying the magic he encounters as well as making up his own magic in response.

On the one hand he learns tricks to participate in the circle, to have something up his sleeve, and to counter the tricks of the others. His incantation is: "To beat an illusion make an illusion." (ibid: 62) And this little wisdom is still pertinent when it comes to the idea of creating truths and alternative truths through poetry. To beat pastoral poetry, its generic effects and the wider discursive function it serves, write pastoral poetry, only make it apotropaic: counter-pastoral. On the other hand, Kinsella also learns of another kind of magic that emerges from his literally marginal writing: "I collated books of tricks and made notes in the margins about the history of a particular illusion. Lacunae and diagrams, marginalia and annotations grew and made their own linguistic tricks. Poetry came out of the magic books." (ibid: 61) His marginal meta-comments thus provided a way to work the magic of these texts for his purposes, but they also wrought a poetic magic entirely their own.

Furthermore, after getting guilty kicks from listening in on conversations that were never intended for him, he finds this experience to be "[t]he same thing as magic, an intrusion into one's perceptions. That's when the author died for me – my poetry had nothing to do with tricking the reader – the tricks were made by the reader him/herself. They did all the believing or non-believing." (ibid: 63) As Kinsella realises how the agency of magic in writing shifts to the recipient, he thus intimates apotropaic strategies of textual subversion – ultimately, an apotropaic theory of textual practices along the lines of Taussig's corn-wolf. And so, the magic circle re/turns spiralling as Kinsella's counter-pastoral writing draws something close to traitorous crop circles in the field of pastoral poetry.

Moreover, the futurity of ficto/critical apotropaic writing is central for Taussig in that it is concerned with its posterity. In his terminology such textual acts always intervene by taking "this one chance, the one permanently before the last" (ibid: 32). This interventionist temporality of ficto/critical writing is pre/post/erous indeed. For example, it is one of Taussig's ficto-*critical* concerns that writing about violence can perversely feed into its discursive reign of terror against one's best intentions. In the "Preface to the Thirtieth Anniversary Edition" of *The Devil and Commodity Fetishism in South America* he reflects this:

> "I struggled to better understand the violence of the atrocities of the rubber boom in the Putumayo region of the Upper Amazon around 1900, and that understanding made me focus increasingly on the talking and writing of terror, coupled with mounting sensitivity as to how most writing on violence makes it worse." (2010a: xii)

He realises that his work of addressing the violence is in danger of perpetuating the discursive system that serves its terror. In a sinister way, thus, even his efforts to expose and condemn the violence still risk backfeeding into the discursive logic that underwrites the terror of violence.

Partly, Taussig's musings on the magic of the corn-wolf and the need for counter-magic are motivated from the practical concern not to fuel the self-perpetuating system of violence, terror, and stories about it, because "[w]orse still, [by writing about violence] you so easily make it worse" (2010b: 28). Many other examples of this back-feeding complex can also be found throughout Taussig's work:

> "Or else I am writing about liposuction and cosmetic surgery as I hear ever wilder stories about these procedures in Colombia among poor young women [...], but what stands out most is the fairy-tale resonance of this endeavor ending in disaster, same as the stories of the devil contracts that I heard in the Colombian sugarcane fields almost forty years ago." (2010b: 28)

Again Taussig is concerned not to re/inscribe the discourse that perversely feeds into the mythologies that perpetuate liposuction. His strategy to counter the magic of such discourses warrants counter-magic that exposes their poetics while harnessing its powers elsewhere.

The same holds true for Taussig's approach to the blood rushing, power-crazed discourses that surround gold, cocaine, or oil and his practical concern for their wider discursive effects:

> "Or else I am thinking of the desperate need for cocaine, the mythologies this rests upon and creates, cocaine that has now made Colombia into a drug colony instead of what it was for four hundred years, a gold colony, and if you don't know or can't feel the mythic power of gold and the fairy tales it has spawned circling around God and the devil, then there is no hope for you." (ibid: 28)

In other words, these ficto-*critical* concerns are at the heart of Taussig's *ficto*-critical take on the corn-wolfing practices of his reading and writing. His re/medial hope is based on the text-practical ideology of what he calls "'penultimaticity', writing as the one permanently before the last" (2010a: xiii). Taussig elaborates this scenario as follows.

> "The writer looks the history in the face at the receiving end of a chain of storytellers and has for a brief moment this one chance, the one permanently before the last, to make this intervention in the state of emergency, before the writer's story is swallowed up by the response it causes." (2010b: 32)

The re/medial hope of apotropaic writing in/formed by this penultimaticity is that "the tension of this interval between your displacing story and the next story that will displace it can create a force field in which the violence can be transmuted into healing" (2010a: xiii).

Against the background of this text-practical ideology Taussig is strategically motivated to *ficto*-critically highlight the mechanisms and means at work in such discourses in general and in his writing in particular. Simultaneously his writing implies our (always already) present reading practices that are no less involved in the self-perpetuation of such discursive systems. The ficto-*critical* aspects of his work are these wider discursive concerns that have sparked the development of *ficto*-critical strategies in writing. "Nervous System writing" is pre/post/erous because it "aims at being one jump ahead of the rules of rulelessness" (2010b: 32). Only agribusiness writing cannot admit to this, while apotropaic writing both explains and exploits this p/re/structuring potential. Apotropaic ficto/critical writing thus hopes to traitorously lead elsewhere when its counter-strategy aims to enlighten and empower the text's recipient about the kind of magic that Nervous System writing works. Ficto/critical textual strategies of this kind are thus traitorous towards their generic origin, apotropaic towards the magic they both counter and continue, as well as pre/post/erous in that they aim to pre/structure our shared discursive post/erity to re/medial effect.

Brief Recapitulation

Over the course of this section two defining characteristics of ficto/critical strategies have been qualified. Firstly, *ficto*-critical textual strategies are marked by traitorous resistance to the generic order from which they emerge because they aim to lead unpredictably elsewhere, that is to a different non-generic reordering, rather than into a marginal order between which could potentially re/turn generic. Secondly, ficto-*critical* textual strategies are marked by apotropaic interventions into the generic effects they target. They harness the constitutive power and means of generic textual practices to re/mediate their effects by way of counter-continuation to re/medial effect. Furthermore, both these aspects of the ficto/critical aim to re/lay the understanding of our textual practices that create such power to begin with. Their mutual goal is to theoretically enlighten and practically empower each individual recipient with regards to the textual acts they are necessarily engaged in at the same time.

A ficto/critically in/formed understanding of our reading and writing practices, in fact, provides the central hinge of the twofold ficto/critical trope, between the realisation of the *ficto*-critical vector and twist and the development of ficto-*critical* edge. Re/theorising our textual acts endows the ficto/critical with im/mediate practical relevance. It is how the ficto/critical manages not to perpetuate the generic practices it criticises. Such ficto/critical theories aim to capture aspects of the Nervous System of our textual practices that in/forms the ideologies of both ficto/critical and generic writing practices. As ficto/critical theories re/configure the constitutive constellational textual frame/work anew, it makes sense to re/conceive of the ficto/critical on the meta-generic level – by re/locating the pervasive notions and terminology of the gap and the space between from the level of the laws of genre onto the level of the laws of the laws of genre. In the following section, two central such ideals shall first be re/traced in primary ficto/critical texts and then be juxtaposed each with a more traditional and conservative understanding.

3.2 PRE/POST/EROUS TEXT-PRACTICAL IDEOLOGIES

At this point in the thesis I shall address the theoretical understanding on the basis of which ficto/critical practices mount textual interventions strategically. In pursuit of this objective, I am going to re/trace specifically ficto/critical ideologies of our textual practices in general. To better understand the parameters, mechanisms, and means by which ficto/critical texts perform and perpetuate interventionist textual acts, I shall re/focalise the paradigmatic situation of our textual practices from a ficto/critical perspective. In particular, I shall focus on the constitutive mechanisms that the ficto/critical sets to work differently from the generic academic practices it resists. In this manner, the current section will re/trace the theoretical frame/work and text-practical ideology that lets ficto/critical writing counter our generic textual practices and their text-practical ideology. As before, the underlying thesis is that our understanding of reading and writing practices indeed guides our performance of such textual work. The point is to clarify how ficto/critical practices capitalise on re/conceiving – on the meta-generic level – of the gaps and betweens at the spatio-temporal heart of reading and writing.

On the one hand, this section aims to identify the crucial theoretical and ideological break that in/forms ficto/critical writing. A first subsection shall re/focus the temporally de/centred understanding of the textual work that spans two agents and their twofold singular textual acts. A second subsection then re/focuses the spatially de/centred understanding of the text that spans both the fixedly inscribed constellation of the manifest object text and the ephemerally recurring re/configurations of the transcendental textual object. On the other hand, this section aims to provide the parameters of the communicative situation of textual representation from which flow the possible *nexi* for harnessing the *ficto*-critical vector and twist to generate ficto-*critical* edge.

To begin with, however, the first part now focuses on the temporal re/conception of our cultural practices of textual communication as an abductive kind of translation, before the second part then shifts the focus onto the spatial conception of our cultural practices of textual representation as a maternally perverse kind of encapsulation. Between them, these two *ficto*-critical theories come to present the core of text-practical ideology which in/forms the strategic pattern of the ficto/critical trope – both its traitorous generic resistance and apotropaic interventionist ambition.

3.2.1 Abductive Writing

> "Commentary and translation are to text as style and mimesis to nature: the same phenomenon viewed in different ways. On the tree of the sacred text they are both mere ever-rustling leaves; on the tree of the profane text, fruit falling at the right time."
> WALTER BENJAMIN/ONE-WAY STREET (2009A: 54)

In this subsection I shall examine how ficto/critical textual intervention is at least partly based on a theoretical understanding of textual communication as constitutively translational. The specific focus here will be on how the constitutive mechanisms of the temporal dimension of the textual work can be conceived of differently with a view to developing ficto-*critical* edge. I shall indicate how the interventionist ambition of some ficto/critical writing practices capitalises on the theoretical insight that the textual work consists of a series of textual acts spread over the realms of con/textual influence of two linguistic-discursive agents. According to this text-practical ideology, each singular textual act facilitates an abductive translational movement between – a phase transition between both con/texts and states of matter – that constitutively re/configures a given textual or discursive constellation. My thesis is that ficto/critical writing sets this re/constitutive re/lay chain of relational mediation within mediating relations to work abductively for its wider discursive ficto-*critical* concerns.

Arctic Flowers of Rhetoric

Aritha van Herk's fourth novel length publication *Places Far From Ellesmere* (1990) creates the potential to simultaneously unsettle her reader's ideas of place and of reading. Specifically, her text mounts a feminist counter-strategy to tackle male inscriptions of womanhood, which she couples with a focus on the mutually influential relation between self and place. Notably, van Herk unites this twofold directedness in an idiosyncratic notion of reading. Her combined principle interest thus lies in the reading and writing relations between self and text as well as between self and place and their mutual interference. In other words, *Places Far From Ellesmere* harbours a theory of how our conceptions of self and place are always already mediated by our textual acts as bi/directionally impacting events.

After her narrator's reflection on her formative years in three south Canadian cities, van Herk lets the development of this theory into strategies of counter-continuation culminate in a journey north, far north, to Ellesmere Island.

The book consists of four chapters, in the first three of which the narrator re/encounters the central places of her life: Edmonton, Edberg and Calgary. The fourth chapter then consists of her re/encounter with an influential novel in a markedly different place: Ellesmere. These two different kinds of re/encounter roughly divide the book in half. The first half re/traces how the narrator has been (in)formed as a woman and academic reader by her social, topological, as well as discursive habitats. The narrator is herself a product of these three places far from Ellesmere, but she also re/produces these places for us in writing on Ellesmere. There, she shifts their formations to the textual realm, where *she* is now the agent of inscription. Having been formed by these places she, in turn, finds a textual form to re/mediate them. The second half of the book – the fourth chapter "Ellesmere, woman as island" (1990: 77-143) – then presents a re/medial approach to reading pre/scribed discursive structures in an enabling con/text and environment. Here, van Herk intersects the narrator's encounter with the otherworldly elsewhere of Ellesmere and her re/reading of Tolstoy's *Anna Karenina.*

The book thus presents the reader with the narrator's protocols of reading throughout – firstly, her re/reading of the formative places (far from Ellesmere), secondly, her "un/read[ing]" (Van Herk 1990: 91) of the formative text (on Ellesmere). Geographic and discursive formations intersect on a number of levels. Most importantly, Ellesmere is indexed to an understanding of reading of which the fourth chapter, which presents this theory, is already a protocol. The place is endowed with an emancipating discursive potential for female reading (and writing) positions. It empowers van Herk's narrator to liberate her/self from received formations – topological as well as discursive – that have become formative. In this sense, Ellesmere is the locus of re/formative reading.

Van Herk's narrator abducts *Anna Karenina*, as an exemplary case, from the con/text within which this book would otherwise affect her into a con/text that is most suitable to a feminist re/reading of it. On Ellesmere she begins "to read this disconnected corpulent Russian novel that pretended for so long to read the essential psyche of the passionate woman succumbing to extreme and impossible passions, infecting all around her" (ibid: 91). Her interest is directed at the poetics of negative influence that *Anna Karenina* has exerted, in our readings, on the notion of womanhood. Her goal is to counter-continue the discursive spell Tolstoy's work casts and to dispel its wider effects on the formation of a female readerly self. On Ellesmere van Herk's narrator comes to realise that "[y]ou are free to un/read yourself, home, Anna, the rest of Canada, all possible text" (ibid: 91). Her con/textual abduction of self and book thus coincides with an un-reading of this canonical text, its main character, Anna Karenina, who is Tolstoy's depiction of womanhood in general, and their combined effect on the (female) reader's sense of (a readerly) self.

The strategy of un/reading that develops on Ellesmere is closely connected to the place because a female reader is "[f]ree here of the graspings of most of ( )man's impositions, his history or fiction or implacable des/scribement, (wo)men either real or invented" (ibid: 113, original ellipsis). In the absence of pre/scribed male structures on the island the narrator is able to conceive of their textual poetics differently and assume agency. On Ellesmere, she is able to re/work such male pre/scriptions by p/re/scribing them, in turn, on the level of text. Her motivation is rooted in "a dazzling dislike for the good intentions of [Tolstoy's] novel, the way they insinuate themselves into a perfectly miserable life and try to cure it, the way they maneuver your reading" (ibid: 104). If reading properly entails *this* for women, then surely it were better to read p/re/post/erously – in a way that p/re/structures these inscriptions for post/erity – in order to prevent the text's wider discursive effects.

Van Herk's narrator is looking for an apotropaic strategy that acknowledges the mutually bi/directional mechanisms of influence between self and text. In light of this, she reminds herself – as much as her reader – of the empowering insight that the only way out is through: "You have read farther than there are pages, travelled farther than there are fictions. You are seduced, a lost woman, reading from within the fiction of all lost/damned/condemned/free women. Knowing that this story, all that is written can be un/read, uninscribed." (ibid: 113) Thus she begins to devise a counter-continuing strategy of discursive resistance by means of reading and writing: un/read Tolstoy's pre/scription of womanhood, protocol this un/reading for post/erity to re/read the formative text; aim thus to p/re/scribe and re/form the text's wider discursive effects.

Addressing the poetics of male pre/scriptions with a view to redressing their wider effects, her strategies of reading and writing become pre/post/erous. For example, she purposively omits some of the text's passages and characters from her reading; most notably perhaps: "Levin, whom you want to avoid, will a/void. He is not here on Ellesmere, although he is in the book. You will not let him out, you cannot stand his fulminating, his pseudo-philosophizing. When you get to him, you snap the book shut, wrap a thick elastic band around it […]" (ibid: 103). Or she abducts characters, like Princes Myagky, from the pages to her con/text on Ellesmere (ibid: 102-3). By creatively engaging the gaps and interstitial spaces of the novel's fictional world she even brings its heroine to comment meta-fictionally (ibid: 112). All in all, she abducts the text from its rigidly established con/text to Ellesmere, where a different, a con/textually abductive reading is possible. Exploiting the constitutive mechanisms of textual communication, van Herk's narrator abducts the discursive structures of Tolstoy's novel. With good reason and a purpose, she de- and re/con/textualises its pre/scribed formations in singular acts of reading and writing.

Van Herk's narrator abducts the fictional character Anna Karenina from the context of the fixedly inscribed text *Anna Karenina* in order to dispel the spell that it holds over our reading as long as we conceive of it as a finished textual work. Much to the contrary, she re/conceives of the reader's textual work as the task to engage with Anna Karenina as the consequential epitome of a male pre/scribed woman reader. Because, throughout, Anna has been "[c]reated by a man, written by a man, read by men, revised by men", van Herk's narrator tells herself that "now, here on Ellesmere, you dare to set her free from the darkness of pages" (ibid: 122). And in this fashion, the text and its characters are deliberately un/read – partly not read, and partly re/read to re/medial effect. The text, which purports to write up the essence of womanhood, is thereby written on in a significantly different direction. Van Herk thus deploys the constitutive mechanisms of textual communication in pre/post/erous fashion for her feminist concerns.

Because Tolstoy mis/read women and inscribed a powerful discursive formation whose effects now haunt our notions of womanhood, van Herk's narrator assumes readerly agency on behalf of Anna Karenina, to whom it is denied in the text, in order to mis/read *Anna Karenina*, in turn. Her mis/readings, in fact, amount to apotropaic un/readings. On Ellesmere a shift of textual agency becomes possible – from the almost holy, pre/structuring text to a profane, maybe even heretic, p/re/structuring act of reading that re/configures the text-discursive constellations with an emancipatory interest at heart. With her concern for female speaking positions in a male dominated and pre/scribed field, van Herk develops a structural metaphor by juxtaposing the wild poppies of the north to the domesticated flowers in the south.

> "The yellow Arctic poppies so much less proper than the wifely blue harebells. Their slender, hairy stems bend to the ink inside their yellow cups, bright against the grey-green ground. Small wells of ink inside their stems, their cups, as if they are flowers of writing, writing themselves strewn over Ellesmere." (ibid: 106)

These poppies are the flowers of pre/post/erous readings that van Herk has in mind. Their agency in this respect stands in the way of their being proper. As a structural metaphor they illustrate the writing that protocols her emancipating readings on Ellesmere.

Crucially, these ficto/critical flowers of writing differ from the closed form of the novel. The poppies' textual agency suggests the future directed principle of writing on, which stands in opposition to the (f)rigidity of a finished form that reproduces only the same sealed-off fictional world. By contrast, there is "[a] bed of Arctic poppies on Ellesmere, and a lover to read their ink" (ibid: 107). The arctic poppies thus become an icon of a female and ficto/critical agency of *receptive* dissemination. Furthermore, as "those flowers pressed against your skin will stain it with their Arctic ink" (ibid: 107) they (p)re/structure the reading self as female by writing back at those male pre/structuring formations. The structural metaphor of the Arctic poppies centrally inscribes these ficto/critical notions of interventionist reading and writing on Ellesmere which thus becomes the place of de/territorialisingly productive reading-writing – the locus of deconstruction even – where writing protocols re/medial readings.

Against this backdrop, van Herk takes particular exception to the fact that Tolstoy seems to punish Anna Karenina for engaging in reading and writing herself. She realises that "Anna makes herself well read in an attempt to unread her earlier passivity" (ibid: 137). Viewed from Ellesmere, "Anna's reading is her act of educating herself, reading herself into an unreading of how she has been read. More notable: Anna writes" (ibid: 137). Fleshing out his fiction in terms of her theory, "it is clear that what Anna is doing when Tolstoy is not looking is writing herself, and the Anna who reads is a front for the Anna writing her own passionate involvement with her own story" (ibid: 137). Moreover, the two are inextricably entwined – on Ellesmere there is only reading-writing. Because "Anna needs a friend, a woman friend, a reader" (ibid: 112), the narrator assumes this agency of reading and writing – for which Tolstoy condemns Anna – on her behalf. Her apotropaic reading-writing permits Anna Karenina to be salvaged, on behalf of women, from *Anna Karenina*. Finally, it is also on behalf of all readers that she "invented the necessity to read her yourself. Despite Tolstoy." (ibid: 81)

Ultimately, the effeminate notion of the reader, too, needs to be salvaged from Tolstoy's cursing approach. Here van Herk's positional feminist and systemic emancipatory ambitions fall into one. She demands "[n]o preconditioned reading" (ibid: 122). The point is that the spell of pre/scription can be broken by reception as p/re/scription. For her narrator, only through this strategy "[t]he real novel (about Anna reading) begins", which is "about you reading Anna, [...] about all Annas and their readings of themselves" (ibid: 132). Ultimately, this ficto/critical ideology of the textual work demands an ethically in/formed, pre/post/erous engagement with text-discursive structures. In pursuit of this, it is indispensable that we de/familiarise and re/conceive of our text-practical ideologies – we need to visit to Ellesmere before we can get there.

Translational Reading-Writing

In the following I shall use the expression "reading-writing" not only for the combined acts of both reading and writing – as in protocols of reading, for example – but also as shorthand for the constituent links of relational mediation that form the re/lay chain of textual communication. In this latter respect, the term "reading-writing" refers to the coinciding movements of de- and re/con/textualisation that constitute our textual acts of reading *or* writing. I deploy this notion, therefore, as a translational trope of re/configuration to explain the communication of discursive constellations via textual structures. In particular, "reading-writing" marks the fact that simultaneous induction and deduction are constitutively at work in both the idealising movements of reading and the manifesting movements of writing. My thesis is that every textual act consists in these coinciding inductive and deductive processes that, between them, work an abductive translational movement of relational mediation – a phase transition from one con/text and state of matter into the next, according to their respectively framing mediating relations.

Qua medium, the text constitutively bridges the communicative divide, which it introduces just as much as our textual practices exercise it. But the text is hardly the only mediating agent in the equation. Rather, the communicative agency is split between writer and reader across the con/textual divide. Because the text-medial interpolation bridges the communicative gap it introduces only at the cost of creating two new such gaps – between text and writer, and text and reader – this bridge is left gaping. The paradigmatic con/textual and representational de- and re/location of a discursive constellation in textual communication is thus effectively doubled: firstly, from the writerly (idiocultural) con/text into a textual form, secondly, from that textual basis into the readerly (idiocultural) con/text. The crucial point is that whereas every such text-communicative act instantiates the trope of reading-writing, ficto/critical ideology embraces these constitutive mechanics – by virtue of which a discursive constellation is relayed only as it is re/laid and thus re/configured – in an abductive translational movement between. By contrast, academic textual practices usually follow a conservatively translational ideal of reading-writing – which text-ideologically prevents their interventionist potential.

Passages of Abduction

John Hughes's collection *Someone Else: Fictional Essays* (2007) highlights the constitutive trope of reading-writing to *ficto*-critical effect when it makes a virtue of the abductive principle. The book comprises a diverse range of unusually composed, yet neatly structured, fictional essays or theoretical fictions – many of which, I want to suggest, examine the poetics of reading and writing in terms of reading-writing. These experimental texts involve authors, artists, musicians, and philosophers as well as their works, themes, characters, and lives. Hughes's imagination and writing thus let the discursive structures that constitute an author – as Michel Foucault has famously argued in "What is an Author?" (1984) – mingle on the same level with the discursive structures that constitute their work. He furthermore lets these epistemic entities mingle on a par with his own personal experience and imagination. His essays incorporate a wealth of inter-textual, but also some intra-textual references, all of which suggests textual grafting as an overriding principle of Hughes's approach to reading and writing.

For example, we find this abductive approach both expressed and performed by the following passage which is tellingly re/deployed both in the "Preface" (which already takes the form of a fictional essay) and as the blurb on the back cover (which serves a framing function not unlike a preface):

> "It was as if I had created a novel in my head, [he said,] the characters would not be still, they rose up from the pages of their different books and argued and fought and merged and grew inside me, but with an autonomy that made them as real to me as you are, sitting here now. I was not alone in this … but […] I was, perhaps, a little more extreme, a little more possessed. I wanted to be haunted." (Hughes 2007a: xv, 208, my square brackets mark two points of minimal divergence)

In the prefatory essay the passage is uttered by a character taken from Max Brod's diary, yet on the dust jacket it introduces Hughes's own method of writing the essays of the collection – including the "Preface" (2007a). Statically performative, his formal re/location of this particular passage thus already instantiates the kind of character abduction it outlines. It epitomises the underlying principle of abducting textual passages or discursive constellations which, once re/con/textualised or re/configured, may serve different functions and effects.

Throughout his book Hughes abducts manifest textual structures no less than textually conceived epistemic entities or discursive formations, such as fictional or authorial characters. In so doing, he highlights a transformative poetics of quotation, grafting, and translation at the heart of our textual acts – one that is favoured by the constitutive mechanisms of con/textual withdrawal and textual re/situation. In terms of text-practical ideology he conceives of the translational trope of reading-writing as the abductive principle of all our reading and writing. Furthermore, he lets the personal pronoun "you" shift between prefatory essay and back cover from intradiegetic reference to extra-textual interpellation of the reader. This extends the text's index finger, if you like, in the form of the *ficto*-critical vector. It aims to illumine always the present textual encounter as real while illuminating its slightly surreal method of writing. Most importantly, however, Hughes's method of transposing passages, characters, authors, as well as his experiences onto the level playing fields of both his literary imagination and the page capitalises on his abductive understanding of textual communication. In the context of this section two aspects of this *ficto*-critical ideology deserve special emphasis.

Firstly, Hughes indicates how reading fiction is still a non-fictional act with real effects. He identifies the border between these two realms as itself an instituted – and hence unmistakably real – fiction. This self-reflexive realisation raises epistemological questions for the reader who, in turn, encounters his musings on the page and brings them to life with her imagination. As the back cover informs us "the stories are fictions. Or are they? Hughes tells us the stories of the figures who live in his mind by making them tell his stories – and doing so engages in an art of literary ventriloquism." (2007: 208) He effectively eschews the dividing line between fictional and non-fictional encounters as he re/lays them as textual encounters. Hughes acquires someone else's discursive constructs – fictional or non-fictional – and slightly re-lays them to relay his own experiences, thoughts, and ideas. Such is what his main character in the "Preface" calls his "imaginative identification" (2007a: xv) which, as he explains, is "the way I viewed myself and the world around me almost entirely through these works" (ibid: xv). This bi/directional relation thus also in/forms *Someone Else*'s fictional and non-fictional, worldly and textual encounters.

But Hughes's collection not only pays homage to those "who had a formative influence on his imagination" (2007: 208), as the blurb on the back cover frames it. The apotropaic strategy of *Someone Else* is much rather to write back at the effects of reading oneself and the world through the works of others. Such is the ficto-*critical* potential of Hughes abductive approach: what happens in his imagination affects his life and idiocultural context – and *vice versa*. In the "Preface" he lets Max Brod analyse the other main character thus: "The only way he could tell the stories of the figures in his head was by making them tell his stories; to create again what was already there by creating something new." (2007a: xvi) Yet, as the fictional and the non-fictional thus intersect, this attempt to "transform taking into a gift" follows not only the circularity of "a vampire, drinking his own blood" (ibid: xvi), but also the spiralling of a re/lay chain that constitutively relays what it relays. This is how Hughes, the vampire, abducts and incorporates discursive constellations, which he fleshes out and re/configures differently, to make them work for his purposes in writing.

In writing, the con/textually translational principle of reading-writing re/constitutes the textual basis on the grounds of which we generate the textual object to begin with, in reading. Seizing this constitutive potential of textual communication, Hughes (counter-)continues the lives of the discursive entities his essays incorporate. Significantly, this marks an ideological shift from the notion that facts and ideas are to be written up and that texts are to be read up, both of which effectively terminate further textual engagement. The ficto/critical ideals that replace them are reading on and writing on, which suggest potentially indefinitely ongoing processes of reading-writing – singular textual acts that continually re/lay the textual work by (trans)posing it, to begin with, anew. Abducting someone else's epistemic entities – fictional or non-fictional – from the pages that have given rise to them, Hughes takes them elsewhere by not only writing on them, but by writing them on.

Secondly, Hughes's approach indicates that both the imagination and the page are level playing fields for discursive structures, irrespective of their erstwhile fictional or non-fictional, worldly or textual provenance. Quite the ventriloquist, he emphasises this kind of boundary crossing in the "Preface" by having the young man who met Brod say that "I could write about these figures who inhabit my imagination as surely as you inhabit my field of vision now" (ibid: xvi). Thus re/laying his experiences via someone else's fictions also changes their mode of existence twice. It takes them from a manifest textual structure into the ideal realm of his "imaginative identification" (ibid: xv) with all its possibilities and back again into a manifest textual form. It subjects the discursive constellations at the heart of this equation – which is also an ongoing equat*ing* – to a twofold re/configuring phase transition, from textual to imaginary states of (reading) matter and back again.

Likewise, Hughes perpetrates twofold textual abductions. As he notes, this practice highlights "the almost febrile world of the works themselves" (ibid: xv), the ephemerally recurring transcendental mode of the textual object as opposed to its manifest basis in the object text. He marks two alternating stages of textual communication: the rigidly inscribed page and the fluidly transforming imagination. He also identifies the regular gaps in-between these stages as realms of potential. Someone else's fluid imagination first lets a fictional world with epistemic things rise from the rigid textual basis and then lets it float with seeming autonomy in their idiocultural con/text. Importantly, these realms of potential unfold along the mediating relations of our textual practices, within the respective con/textual gaps between object text and textual agent. Their potential is then exercised in singular acts of relational mediation that interpret the constitutive trope of reading-writing either conservatively or abductively.

In this respect, Hughes addresses, firstly, how we construct an imaginary world from the page, secondly, how this world takes on a life of its own within the context of the reading imagination and, thirdly, how that imaginative faculty is at the same time operational in (re)directing the reading self in a worldly con/text. Mindful of this bi/directional relation at the intersection of linguistic-discursive and wider discursive practices, Hughes's narrator of the "Preface" summarises his abductive take on textual and worldly encounters as follows:

> "For my part, I can only say these [diary] accounts of [Max Brod's] conversations with the young man in the café have penetrated me like an actual life, and they are now so enigmatic and familiar to me that it seems they have been mental possessions of mine from the moment when I first began to accommodate human beings entirely in my mind, in order to arrive, time and again, at a fresh understanding of them." (ibid: xviii)

Likewise, Hughes abducts characters and other epistemic entities from their respective (con)texts into his idiocultural con/text to make them (part of) *Someone Else* and have real effects elsewhere. In ficto/critically pre/post/erous manner, he seizes the constitutive *ceteris paribus* mechanism which encompasses the entire problem of de- and re/semanticisation in textual communication from one linguistic-discursive agent, via text, to the next.

It is an architectural hallmark of Hughes's essays that he, firstly, re/lays and mixes textual or discursive constellations from primary works with textual or discursive constellations from secondary literature – which may deal either with an author or their work – and, secondly, lets his idiocultural con/text and personal experiences guide this imaginative relocation. His *ficto*-critical point is that all these discursive formations mingle in the realm of fluid potential that is his readerly imagination before they are fixedly re/arranged, in turn, as a textual structure on the equally level playing field that are the pages of his essays. Hughes, I want to suggest, identifies in these movements of the imagination and these intervals of textual stasis the constitutive mechanics of reading-writing – the phase transitions between rigid and fluid states of discursive matter according to the tact of these acts – and he interprets them abductively. His textual strategy highlights these insights *ficto*-critically, exploits them ficto-*critically*, and re/lays them to likewise empower his readers.

Conservative vs. Abductive Translation

The translational condition of the im/possibility of textual communication has here been presented in terms of two different text-practical ideologies. On the one hand, there is the academic ideal that emphasises the possibility of essential translation in order to conserve the textually inscribed discursive constellation across the equation. This model stresses that the medium effectively bridges the con/textual divide to form a textual juncture. On the other hand, there is the ficto/critical ideal that emphasises the impossibility of essential translation in favour of both the abductive necessity to re/configure the discursive constellation in each textual act and the concomitant abductive potential to re/mediate to re/medial effect. This model stresses that the medium bridges the communicative divide only by way of a gaping bridge. While this is a crucial ideological difference in the kind of relational mediation that our textual work should aspire to, both theories depart from the same given parameters of the framing mediating relations that present the non-transcendental condition of the im/possibility of textual communication.

No doubt, our default approach in everyday reading and writing is to aim for the essential perpetuation of discursive constellations, but ficto/critical strategies sometimes turn the impossibility of essential translation into a virtue for their wider discursive concerns by turning their reading and writing abductive. The *ficto*-critical theory of translational reading-writing promotes a motivated shift from the conservative and faithful to the abductive and traitorous, which creates considerable interventionist potential for ficto-*critical* concerns. Abandoning the conservative ideal of fidelity, which lets a pre/scribed discursive structure reign supreme over the individual's textual act, ficto/critical strategies pursue the traitorous ideal of abduction from discursively concerned positions. Because this theoretical re/assessment of the first principles of textual communication creates a practically empowering perspective, it amounts to an enlightening text-practical ideology. Ficto/critical theories re/conceive of the constitutive gap in each mediating relation as an opportunity to build a communicative bridge elsewhere by way of relational mediation.

Ultimately, the juxtaposition here is between the textually arresting principle of reading-writing up and the discursively liberating principle of reading-writing on, which Benjamin's epigraph to this section so finely anticipates. The ficto/critical insight is that the constitutive translational re/lay chain of textual communication relays only as it re-lays – a notion that is then both highlighted *ficto*-critically and exploited ficto-*critically*. In this sense, ficto/critical strategies of textual communication keep their bridges gaping with an enlightening as well as empowering ambition in mind and a practical concern at heart.

3.2.2 Perverse Writing

> "Anyone seeing the sun come up in front of him while awake, dressed – out walking, say – will retain throughout the day above all else a sense of the sovereignty of an invisibly crowned king, and anyone having the day break over him at work will feel, around noon, as if he had crowned himself."
> WALTER BENJAMIN/ONE-WAY STREET (2009A: 82)

> "Like ultraviolet radiation memory shows all of us, in the Book of Life, writing that invisibly, prophetically, accompanies the text as a gloss."
> WALTER BENJAMIN/ONE-WAY STREET (IBID: 108)

In this subsection I shall examine how ficto/critical textual intervention is at least partly based on a theoretical understanding of textual representation as constitutively encapsulated. The specific focus here will be on how the constitutive mechanisms of the spatial dimension of the textual work can be conceived of differently with a view to developing ficto-*critical* edge. I shall indicate how the interventionist ambition of some ficto/critical writing practices capitalises on the theoretical insight that the textual object is continually re/constituted in the readerly act of generative textual triangulation on the basis of the given object text. According to this text-practical ideology, each singular textual act effects a perverse, encapsulated projection – a phase transition between both states of matter and con/texts – that constitutively re/configures a given textual or discursive constellation. Ultimately, my thesis is that ficto/critical writing sets this p/re/structuring re/lay chain of relational mediation within mediating relations to perversely re/work any p/receding structures for its wider discursive ficto-*critical* concerns.

Lightful De/icing on the Lake

Complementing the arctic poppies, Aritha van Herk deploys at least two more structural metaphors in *Places Far From Ellesmere* that combine to parallel the poetics of her un/reading. For a start, she juxtaposes the light and darkness of different places in terms of reading practices. Building on this, she also allegorises the phase transitions of Lake Hazen into a poetics of textual encapsulation. In the following, my reading is going to elaborate the theoretical significance of these imageries for the spatial dimension in a ficto/critical theory of textual representation.

Firstly, van Herk opposes the endlessly persistent natural light during the northern summer, which her narrator encounters on Ellesmere, to the darkness of the south Canadian winter, which she associates with her formative years in Edberg, Edmonton, and Calgary. She also connects the aligned north/south and light/dark divides to principles of engaging with text. On Ellesmere the narrator finds "[r]eading in this clear green light an act different from reading south under the sanctimonious permission of fluorescent and incandescent fixtures" (1990: 123). She realises that her "[r]eading changed by the quality of light it partakes of" (ibid: 123). In addition to its barren geographical formation – un/inscribed compared to the places far from Ellesmere – the favourable light on Ellesmere, too, advantages the readerly mechanism of situational abstraction differently. Ultimately, she thus contrasts her formative experiences of male discursive heteronomy, or writerly pre/scription, in the south with her re/formative anticipation of female discursive autonomy, or readerly p/re/scription, in the north.

The imagery lets Anna Karenina's reading appear in a different light, too: "She is understandably fascinated by her own story, but her reading in the darkness is Tolstoy's representation." (ibid: 135) His text lets Anna read, but he also pre/scribes the course and consequences of her reading – just like he aims to pre/scribe our reading, too. The way out of this double bind, which van Herk's narrator entertains for Anna as much as her reader, is that "[s]he reads her way toward Ellesmere, where you will read her, where she has never been read before, you are willing to wager that uniqueness, where in perpetual daylight you un/read Tolstoy's reading of her reading" (ibid: 135-6). On bright Ellesmere the encapsulated contrast becomes the readerly solution: "Anna cannot escape darkness. You cannot escape light. She reads. You read." (ibid: 136) Anna's reading may be heteronomously pre/structured, but van Herk, her narrator, and future readers do have the autonomy to p/re/structure this discursive formation in reading-writing. Such is her antidote to Tolstoy's detrimental inscription of reading women.

With regards to Anna, who the narrator wants to salvage from Tolstoy's pre/scription as a signifier of womanhood, she ponders: "And if you were a character in the implacable mote of a reader's eye, then would you live within white nights? Or dark pages? Which would be preferable, the cage of book, the open glare of the sun?" (ibid: 80) In light of Ellesmere's principles of reading, of course, no text is ever fully written up, no fictional world ever entirely sealed off. Instead, they are opened in unimpeded readings, facilitated by the excellent light that makes it possible to read on and on; and then write on, too, so as to manifest elsewhere what one encounters differently in thus reading. Whereas "Edmonton" to her is "still the darkness of winter and buildings, of enclosed cold" (ibid: 52), she derives warmth from the northern summer light that facilitates her re/configuration of textually enshrined discursive formations. While the places in the south are, to her, enveloped in the darkness of closed books, Ellesmere is the locus of resisting – maybe even re/medial – reading.

The apotropaic magic of Ellesmere's northern light is that it can help to break up pre/structuring formations in reading and allows to p/re/structure them in turn. The light on Ellesmere thus harbours emancipating reading potential, an escape route from detrimental discursive orders. This is very different from the artificial reading light the narrator associates with the south Canadian wintery darkness, which further limits the options in an already heavily pre/scribed discursive environment. In this sense, the island's distance from her formative environment in Alberta matches the difference that reading a map can make to being lost. By way of her tropical depiction of arctic Ellesmere Island van Herk aims to instigate the poetics of readerly intervention in her readers.

Secondly, van Herk leads the analogy of readerly light into another structural metaphor. "Warming" under the influence of the sun, her narrator realises how "the puzzle-ice in the lake begins to melt itself into open patches, push itself around" (ibid: 93). And this imagery of phase transition between de- and re/frozen states of matter is recurring:

> "In the distance Lake Hazen riffles through every version of blue. The first day it is no more than a textured conglomeration of white, knobbled ice butting against itself. Slow cracks, the blue between creep imperceptibly every day wider, a stretching of the lazy water, azure. The puzzle pieces are scattered farther, stirred apart on the blue board of the lake by a huge finger of sun, still caught in its implacable rotation, only slanting low between three and ten before it describes an arc upwards again. Lake Hazen a carelessly broken jigsaw abandoned after a lazy Sunday dinner. There are huge sheets of ice left, almost square, and hundreds of tiny pieces orbiting in endless float." (ibid: 111)

The light de/freezes the lake, which breaks into so many elements, shifts its constellation slightly, only to eventually freeze over again, albeit newly re/configured. The narrator calls this "[s]ummer on Ellesmere. Thaw, a pure reading." (ibid: 93) Importantly, these de- and re/territorialising processes closely parallel the modal itinerary of a discursive constellation in reading-writing – especially the narrator's un/reading of *Anna Karenina*.

The trope of Lake Hazen thus presents a partly fluid phase between two solid formations, which represents the potential for re/configuration and re/inscription. "This ice picture" is furthermore characterised as "enigmatic, fascinating, a portrait of Anna herself" (ibid: 111). The re/formations of the ice under the summer sun thus parallel those of Tolstoy's text in the narrator's reading on Ellesmere, in which "[t]he words are stirred, mixed, like pieces of a jigsaw, broken up into their separate shapes and the whole picture lost, left to be reconstructed by another, a different hand" (ibid: 113). Her agency as a reader re/configures the discursive constellation enshrined in *Anna Karenina* to begin with, but she further opts to re/lay her actively benevolent re/configuration in a protocol of reading, which is her writing in *Places Far From Ellesmere*. In so doing, her reading effects a counter-continuing warm spell not only on Anna Karenina but also on the discursive order that has given rise to her. As we have seen, the narrator disrupts the text, omits passages and characters, writes new scenes and so on – yet she thereby not only re/configures the order of the textual basis, but furthermore re/adjusts the (wider) discursive order it has come to represent.

This scenario of melting formations and floating fragments has already been anticipated *en route* to Ellesmere. As the narrator realises on her flight, the north Canadian islands appear from above – as they do on a map – as a lose conglomerate, broken off from the solid southern landmass:

> "The ocean here, Cornwallis Channel, one huge jigsaw. The ice pieces laid out on a giant board waiting for winter to put them together again. Puzzle-ice. Mesmerizing, its slow wash and float, its conundrum melting and reappearance. The chunks themselves islands and the arctic ocean between a liquid light." (ibid: 87-8)

Again place and light, topology and lines of flight intersect to form – or in this case anticipate – the trope of reading-writing that becomes one with the local geography on Ellesmere. Even the flight north is already suggestive of a transcendental movement of situational abstraction underneath which rigid formations fragment, float, and re/arrange much like shelves of ice – or, in fact, as if on a parable flight. In this con/text, a textual constellation only ever functions as an iconic map of the differently re/configured discursive constellations we actually read from it. Accordingly, text's indexical relation to our readings ultimately ought to be conceptualised as one of discursive iconicity.

In any case, the combined structural metaphor of northern summer light and the ice on Lake Hazen captures the constitutive processes of de- and re/territorialisation in reading and writing which the ficto/critical credits with a pre/post/erous potential to counter detrimental discursive pre/scriptions. The de/icing and re/freezing lake, in particular, illustrates a poetics of reading-writing that is p/re/structuring textually encapsulated representations. It undergoes re/configuration just like a textually structured discursive constellation that is re/constitutively p/re/structured in protocolled acts of reading-writing-*before* – always the one before the last. In this manner, van Herk inscribes the discursively re/medial potential of reading and writing ficto/critically on Ellesmere by way of locally in/formed structural metaphors. If you like, the lightful de/icing on the lake is also the delightful icing on the cake of her ficto/critical theory.

Perverse Reading-Writing-*Before*

Building on my earlier terminology, I shall henceforth deploy the somewhat contrived expression "reading-writing-*before*" as shorthand for the necessity in our textual acts to constitutively re/configure the discursive constellation across the representational divide. In this respect, the term "reading-writing-*before*" refers to the perpetual modal transformation between rigidly (re)inscribed textual structures and our more fluid understanding of discursive structures. I deploy this notion, therefore, as an encapsulating trope of re/configuration to explain the representation of discursive constellations via textual structures. In particular, "reading-writing-*before*" marks the fact that each phase transition, spatially separating the manifest object text and its transcendental textual object, also temporally separates these states of matter by way of the translational trope of reading-writing – to perpetually begin with again. Hence, to avoid an anachronistic perspective, the spatial between of encapsulated textual representation is best captured by the temporal before of our textual work. The thesis is that such textual acts consist in either enshrining or decrypting processes that follow the logic of encapsulation in their framing mediating relations – from one state of matter and con/text into the next, according to their respectively directed work of relational mediation.

Qua medium, the text constitutively bridges the representational divide that it introduces as much as our textual practices exercise it. Thus, the text is hardly the only mediating agent here. Rather, the agency is split across the representational divide between the text and the idiocultural con/text that encounters it. Because this text-medial interpolation bridges the representational gap it introduces only at the expense of creating a new gap in turn – between this re/configured constellation and *its* recipient – this bridge keeps gaping. The paradigmatic medial, transcendental, and con/textual de- and re/location of a discursive structure in textual representation is thus effectively generative: between a textual basis and the readerly (idiocultural) con/text a textual object is created just as, *vice versa*, textual form is created between a writerly object and the medium. The crucial point is that whereas every such text-representational act instantiates the trope of reading-writing-*before*, only ficto/critical ideology embraces these constitutive mechanics as potentially re/generative. By contrast, academic textual practices usually follow a conservatively encapsulating ideal of reading-writing-*before* – which text-ideologically prevents their interventionist potential.

At this point, Heather Kerr's instructive essay "Perverse Writing – Maternity and Monarchy: Fictocriticism and Exorbitant, Plural Bodies" (2002) presents a helpful ficto/critical understanding of the text's twofold spatial positioning across the representational divide. Following her example, I shall first qualify the constitutive encapsulating principle of reading-writing-*before* as perverse on account of its plural corporeality, and then juxtapose a transcendental and a material ideal of this model in terms of the monarch and the mother. With these polar archetypes Kerr finely captures the modal *aporia* of textual representation: the spatial condition of the im/possibility that academic and ficto/critical principles emphasise differently.

Kerr sets out "to explore the possibility that fictocritical writing in the academic context is an instance of the perverse" (2002: 148). In particular – and this includes her own piece – she aims at "a feminist engagement with the essay as a potentially 'perverse space'" (ibid: 148). Kerr uses the terminology of perversion for instances of a twofold corporeality, two examples of which draw her particular attention. On the one hand, "[i]n the case of kingship the so-called 'body natural' (the finite, material body) incorporates the 'body politic' (understood as a perpetual ideality)" (ibid: 148). On the other hand, "[i]n the case of the maternal body in patriarchal culture, her plurality is by contrast the mark of a (doubly) inescapable materiality (as woman and as mother), birthing an unavoidable scene of grotesque abjection" (ibid: 149). While the monarchic principle incorporates a transcendental body within the material body, the maternal principle generates a material body from a material body.

Notably, Kerr's feminist "interests in this essay have less to do with the phenomenology of 'lived experience' of maternity and more to do with its poetics" (ibid: 149). In this respect, the (f)rigid poetics of monarchic corporeal doubling extend in a transcendental dimension, while the re/productive poetics of maternal corporeal doubling extend in a material dimension. Furthermore, Kerr knows that, when it comes to writing, "we are still in need of ways of understanding the 'spaces' and 'gaps'" (ibid: 151), not least on the constitutive level of textual representation. Her goal is thus "to trace the contours of a writing practice that would do justice to […] the grotesque literalism of plural embodiment" (ibid: 150), one that would re/constitute the transcendental textual object from the manifest object text. Her strategy to achieve this is to "deploy the maternal as a monster proper to the monarch" (ibid: 150), to juxtapose the transcendental and material principles of reading-writing-*before*.

Kerr investigates "the conjunction of the monarch and the mother via a structure that [Ernst] Kantorovicz regards as a literalizing of the King's two bodies: the late medieval double tomb" (ibid: 156). She develops this imagery into a structural metaphor – or "postmodern allegory" (ibid: 156), as she prefers to call it – for textual representation. The point is that "[t]ypically the prince is 'buried in a tomb showing the body in corruption below the effigy in glory'" (ibid: 156). According to the tomb "[t]he sublime body politic literally depends upon the abject body natural, figured as the cadaver, death itself" (ibid: 156). The royal body's significance is here thrown in relief from its base, which yet embodies it. And likewise for text: the significance enshrined in a text corpus needs to be de/crypted from its manifest in/scription. Not only Kerr's imagery is thus spot on, but also its semantic realm – which Maud Ellmann has brilliantly developed at length with regards to writing in *The Hunger Artists: Starving, Writing, and Imprisonment* (1993).

By following the transcendental principle, "[t]he tyrant mistakes his monstrosity for an ideal, self-generated unity" (Kerr 2002: 162), whereas the mother capitalises on the monstrous perversity of her body: leaking into and out of, giving birth, she ultimately transfigures part of her body into another corpus. The monarch's (f)rigid corporeal doubling follows a golden ideal of autocratic rule. But the mother's potentially unfaithful corporeal doubling, or re/production, anticipates a purple patch of fluidly productive, emancipating reception. The monarchic trope thus emphasises the constitutive mechanism of reading-writing-*before* as transcendentally directed, the maternal trope as materially directed. For Kerr, reading-writing ficto/critically "would be to consider the body as a point of departure for a desiring movement in 'the spaces between', a queer allegory" (ibid: 162). On the level of our textual practice the ficto/critical point is that there is not one transcendental object to match the corpus. The movements of relational mediation in the spaces between mediating relations instead generate multiple such objects. These, however, register only manifestly as further corpora.

Against this backdrop, Kerr formulates two insights that have in/formed my approach. Firstly, when she warns that "we must not fetishize the aesthetic surface of our writing: it cannot guarantee ethical effects" (ibid: 164), she is aware of the dangers of generic resistance. She already knows that the ficto/critical is a strategy, not a form. Secondly, Kerr effectively re/locates the notional significance of the gap and the in-between space as fictocritical tropes on the constitutive level of our textual practices. She already knows that *ficto*-critical strategies flow from the constitutive parameters of reading and writing. In the spatial dimension of textual representation Kerr re/locates the significance of the text's twofold situatedness across the representational divide with its concomitant potential to re/configure an enshrined discursive constellation across the communicative divide. Ultimately, she thus turns the tables on the (f)rigid spatial dimension of textual representation by circumventing its monarchic regime via the fluidly receptive and unfaithfully re/productive temporal axis of textual communication – which is precisely the gist of maternal reading-writing-*before*.

It is important to remember that these two principle interpretations of perversely twofold corporeality are text-ideologically polar aspects of a constitutive complex. Towards the end of her essay, Kerr carefully re/emphasises the *aporia* of her juxtaposition in terms of genre.

> "If we deploy these elements to model perverse (academic) writing we must notice that what is perverse in terms of organic life is precisely that which is rewarded in academic life. Clean and proper writing, the essayist's equivalent of the (imaginary) closed, classical (in fact masculine) body, cannot face its monstrous other in the embarrassingly open, messy, and grotesque practice of 'pregnant' cyborg, fictocritical writing. Similarly, perverse fictocritical writing must not turn away from the fact of its being hinged to an anorexic other." (ibid: 163)

The *aporia* between these principles of textual encapsulation thus needs to be acknowledged and strategically balanced in motivated singular acts of reading-writing-*before*. Although Kerr ascribes the transcendental doubling of the text to academic writing and its material doubling to the ficto/critical, both are constitutive principles of all our textual encounters – albeit only the maternal ideal harbours text-interventionist potential for ficto/criticism.

Ash, Smoke, & Shadows

In his piece "Translations" (2007b), John Hughes focalises a structural metaphor that he finds expressed in Paul Celan's writing, starting with this epigraph: "In a late Notebook entry, Paul Ancel (formerly Celan) attempted the following translation. He had come to view translation as a shadow that was also, somehow, the light that threw it; a fire that leaves, like ash in the new language, a trace of the original…" (ibid: 183). The terminology of fire, shadow, and ash deployed here to describe Celan's surprising ideal of translation harbours an important insight into the indexicality of our textual encounters. More precisely, I would like to suggest that Hughes's focus on this terminology provides a structural metaphor that explains the indexical division between the object text and the textual object across our textual acts that comprise the textual work.

It is worth noting that, in typical fashion, Hughes has already (re)deployed this abducted terminology in the "Preface", where the curious character we encountered before is "obsessed with Paul Celan who, he claimed, spend his whole life trying to translate his poetry from German into German" (2007a: xii). This scenario thus depicts a man "translating all the time, but without a change of language" (ibid: xi). In a trademark intra-textual reference Hughes lets the man write the following observation:

"A good translation is a fire that leaves, like ash in the new language, a trace of the original. It creates a kind of language, a style, that has not existed until that moment and could not be created ab novum by a writer. Every word in a good translation is like an echo, a shadow that is also, somehow, the light that throws it." (ibid: xi)

For the purposes of this section the two relevant points of this analogy are, firstly, its counter-intuitive perspectival shift and, secondly, the indexicality it suggests for the textual work.

Firstly, how to understand translation as both a shadow and the light that throws it? Before properly translating a text, one needs to understand it. But if the constitutive trope of reading-writing is translational, so is this first understanding. Hence, even the original work appears to us, to begin with, only in the guise of an original translation. This original de- and re/con/textualisation is the *sine qua non* of perceiving the textual object. Ultimately, this is where re/semanticisation and radical interpretation intersect in reading. Understanding a text, the reader has always already translated its textual structure into her discursive idiocultural con/text. Translating a text then transposes this resultant discursive structure, again, into the linguistic con/text of the target language. A translation that changes linguistic code is thus dependent on a prior translation that does not, yet both transpose an encapsulated discursive structure from con/text to con/text. Paradoxically, we can properly translate only on the basis of this primary translation. Translation proper is thus cast as a shadow only in light of this initial translation.

Secondly, because it is expressed in terms of ash and smoke, this scenario has significant implications for the indexicality of the textual work, which I would like to pinpoint as follows. From the writerly perspective the co-presence of the textual object and the object text is like a fire and the smoke it emanates. The indexical relation of simultaneity between them makes the object text a signal of the textual object. Paradigmatically, we write texts as smoke (text-as-signal) because for the writer they are co-present to the idea that gives rise to them. From the readerly perspective, however, the initial absence of the textual object from the object text renders the latter ash, perhaps ember, from which to rekindle (an/other) fire. The indexical relation between them makes the object text a trace of its textual object. Paradigmatically, we thus read texts as ash (text-as-trace) because for the reader they are not the fire that is absent but what is present to rekindle it. The indexicality between the object text and its textual object is constitutively routed through the respective agents at work on the text. Importantly, thus, not the truth relation of the text establishes meaning, but the subject relation of the textual work.

Paradigmatically, we write text as signal but we read text as trace, and the indexical mechanics of these constitutive perspectives work very differently. Especially for the readerly position the concrete presence of the object text does not coincide with an equally manifest co-presence of its textual object that, after all, is only the result of generative textual triangulation by way of twofold con/textual withdrawals. The structural metaphorics of ash, smoke, and shadows that Hughes identifies in Celan's writing capture not only these constitutive mechanics but also connect what we could now call his *ficto*-critical insight with his main ficto-*critical* concern. The crucial point is that part con/textual loss is the constitutive violence of our text-cultural practices, nowhere more so than when it comes to the reaction, in writing, to violent and traumatic events.

Importantly, their different background concerns can explain that while van Herk aims to set the abductive re/lay chain of textual relations to work for her discursive agenda, Celan highlights the danger of con/textual loss that is a constituent part of this otherwise enabling mechanism. Although they highlight complementary – possibly even opposed – perspectives onto the same constitutive mechanism, both do so to develop ficto-*critical* edge. While there may be too little abductive re/configuration in our readings of the canonical discursive constellations that affect our conceptions of womanhood, there may be too much of the kind when it comes to collective memory and its discursive treatment of traumatic loss. Because some constitutive mechanisms are variably deployed in our textual practices to serve certain functions, different *ficto*-critical and ficto-*critical* strategies are required to highlight detrimental practices and counter-continue their complicity in the wider discursive formations that are still ongoing.

Monarchically vs. Maternally Perverse Encapsulation

The encapsulating condition of the im/possibility of textual representation has here been presented according to two different text-practical ideologies. The academic ideal emphasises the possibility of essential encapsulation (text-as-signal) in order to conserve the textually inscribed discursive constellation. This model stresses that the medium bridges the representational divide to form a juncture of receptive re/production. The maternal ficto/critical ideal emphasises the impossibility of essential encapsulation on account of the constitutively perverse, twofold corporeality of text (text-as-trace) and its concomitant potential for productive re(con)ception. This model stresses that the medium bridges the communicative divide only by way of a gaping bridge. While this illustrates a crucial ideological difference in the assumed frame/work of mediating relations, both theories yet agree that acts of relational mediation present the communicative condition of the im/possibility of our practices of textual representation.

In everyday reading and writing, of course, we operate on the academic assumption of text as signal, but ficto/critical strategies often turn the impossibility of this monarchic perversion into a virtue for their wider discursive concerns by turning their work of reading and writing maternally perverse. The *ficto*-critical theory of perverse reading-writing-*before* promotes a motivated shift from a sacredly celibate perversion to the perversion of unfaithful fertility, which creates considerable interventionist potential for ficto-*critical* concerns. Thus abandoning the conservative ideal of fidelity, which lets the pre/scribed discursive structure reign autocratically over recipient re/production, ficto/critical strategies pursue the traitorous emancipatory ideal of productive reception from concerned positions. Because the theoretical re/assessment of this first principle of textual re/presentation creates a practically empowering perspective, it amounts to an enlightening text-practical ideology. *Ficto*-critical theories re/conceive of the constitutive gaps in the frame/work of our mediating relations as an opportunity to build representational bridges elsewhere by way of relational mediation.

Ultimately, the juxtaposition is between the textually arresting principle of reading-writing up and the discursively liberating principle of reading-writing on. The ficto/critical insight is that the constitutive encapsulation of textual representation turns circular transcendental reproduction into a spiralling materialist spin-off productivity – an understanding that is both highlighted *ficto*-critically and exploited ficto-*critically*. In this sense, ficto/critical strategies of textual representation keep their bridges gaping with an enlightening as well as empowering ambition in mind and a practical concern at heart.

Brief Recapitulation

The underlying theoretical move in this section has been to re/conceive of the ficto/critical as theoretically in/formed text-practical ideology. The ficto/critical and its academic other conceive of constitutive features in our textual practices to contrary effect. Whereas we traditionally take these mechanisms as conditions of the possibility of textual representation and communication, *ficto*-critical theory harnesses them as conditions of their impossibility. Thus, the translational aspect of textual communication is utilised not as faithful but as abductive reading-writing. Likewise, the encapsulating aspect of textual representation is utilised not as monarchically but as maternally perverse reading-writing-*before*. While the former interpretation favours a conservative, the latter promotes an interventionist stance in reading and writing. Due to their practical relevance these differing theoretical perspectives amount to two sets of text-practical ideology: one conservatively academic, the other radically ficto/critical in outlook. Moreover, whereas the traditional ideal of our textual practices serves the wider discursive structures that be, the ficto/critical ideal promotes variably positionally deployed generic resistance and textual intervention against such systemic effects.

The foregoing two sections have illustrated how (slashed) ficto/critical text-practical ideology emphasises these constitutive parameters and mechanisms according to an interventionist principle that in/forms ficto/critical writing as strategically traitorous and apotropaic. This combined and refined ficto/critical theory finally presents the nexus between the realisation of the *ficto*-critical vector and twist and the development of ficto-*critical* edge.

3.3 ARTFUL THOUGHT-EXPERIMENTAL WRITING

Artistic and artful experimentation often converge in ficto/critical strategies. Based on this observation I shall now venture to re/formulate my theory of the ficto/critical. Specifically, I am going to re/conceive of the ficto/critical in terms of experimental writing. Firstly, the *ficto*-critical side of traitorous generic resistance will be re/formulated in terms of artistically playful experimentation. Secondly, the ficto-*critical* side of apotropaic textual intervention will be re/formulated in terms of artfully pre/scribed thought experimentation. Both of these aspects furthermore share the epistemic curiosity of scientific experimentation, albeit from a ficto/critically motivated perspective. I shall thus avail myself of the terminology of experimentation in a threefold sense in order to capture the complexities of the strategic two-step pattern in my theory of the ficto/critical. Without pretending to investigate these dimensions exhaustively, I shall now very briefly re/trace some central features as well as the epistemology of scientifically exploratory experimentation, the avant-garde artistically experimental, and philosophic thought experiments.

Firstly, scientific experimentation classically creates controlled and repeatable scenarios in order to gain information to either refine and improve or falsify and replace a given theory. The environment and setting of such experiments is heavily pre/scribed. In turn, the results are written up for a scientific community that shares the same discourses and interests. Apart from discovering new facts about the world, such actual experiments have a further layer of non-fictional significance by way of the theories and discourses they put to the test. Their results require intermediation between induction and deduction, between a theory and its observable basis in fact. Although their hermetic and controlled setting makes them rather low risk exercises, scientific experiments transgress what is securely established so as to generate and order what is not yet. Their epistemological significance can thus be tremendous.

Secondly, the artistically experimental, by contrast, implies riskier and less predictable exercises that are often characterised by an anything goes attitude. Such singular acts often puzzle and confuse our set ways of approaching art in order to generate a new outlook. The artistically experimental thus either forces modifications onto the frame/work with which we approach it as art or forces us to reject it. The experimental in art presents transgressions of what is acceptable, recognisable, and ordered in a certain way. Its epistemological significance lies in its purposive unpredictability that challenges existing artistic theories and practices. Just like scientific experiments, the artistically experimental can be written up retrospectively. Notably, however, the artistically experimental consists in unpredictable events and performances whose experiential point can only be captured by writing that turns itself textually experimental – and such writing on would make our textual performances of read*ing* and writ*ing* the main event.

Thirdly, and much less clear-cut, there are thought experiments of scientific, philosophic, or literary provenance. Scientific thought experiments stipulate impracticable experimental settings and then deduce, even calculate, their outcome from this set of hypothetical givens. Philosophic thought experiments consider hypothetical or counterfactual scenarios that aim to precipitate revisions of targeted background theories, axioms, and theorems. Literary thought experimentation is surprisingly different again because the same textually prescribed scenario can be received to very different effect in singular reading performances, which may or may not lead to significant revisions of certain notions, attitudes, or even worldviews.

All thought experiments are speculative and rhetorical exercises. Written out – sometimes artistically, sometimes artfully – they conduct the reader to conduct the thought experiment: they lead the reader along a line of thought into considering the non-fictional implications of a fictional scenario. They often present a curious type of text between argumentative relevance and narrative lure. They are rhetorical devices of ultimately epistemological, sometimes even ideological, significance. Textually conducted thought experiments are generally pre/scribed, socially shared, yet singularly conducted. They are textual exercises that aim to re/arrange our theoretical understanding in a certain direction. In all of these aspects, textually conducted thought experiments are, in fact, not entirely unlike ficto/critical writing.

Ultimately, I would like to suggest that ficto/critical writing participates in the three main directions of (thought) experimentation to a degree. Taking the non-fictional significance of fictional textual practices seriously, they pursue the epistemological exploratory curiosity of scientific experiments. Deploying literary means in pursuit of theoretical considerations, they also couple the artistically experimental with the artfully thought-experimental. The ficto/critical is experimental writing in an artistically avant-garde sense, but it is also thought-experimental pre/scription in a sense that is both literary and philosophically rhetorical. Based on this layered, constellational understanding, the following two readings in the next subsections shall contribute further to qualifying the ficto/critical as artfully thought-experimental textual practice.

3.3.1 Pre/scribed Derailment & Railroaded Lines of Flight

Although MY WINNIPEG (Maddin 2007) is not a text *sensu stricto*, I shall argue in this section that its strategy functions analogous to ficto/critical textual practices for the equally post-auratic medium film. Luckily, Guy Maddin also wrote his filmic project on by releasing the lavishly supplemented script book *My Winnipeg* (2009) to which I shall give my references here. In the following, I am going to read MY WINNIPEG in terms of the experimental because its ficto/critical approach unites central aspects of the three previously outlined strands. My thesis in this respect is that MY WINNIPEG is perhaps best understood as a filmic thought-experimental train journey. Maddin's narrator, who we are encouraged to identify with him, takes us along on his flight from his personally haunting, almost psychotic Winnipeg. To loosen the city's grip on him, he has to re/visit and revise past experiences that are forever located in its psychogeography. As a true Winnipegger the narrator, of course, takes the train out of town. And as Maddin thus gets his artfully pre/scribed thought experiment on track we, too, are taken for a ride.

"All aboard!" (Maddin 2009: 9) is the narrative film conductor's first call from the off, before the rhythmically hypnotizing, mantra-like, and quasi-poetic voice sets the scene and announces the subsequent filmic quest:

> "Winnipeg. / Winnipeg. / Winnipeg. / Snowy, sleepwalking Winnipeg. // My home for my entire live / My entire live. / I must leave it. / I must leave it / I must leave it now. // But how to escape one's city? / How to wake oneself enough for / the frightening task? / And how to find one's way out?" (ibid: 9)

In response to which the soliloquising narrator then speculates: "What if ... / I film my way out of here?" (ibid: 29) From this point onwards, it is clear that he is both fleeing by train intradiegetically and filming his way out of his Winnipeg from a meta-perspective. As reel and rail thus intersect, this sets the frame for the cinematically experimental collage of events to follow. Several curious episodes then reel off as much as they roll by the narrator's train compartment window which is, in fact, another movie screen. This intradiegetic movie screen is furthermore cleverly blended into and out of congruence with the one the film's audience is watching. The train's window thus leads onto the intradiegetic world of the narrator's Winnipeg only via filmic re/presentation, precisely the mode by way of which, firstly, the narrator wants to leave it behind and, secondly, we encounter it to begin with. Analogously, the train compartment also encapsulates the cinema space occupied by the film's audience. As Maddin thus lets his narrator attempt to flee on the locally specific means of transport, he lets this intradiegetic train line of flight coincide with the filmic medium that carries the entire picture.

Maddin's artistically experimental film and his narrator's intradiegetic, ostensibly exploratory, filmic experiment thus approach congruence to present the viewer with a challenging speculative thought experiment on film. In an equally meta-fictional and meta-documentary twist, the subsequent collage of archival documentary footage and fictitious mockumentary elements that flashes past both systematically and systemically questions the film's referential status and relation further. Thus framed, the epistemological uncertainty of the film's self-proclaimed categorisation as "a docu-fantasia" (ibid: 164) further connects, on the meta-level, to the paradigmatic representational and communicative situation of its medium. The linear track of Maddin's pre/scribed filmic journey, the train of thought he conducts and we ride, does not lead anywhere so much as it purposively ties a knot into the generic referential poetics of its medial basis. Arguably, this is how MY WINNIPEG sets the viewer on course for the derailing itinerary of a ficto/critical vector.

Likewise, the narrator's poetic voice from the off guides us in a somnambulistic stream of consciousness whose framing function is visually emphasised by writing interspersed on screen – a means that enhances as well as foregrounds the narrative control imposed on the often unlikely footage we encounter. The repetitive rhythm of the voice figures the film's further leitmotif of a doubling sameness. It conjures a train journey over old tracks, whose joints make that characteristic sound pattern of first hitting the front wheels of the carriage, then hitting the rear wheels of the carriage. The film's narrative conductor thereby evokes the sleep inducing soundtrack of a train ride and, before long, the viewers find themselves "sleepwatching" (ibid: 144). Meanwhile, the train journey functions as the central structural metaphor of the *ficto*-critical thought experiment that is MY WINNIPEG. The filmic medium and its narrative frame artfully railroad our experience of the artistically experimental episodes. Even as we are on course for the purposive derailment of a *ficto*-critical vector the entire thought-experimental exercise is as carefully conducted as it is firmly pre/scribed by this filmic railway- and its soundtrack.

For the goals of the present section it can be furthermore productive to read the film's meta-perspective in conjunction with one particular episode about "the forgetfulness of snow" (ibid: 77) whose obliteration of traffic regulating lines figuratively parallels Maddin's genre-blurring. In the narrator's words: "When the snow starts falling, / the city starts to feel lawless. / Lawless but safe. / All the painted lines on the street are erased / by snow and anything goes." (ibid: 75) These volatilising lines give way to potential lines of flight. Yet they contrast with the filmic and narrative train line by way of which the narrator attempts to escape and to which the viewer is tied. While one set of pre/scribing lines disappears under an oblivious sheet of snow, a figurative *carte blanche* for p/re/scription, this imagery is yet in turn pre/scribed by another set of lines that conduct the recipient through the filmic thought experiment. Paradoxically, the thought-experimental exercise thus performatively contradicts Hannah Arendt's figurative notion of "thinking without a banister" (1979: 336) while yet advocating it. Chained to the rail of the reel the viewer is bound to follow the train's figures of thought, is bound to consider the fleeting traffic lines as a potential for lines of flight.

Moreover, in another episode we are warned that "[i]n Winnipeg, every / day is If Day" (Maddin 2009: 117). And Maddin's MY WINNIPEG indeed confronts us with a startling constellation of ifs. Throughout the episodes he plays off an incredulous as if against an immersing as if. Representational immersion, of course, is successful when disbelief is suspended and it briefly feels as if (events depicted were the case). But in MY WINNIPEG this perception is never experienced without its accompanying flip-side, the doubtful suspicion as if (that really was the case), which reinjects suspense into representation. From these contradicting as ifs a more speculative, thought-experimental what if then arises to let us consider what the implications were if something was the case. Remaining on track, the recipient is thus subjected to film-conjectural experiences, lead to question their epistemic status as documentary or fiction, and conducted to consider both their poetics *ficto*-critically and their wider discursive implications ficto-*critically*. Frictioning our epistemic relat*ing* to the scenarios we encounter on screen, MY WINNIPEG ultimately highlights this receptive work on representations as active work on the self and its wider discursive positioning. Whatever their origin and epistemic status, our encounter with these images *is* a non-fictional event.

The film's poster with the iconic frozen horses advertises the patchwork of archival documentary footage, fictional (re)creations, meta-fictional elements, and cartoonish passages as "a docu-fantasia" (ibid: 164), but Maddin also toyed with the quasi-subtitles "Stranger than Fact" (ibid: 164) and "The Truth is Relative" (ibid: 165). The mockumentary overlap of fictional and non-fictional footage ensures that these representational modes of the filmic object blur. A short warning preceding the script book makes this even more explicit: "The film *My Winnipeg* deliberately blurs the line between fact and fiction. No attempt has been made to distinguish the two, and so there may be significant factual errors in the script, narration, and essays. Please don't read this book as historical truth." (ibid: 4) Right, as if we would! Well, what if we did? In any case, the ficto/critical point is neither for the viewer nor for the reader to trace and ascertain or falsify the either fictional or non-fictional origins, kernels, and additions of each episode. Much rather, and in keeping with the artistically experimental, the episodes' epistemological uncertainty *is* their *ficto*-critical point: our discursive frame/work of assuming referential relation and status differently for documentary and fiction are made perceptible by the artful thought experiment that is My Winnipeg.

From a *ficto*-critical perspective, the film's pervasive trope of repetition also reverberates on the meta-generic level of the laws of the laws of genre. From this vantage point, Maddin also addresses a number of his ficto-*critical* concerns. For example, with regards to one's formative years and how to remember them, the wittily empowering message is to "[n]ever let your upbringing bring you down" (ibid: 165) because even such powerfully in/scribed formations are still always open to playful de- and thus p/re/scription. Another central concern is the gaping discrepancy between the inbuilt logic of modern cityscapes, which the narrator calls a "horrific chain reaction of architectural tragedies" (ibid: 81), on the one hand, and the psychogeographic environment that people actually live and feel at home in, on the other. Maddin's apotropaic strategy to both artistically and artfully p/re/structure the psychogeography of a detrimentally pre/structured geography is aptly captured by this further empowering witticism: "Home is where the ~~he~~art is" (ibid: 164).

On the whole, My Winnipeg presents an artful ficto/critical thought experiment that lifts the epistemological question from the level of generic form onto the meta-level of its post-auratic medial form. Creating My Winnipeg by filming his way out of his Winnipeg by train, Maddin's narrator puts his line of flight firmly on track for the viewer. While this medially pre/scribed train of thought provides the film's framing structural metaphor, it is also only the first of many such ficto/critically deployed means in its multilayered experimental dimension. As an artistically thought-experimental film My Winnipeg may be speculative and counterfactual, but it still presents an exploratory experiment of non-fictional relevance because it *ficto*-critically interpellates the recipient agency by frictioning the discursive practices of meaning, other, and self-formation at work in relat*ing* to filmic representations. Maddin's *ficto*-critical filmic strategy of thought-experimental derailment is intradiegetically anchored, post-generically executed, and medially railroaded. Additionally, its artful composition also develops ficto-*critical* edge by raising connected concerns of potential wider discursive significance via this im/mediate and performatively self-reflexive awareness. Ultimately, of course, My Winnipeg is a ficto/critical film because the various non-fictional concerns it addresses ficto-*critically* in its wittily idiosyncratic lament on the city are related to our (film) discursive practices which it addresses *ficto*-critically.

After my reading in this section has perhaps rather more focalised the *ficto*-critically experimental dimension, the next section shall now, in turn, shift focus slightly more towards the ficto-*critically* experimental dimension.

3.3.2 Ordinary Affects & Special-Effect Writing

Kathleen Stewart's announcement at the beginning of her book is straightforward: "*Ordinary Affects* is an experiment, not a judgement." (2007: 1) She furthermore distances her project from experiments that are designed to corroborate a given theory: "Committed not to the demystification and uncovered truths that support a well-known picture of the world, but rather to speculation, curiosity, and the concrete, it tries to provoke attention to the forces that come into view as habit or shock, resonance or impact." (ibid: 1) Thus reading our affective relating in the world through such situations and experiences, Stewart then writes what she calls "still lifes" (ibid: 18-9), provisional fragments that abstain from both premature judgemental intrusion and preconceived theoretical assimilation. Specifically, the experimental arrangement of the text is not designed to resolve notional frictions within an already given theory. And yet, I want to argue in this section, her experimental writing is still very much theoretically operational when it aims to both register affect and precipitate ficto/critical effects textually.

Convinced that "[t]he vagueness or the unfinished quality of the ordinary is not so much a deficiency as a resource" (ibid: 127), Stewart proclaims to write (and thereby claims to be read) "not as a trusted guide carefully laying out the links between theoretical categories and the real world, but as a point of impact, curiosity, and encounter" (ibid: 5). Far from writing up her subject matter, her mode of textual engagement with the real is thus to write it on by generically other means: "Each scene begins anew the approach to the ordinary from an angle set off by the scene's affects. And each scene is a tangent that performs the sensation that something is happening – something that needs attending to." (ibid: 5) With regards to such "complex and uncertain objects that fascinate", her aim is "to fashion some form of address that is adequate to their form" (ibid: 4). For her writing that "means pointing always outward to an ordinary world whose forms of living are now being composed and suffered, rather than seeking the closure or clarity of a book's interiority or riding a great rush of signs to a satisfying end" (ibid: 5). Ultimately, Stewart's reading-writing in *Ordinary Affects* aims at textual experiments of extra-textual epistemic significance.

Across the book, Stewart's deployment of the term "experiment" endows it with a multi-layered extension, not least because she appears to apply the notion to her writing and the events she witnesses alike. Potentially, I want to suggest, her understanding of the experimental arrangement of *Ordinary Affects* even includes, firstly, the unpredictable scenes she experienced, secondly, her artistic act of writing them on, thirdly, our thought-experimental act of reading her text and, fourthly, the unpredictable follow-up acts and affects it effects. These possibilities, of course, identify the four paradigmatic acts of reading-writing that, between them, comprise the textual work by way of which reader and writer, as the principle discursive agents involved, re/lay the textual work between them. Notably, these are also the four crucial re/lay stages for currents of affective charge across textual representation and communication, within the parameters of which, I want to suggest, Stewart produces artistic special-effect writing in order to highlight and re/focalise the overall poetics and epistemology of ordinary affective re/lays, both im/mediate and textually. "Ordinary affect", as Stewart clarifies, is "not about one person's feelings becoming another's but about bodies literally affecting one another and generating intensities" (ibid: 128). And clearly, in the encounter with *Ordinary Affects* one of these bodies happens to be a text corpus with its concomitant poetics and epistemology of literally affective re/lay.

Stewart's strategy to endow her thought-experimental text with a *ficto*-critical perspective from which to develop some ficto-*critical* edge, I want to argue, departs from the latently perceptible discrepancy between the affective charges alive in the situations depicted and their re/layed effects as communicated representations on the reader. What becomes strikingly perceptible is that while the affective charges at the root of Stewart's experiments trigger affects in her readers, they yet only ever do so through the re/layed detour of her (as much as the reader's) textual work and *its* effects. Insofar as Stewart's *ficto*-critical strategy highlights the difference between the affects depicted in writing and the affects triggered in reading, her still lifes performatively illumine something else than they ostensibly illuminate. Notably, at the same time as she highlights an experiential remainder she also generates some theoretical surplus. As her textual fragments discursively re/lay situations full of affective charges, she skilfully creates a (meta)circuit between them. What is more, her set of still lifes does harbour a dispersed theory, after all, namely of the connectivity that re/lays both discursive structures and affects. The episodes are frequently interspersed with almost literary definitions of vocabulary that yet creates theoretical potential. They are furthermore framed by two explicit meta-passages that outline the project. Although there is no overarching narrative to this neatly composed text, it is certainly driven by an underlying theoretical frame. In this manner, I want to argue, *Ordinary Affects* provides a *ficto*-critical twist when it illuminates a poetics of textual affect while aiming to illumine a *ficto*-critical vector to this effect.

In the last instance, the reader with her textual as well as wider discursive practices is the text's *ficto*-critical subject, by way of which Stewart aims at the interface between the discursive and affective. Or, to turn it around: Stewart addresses her wider discursive concerns ficto-*critically* by way of im/mediately interpellatory writing with exploratory non-fictional significance. Because thought-experimental work on the text is in equal measure work on the self, she can, ultimately, even hope to re/medially re/lay some of these concerns. But the *ficto*-critical direction of her writing also has an important non-transcendental purpose in so far as it is a discursive intervention in our affective relation to the extra-textual, which emphasises "the need for a speculative and concrete attunement" (ibid: 128). "[T]hought", for Stewart, is "something that takes off with the potential trajectories in which it finds itself in the middle" (ibid: 128). And to p/re/structure these potential trajectories, I want to suggest, is the ficto-*critical* task of her project. In this sense, *Ordinary Affects* is also a ficto-*critical* experiment because it is concerned with an unceasing curiosity for speculative as well as exploratory understandings of one's concrete surrounds which ultimately hopes to facilitate perpetual re/negotiation of one's experiences and sense of self.

Because the discursive is operational in the creation, reception, and effective impact of affective charges – at the interface between the ideal and the corporeal – Stewart ponders the reading-writing possibilities to re/lay ordinary affects to special effect. And her text challenges us, her readers, to do likewise on the back of the theoretical understanding and experimental impulses that it circulates at the same time. For example, her terminology of re/lays provides a model for the, always current, discursive as well as affective conduits and circulation at work, in which intermittent agents of transmission function also as mediators that effectively re/lay the transmitted relational structure. She further contends that it is possible to conceive of these mechanisms as entirely corporeal (ibid: 128). Just like there are impulses generated and forwarded through the body by im/mediate experiences, so there are impulses generated and forwarded through the (social) body by experientially encountered or textually mediated experiences. In any case, Stewart (re)works these mechanisms ficto-*critically*. Eventually, the epistemic things in question are going to change, as does the self that sets itself in relation to this re/medially re/layed subject matter from a *ficto*-critically in/formed angle.

Ordinary Affects promotes a non-transcendental project of continually re/conceiving of our lived world anew. And yet the non-fictional significance of its ficto-*critical* textual experiments lies not in the exploratory acquiescence of new information about another subject matter so much as in the speculative re/arranging of our text-epistemological access patterns to its re/layed medial fictions. Because "[t]he ordinary is a shifting assemblage of practices and practical knowledges" (ibid: 1), Stewart's *ficto*-critical interest is how affective charges are conducted discursively, but her ficto-*critical* concern then lies with the people who act on the basis of such current discursive formations in everyday situations. Part of the experiment is to observe her textual re/lays reverberate, to make perceptible not only how they work but also whether and where they perhaps make a difference. Even though we sometimes indulge in treating discourse as an end in itself, it still constitutively pervades reading individuals and their world. Stewart's thought-experimental writing makes both the mutual dependence and potential liberation of discursive and affective textual work perceptible. Her suggestion is not to substitute discourse for the world, but to understand it in its essential epistemological function *sine qua non* and operate its levers with a more consciously practical and less transcendental direction.

Ultimately, such ficto-*critical* experiments aim at changing our understanding of the world by putting the linguistic-discursive side of our epistemological access at stake. Rather than corroborating or falsifying a theoretical construction by induction and deduction, their aim is to instil a self-reflexive meta-awareness that abductively re(in)forms the self at work in the experiment. After all, the readerly self thus interpellated sets her/self in constitutive relation to the world and the text via the same interpretive persona. While scientific experiments administer theory to the world from the removed position of an abstract observer, ficto-*critically* experimental art and literature brings the underdetermined individual position of the always current recipient agent at work back into the equation. Ficto-*critical* writing no longer excludes the person encountering it, by abstracting from her individual position into a transcendental subject, but establishes an operational systemic connection for the readerly position between the writing and the act of read*ing* under way. In this manner, what I have previously defined in the second chapter as the self-reflexively im/mediate and performative realisation of the *ficto*-critical vector and twist is harnessed to develop some ficto-*critical* edge, which will subsequently be the detailed subject of the fourth chapter.

All in all, *Ordinary Affects* is *ficto*-critical because its artistically experimental form re/lays scenarios full of affective charge interspersed with theoretical musings on the representational and communicative connectivity and circuitry of affect, both corporeally and discursively. Stewart's special-effect writing which contrasts with the ordinary affects it depicts – throwing in relief the im/mediately corporeal and textually mediated modes of re/laying affect – steers the reader towards realising the *ficto*-critical vector. The text furthermore presents its readers with an artful thought experiment whose textual nature highlights the discursive mechanisms of affective charges ficto-*critically*. Re/laying affective charges textually, it experimentally explores challenges to our discursive practices that effect the conduits of affect. *Ordinary Affects* is thus ficto-*critical* because it takes discursive formation and practices seriously as im/mediate and non-fictional events. In this regard, Stewart's particular concern lies with the ways in which our practices of meaning, other, and self-formation differ and interfere between the linguistic-discursive and socio-corporeal fields. Throughout, she privileges the non-transcendental and advocates a continually re/adjusted primacy of the affectively registering world of matter that also – yet not exclusively – matters because it affects us.

Brief Recapitulation

The foregoing reading of the ficto/critical in terms of experimentation highlights how the *ficto*-critical vector and twist are rooted in the artistically experimental side of such textual practices and how ficto-*critical* edge is developed by their artfully pre/scribed thought-experimental side – both of which in combination gain the significance of exploratory non-fictional experiments. This layered notion of the experimental can capture the simultaneously playful and purposive aspects of ficto/critical textual practices. But its nodal structure is also entirely suitable to formulate the nexus point on which the two-step trope of the ficto/critical hinges and at which our text-practical ideals matter. A text is *ficto*-critical if its artistic experiments make our generic frame/work of approaching texts perceptible (*ficto*-critical vector) and if it simultaneously experiments with framing this work differently (*ficto*-critical twist). A text is furthermore ficto-*critical* if it connects its wider discursive concerns to such *ficto*-critical insights to endow its textual thought experiment with im/mediately non-fictional significance (ficto-*critical* edge) for our textual frame/work*ing* practices. Ultimately, a text derives ficto-*critical* edge by interpellating the reading agent who is at work in the textual practices under critique which the text also illumines and illuminates via the *ficto*-critical vector and twist.

4. Developing Ficto-*critical* Edge

Issues & Practices of Ficto/critical Concern

Structurally abutting on the second chapter, which has established what qualifies texts as *ficto*-critical, this fourth chapter shall now ask what qualifies such texts as also ficto-*critical*. My overall thesis is that where ficto/critical practices realise the *ficto*-critical vector and twist they sometimes give additional practical direction to these im/mediate textual experiences by way of the wider con/textual concerns they also feature. In this manner, the im/mediate textual experience of the *ficto*-critical vector and the realisation of the *ficto*-critical twist – with their performatively immersed and explanatorily distanced aspects – gain a broader practical significance which is directed by the text's constatively raised concerns. Of ficto/critical interest are those thematic complexes in which a text's ficto-*critical* concerns relate to – as much as they flow from – its *ficto*-critical insights. The point of the two-step trope is to indicate that constitutive mechanisms of our textual practices are implicated in the wider discursive issues under critique. The ficto/critical pattern illumines and illuminates them via *ficto*-critical vector and twist at the same time as it links them to a critique of wider discursive issues. A text's concerns are ficto-*critical* in so far as they have a *ficto*-critical point of origin. Ficto/critical texts connect their im/mediate and theoretical insights into our textual practices to the wider discursive concerns they mediate – which is how they develop ficto-*critical edge*. In the following, I am going to re/trace the main ficto/critical nexus in two exemplary ficto-*critical* texts in order to explicate, illustrate, and define the crucial tropical pattern further.

Ultimately, though beyond the scope of the present thesis, it will be productive to identify clusters of both *ficto*-critical insights and ficto-*critical* concerns that, in relating to their respective counterparts, instantiate conspicuous patterns of the fully-fledged trope. In this manner, a systemic *ficto*-critical theory of our textual practices could eventually become an ordering principle of different ficto-*critical* impetus across the re/drawn 'field'; to which project this chapter is prolegomenon.

4.1 FICTO/CRITICALLY TURNING "THAUMATROPES"

A worthy ficto-*critical* counterpart to Stephen Muecke's *ficto*-critically exemplary "The Fall" is Gail Jones's "Thaumatropes" (1998). Similar to Muecke's piece, I want to argue, Jones's essay presents a fine instance of a text that condenses into structural metaphors the central representational and communicative mechanism of concern in and to her writing. Although her structural metaphors are filmic their crucial insights extend to writing *qua* post-auratic medium. Jones's effort, however, further compliments the performative, self-reflexive, and im/mediate interpellation of her reader and the poetic explications of her imagery with a practical concern over the function such post-auratic projections serve within wider discursive formations. She thus endows her text's potential for the *ficto*-critical vector and twist with ficto-*critical edge* by further relating them to her concerns with cross-cultural (ethnographic) projection.

Jones's essay is divided into seven sections of very roughly similar length and there is a structural element to the composition of these fragments that is worth considering in light of the theoretical suggestions it presents. While the first fragment describes a remembered experience, written up after the event, this picture then becomes the subject of the following six sections that work theoretically to shift perspective not only on the initial scene presented, but also on its kind of textual presentation. Reading the essay is, thus, to engage with Jones's self-reflexive meta-commentary on her writing at the same time as relating this to the opening scene which we encounter mediated by her writing. Hence, Jones's carefully structured text consists of writing that aims to partly (re)contextualise itself.

A Cinematic Textual Turn (*Ficto*-Critical Vector)

It is worth considering Jones's two opening sentences, because they indicate her *ficto*-critical strategy, anticipate her structural metaphors, and establish her main ficto-*critical* concern:

> "Picture this: a single white woman sits embraced within a community of Aboriginal people – of the tribe Bardi – to watch a movie projected outside on the whitewashed wall of the school. It is a windy night and the audience is bound together by a breeze from the sea that circulates between them and brushes, phantom-like, at their hair and their faces." (Jones 1998: 98)

Firstly, the framing demand to "picture this" creates a *ficto*-critically striking encapsulation of the intradiegetic scene and our textual access to it. Secondly, the wind enters the scene as an all-pervasive force around whose metaphoric potential

Jones is then going to structure the narration of her *ficto*-critical argument on ethnographic projection. Thirdly, the Aboriginals' embrace of the observing narrator presents a communal counterpoise to the general embrace of the wind. Building on this early metaphorical constellation, Jones then proceeds to endow her cross-cultural concern with ficto-*critical* edge.

Before scrutinising these three aspects in greater detail it is helpful to cast a glance at Jones's reasons for her theoretical reflections and concomitant shift in perspective. On second reading she scrutinises the speaking position and interpretive gesture of her own writing: "The tonal authority achieved by the third-person narration is [...] purely fraudulent: the collapse of cultural certainty at the end of the story allegorizes the position non-indigenous scholars frequently enact in cross-cultural encounters" (ibid: 100). Her proximity to dominant academic perceptions and depictions of self and other across cultures in writing is thus of central concern to Jones's writing.

Because her critique is concerned with the dangers and potential of our textual practices, and because she does not want to replicate any detrimental structures, Jones wonders, "What position might I take to comment on my own experience [...]?" (ibid: 99) In classic fictocritical style she then brings the personal into academic discourse by pondering, "To what extent is my difficulty in finding a speaking position an elaboration of this childhood confusion of the bodily and the social and the wish to recover, in any case, a utopian possibility of alterity?" (ibid: 108) She thus marks the fact that her quest for an appropriate speaking position originates from dissatisfaction with available models as well as her recognition of the significance of singular personal experiences. These motivated concerns underwrite her subsequent self-reflective meta-commentary on the opening scene. Her writing thus presents a protocol of re/reading the initial fragment at the same time as it is already a ficto/critical exercise of its self-reflected counter-continuation.

"Thaumatropes" also aims at a performatively self-reflexive realisation among its readers. Jones creates the potential for a *ficto*-critical vector from the recoiling structure of her re/reading. Right from the outset her text establishes a connection between the filmic medium it investigates and its underlying textual medium. "Picture this" is the initial call to the reader, followed by a three paragraph descriptive passage infused with metaphorical potential on which the theoretical development of the entire essay feeds. Jones launches her text as an exercise in pre/scription, a thought experiment, a program to be run on the reader just as much as a program for the reader to run through. By identifying our read*ing* performance in filmic terms she cleverly frames the story of an Aboriginal tribe's cross-cultural filmic reception. She figuratively encapsulates these two kinds of medial projection.

Pushing this idea, a little, I want to suggest that Jones's text – *qua* thought experiment – even amounts to a motion picture in its own right, on our mental screens. Her initial address to the reader presents a cinematic textual description of a scene containing the movie picture at its heart. The interpellatory address sets the stage for her medial considerations to follow just as much as the descriptive fragment then sets the scene of the example to be investigated. From the very beginning, "Thaumatropes" introduces an internally (re)coiling movement that prepares the way for its considerations of the filmic medium to hit home in relation to its own textual basis. The opening phrase establishes a link to the central medium of the scene, which is depicted in a way that allows its theoretical commentary to feed back into an understanding of the medium text. The figurative medial intersection at the beginning of the text demands a re/consideration of its text-medial basis in light of its subsequent assessment of the filmic medium and our representational and communicative relat*ing* to it. Figuratively apt, it brings the reader into the picture and thus possibly sparks an im/mediate realisation of the *ficto*-critical vector.

Additionally, Jones's focus on the Aboriginal community's reception of THE SHOOTIST (Siegel 1976) enhances the self-reflexive challenge of her meta-commentary for the readerly performance. On the one hand, the medial "image that appears on the wall has the firmest of boundaries. It is an immutable box, a stiff rectangle. And within it the visions are sharp and windscreened: this is a virtual reality detached from the weather." (Jones 1998: 98) It is thus not unlike the written page. On the other hand, this detached vision finds its counterpoise in the audience, which "is responsive and extra attentive" (ibid: 98). There is "a kinesis in the audience, a refusal to be passive" (ibid: 99), and this receptive attentiveness during the screening is then followed by a collective cultural response to the film. The Aboriginal community enters a mourning ritual related to the film because of the screen death of its John Wayne character, J. B. Books.

The Bardi community in their specific take on the film not only treat the post-auratic artwork auratically within their idiocultural con/text, but furthermore approach the events on screen thoroughly within their own con/text as real. Because *they* have encountered and were presently affected by the film, they fully embed its narrative within their cultural con/text by reacting to the screen death with traditional mourning. By contrast, for Jones's presumably Western-educated readership with its own tradition of film receptive practices "[t]o grieve for John Wayne is insubordinate; it is a reclamation of social consequence from mere simulacra; it is a conversion of the specular into the performative" (ibid: 102). For Jones the

Aboriginal response amounts to "consubstantiation, an insistence that the sign somewhere connects with bodies and with souls" (ibid: 102). And this "somewhere" she thus firmly locates on the *readerly* side.

Jones's move re/admits auratic elements into her theory of relat*ing* to post-auratic media such as film and text. As she acknowledges, "by communal reception, audiences may reconstitute a sense of authority associated with auratic art. The Aboriginal audience participated, one might say, in this communalized assertion, this refashioning reception." (ibid: 103) Their communal reading of the post-auratic film presently restitutes an auratic character. Jones draws on Benjamin's famous distinction between auratic and post-auratic artworks in "The Work of Art in the Age of Mechanical Reproduction" (2009b) to effectively relocate the aura of art in our framing work of relat*ing* to it.

The Aboriginal community's shared idiocultural con/text and practices in relation to film have effectively overruled the dominant Western assessment of the medium's epistemology: "Rather than indicating submissiveness and cultural defeat, the mourning ceremonies can be read as an assertion of the primacy of tribal epistemology over Western meaning. It can be read, that is, as abrogative and counter-discursive." (Jones 1998: 102) A general consequence of this insight, which ultimately implies Jones's readership as well, is "that audiences are capable of mobilizing symbolic effects that are counter to, and in contradistinction with, conventional and predisposed significations" (ibid: 103). Notably, she reminds her reader of this via a scenario that emphasises "the *transactive* nature of cross-cultural screen engagement" (ibid: 103, original emphasis). Jones's meta-commentary on her own cross-cultural observations and assessment thus appears in a different light, too, and with it the anthropological reading situation *per se*.

As it turns out, because "the Pallottine brothers had a history of showing movies to the community […] including ethnographic footage of Bardi life earlier that century" (ibid: 105), the Aboriginal community at the screening already had its own reception history of film firmly established. They have previously been "inducted into varieties of filmic knowledge, the generically specific (slapstick, Western) and the putatively mimetic (ethnographic)" (ibid: 105). Significantly, "[t]he ethnographic material was under restriction and regulation, since it was regarded as spiritually improper to show images of people who were known and deceased" (ibid: 105). Thus, not a previous absence of filmic experience but their long established idiocultural tradition of film reception has given the Lombadina community reason to conduct themselves in relation to the events depicted in the way they did.

What seems, perhaps, surprising or curious at first is, in fact, a different approach to the medium, its referentiality, and epistemology. In their reaction to THE

SHOOTIST the Bardi people continue their own tradition of filmic encounters, especially because the narrative focus of the film is likely to have resonated heavily with the significance of kinship in the tribe (ibid: 110-1). Jones contrasts this with one Western discourse in particular: "The synchronic pretence of ethnography – its paradoxical manoeuvre to fix in an atemporal present that which is simultaneously regarded as always past – was here clearly refused: the Aboriginal community simply *assumed* the historical entailment, disposition and consequentiality of the film." (ibid: 105, original emphasis) Indeed, through their cultural con/text the Aboriginals had very good reason to bring their idiocultural interpretive resources to bear on the film like this. Realising this, Jones, too, finds good reason to avoid the pretentious voice of her opening fragment.

As she continues to paint the picture in which "the community at Lombadina may have responded in part to the problematic logic of the medium itself" (ibid: 105), Jones presents a more and more sophisticated constellation that throws in relief the in/formed expectations of the different idiocultural con/texts and practices in relation to the medium. Furthermore, she notes that the cross-cultural perspective exacerbates the contrasting practices towards "a medium that, while pretending process and materiality, adumbrates most profoundly closure and loss" (ibid: 106) – at least to Western eyes. To the Aboriginal community by contrast "[t]his is film as séance, medium as medium" (ibid: 106). Clearly, what is at stake here are the cultural practices of medial reception, and Jones *ficto*-critically brings those of her reader into the picture.

In this way, Jones aims to induce a *ficto*-critical vector by figuratively intersecting the present text with the filmic medium ostentatiously at the centre of attention. Her perspectival shift from (essential) medial characteristics to (performative) practices of medial relat*ing* has implications for our act of read*ing* from within which we access her text's considerations. She makes the constitutive possibility of accessing the post-auratic medium auratically her text's subject at the same time as she lets the Aboriginal community's cross-cultural reception of THE SHOOTIST contrast with the (potentially) stifling cross-cultural embrace of Western anthropology in particular. In a second move, Jones then reaps the metaphorical potential she sowed in her original fragment.

Turning Windy, Taking Breath (*Ficto*-Critical Twist)

The initial imagery of the textual motion picture heralds the crucial significance of imagery throughout the essay. Jones skilfully develops a further structural metaphor of wind/breath to contrast different principles of both post-auratic projection and the cross-cultural embrace. Ultimately, she converges all these images in the figure of a cinematic toy, namely her thaumatrope.

Re/reading her own account in the first fragment, Jones realises "that the mysticism of the narration, the bizarre wind, is at once a naturalizing, an authority, and a kind of radical pyrrhonism, a flight into bewilderness" (ibid: 101). In the third section "West wind" (ibid: 101-4) she aligns this kind of wind, which is the pervading presence in the opening scene, with Western anthropology. Jones reflects the initial speaking position of her narrator in this manner: "She finds herself at the margins. She feels the wind from the sea blow directly through her body. She feels finally no more or less than this wind: it identifies her sense of insubstantiality." (ibid: 99) She thus marks herself as marginally positioned in a way that suggests the ideal of an omnipresent observer, an absently present speaking position that relays without re-laying. "In ethnographic terms", she observes, "this is a classic dilemma of social positioning, a 'being there' [...] which affirms, paradoxically, both the *authority* of the Westerner and her *incorporeality*" (ibid: 101, original emphases). Her position in the depiction thus matches the anthropologist's writing position. Notably, this removed positioning is further naturalised by the textual medium and exercised by our textual practices.

In particular, Jones notes a transcendental bend in her description that would suggest her pervasive as well as pervading position as the narrator. On re/reading, this makes her uneasy. She is concerned about "the anti-materialist rhetoric implicit in [her] telling of the movie tale" (ibid: 100) and wonders, "whence does this metaphysical impulse derive" (ibid: 100), this flight into "the textual ether" (ibid: 101)? Problematically, this "textual ether" coincides with her depiction of her/self as "the normative in a story about the loss of normatives" (ibid: 99), which coincides with the medial necessity to project the other in one's own con/text. She highlights filmic vision and the textual ether as transcendentally sealed-off generalities by virtue of their post-auratic medial bases, whose socio-corporeal and practical significance she would now like to analyse, revise, and deploy differently, ficto-*critically*.

Jones then juxtaposes her personal motivation and positioning to the ethereal West wind. Her twofold imagery of wind/breath relates to different principles of post-auratic projection, both of which operate the same constitutive filmic mechanism captured by the thaumatrope. The impersonal West wind pervades Jones's opening depiction of the Lombadina screening, while her intimate breath animates the cinematic projection of her childhood toy. While she aligns the West wind with the general cross-cultural embrace of anthropology, her breath on the thaumatrope not only represents the constitutive mechanism of filmic projection but also figures her subjective motivation to write ficto/critically. At the end of the essay, Jones favours her own breath to operate the thaumatrope together with its particular figuring of the cross-cultural embrace. Her turn from the West wind to her breath highlights the profound shift of her perspective and approach over the course of the essay.

Jones counter-continues the metaphysical West wind by introducing the intimate and subjective, for example, by telling us that "[a]s I read my movie tale, I know that the body I wish to recover is really very young; it is the child who spent years visiting the Sun Pictures in Broome, enwrapped in the many-coloured arms of her friends" (ibid: 107). Writing like this she breaks ranks with the generic and opts for the kind of subjective textual conduct that is still often sanctioned in academia. The personal experience of a cross-cultural embrace becomes her ideal of textual representation and communication. She also explicitly wonders, "To what extent is my difficulty in finding a speaking position an elaboration of this childhood confusion of the bodily and the social and the wish to recover, in any case, a utopian possibility of alterity?" (ibid: 108) Jones intimates a personally inflected, ethical motivation at the heart of her self-reflexive meta-commentary on our reading and writing practices. By way of its purposive playful brilliance "Thaumatropes" is thus indeed a ficto-*critically* driven text throughout.

From this perspective, it is significant that Jones describes the children's section at Sun Pictures as "an area interracial, libidinal, deterritorialized and blent with the exotic of the Hollywood imagery. Rained on. Screen lit. Star bright. *Wind swept.*" (ibid: 108, original emphasis) But this is a different breeze from the West wind. Her memory juxtaposes the adult segregation in the cinema with this child enacted cross-cultural utopia, which further parallels the conflation of corporeal arrangements with the filmic image conflation of the thaumatrope. Most importantly, these memories generate Jones's desire to write in a way that would match her breath on the thaumatrope: to replicate in writing the benevolent, corporeal, and reciprocal cross-cultural childhood embraces at Sun Pictures rather than to follow the West wind with its transcendentally removed, and yet stifling, cross-cultural embrace of (academic) anthropology. In exemplary fashion, Jones's windy structural metaphor of the breath that operates the thaumatrope unites her text's theoretical insights with her ethical concerns – the constitutive mechanism of post-auratic projection with her cross-cultural childhood memory turned writer's wish.

Moreover, Jones's realisation that "we project these desires onto the screen-shaped spaces that hang, gently flapping, between experience and interpretation" (ibid: 109) identifies the constitutive medial level of post-auratic reception on which the Bardi people's and her own practices converge. Located *between experience and interpretation*, post-auratic medial reception already relies on idiocultural capital, which may or may not opt to presently restitute an aura to the artwork by way of its fram*ing* work of art. The imagery constellation of wind/breath and thaumatrope evokes both the juxtaposition of principles and their convergence in the constitutive mechanisms of filmic projection. It aims to deconstruct the academically instituted hierarchy between the two principles. The same constitutive mechanism throws in relief the ethnographic ideal of reception and a ficto/critical ideal of how other recipient practices are possible. Jones achieves this in tune with her theoretical considerations which privilege the recipient's position over fixed medial characteristics.

This is the *ficto*-critical capital of Jones's imagery. However, she proceeds to capitalise on this ficto-*critically* by feeding this imagery into the difference between the two cross-cultural filmic encounters at the beginning and the end of her essay – her insubstantial presence in narrating the screening at Lombadina and her embodied, animating wish in blowing the thaumatrope. In this fashion, then, the text provides the potential for a *ficto*-critical twist when it constatively presents a poetics of film – which *qua* post-auratic medium also applies to text – that manages to combine the self-reflexive performative awareness provided by the *ficto*-critical vector with the explanatory force of the structural metaphor combining wind/breath and thaumatrope.

Thaumatropical Cross-Cultural Turns (Ficto-*Critical* Edge)

"Thaumatropes" develops ficto-*critical* edge because it endows the explanatory poetics of its structural metaphor with im/mediately significant practical direction. It intersects the aesthetic imagery of the winds and thaumatrope with the ethical concern that pervades the text both as subjective narration and meta-ethnographic consideration, namely the cross-cultural embrace. Against the backdrop of her concern with cross-cultural interpretation Jones thus combines a poetics of post-auratic media – the subject of her text's *ficto*-critical vector and twist – with the ethical motivation for her protocol of re/reading the initial fragment. This is how she lets her accumulated constellation of structural metaphors culminate to ficto-*critical* effect:

> "I possess a small antiquarian scientific toy called, somewhat ostentatiously, a thaumatrope. Despite its fine name, it is blithely simple, consisting of a series of cardboard discs strung on a string. When the discs are rotated, by breath or manipulation, images on either side are visually combined. On one side, for example, is a black Mummy figure, on the other a white baby; [...] when the disc spins around the woman appears to hold the baby." (ibid: 112)

The figure of this little toy thus converges the *ficto*-critical and ficto-*critical* aspects of Jones's text in a single, deceptively simple, image.

At a basic theoretical level, "[t]he thaumatrope is a device [...] notable for its discovery and illustration of the principle of the persistence of visual impression, that fortuitous ocular capacity upon which the technology of film relies" (ibid: 112). Jones's fascination with it comes partly from "the pleasure of seeming to contain, so very modestly, something of the originary logic of film itself" (ibid: 112). And yet, this interest also pertains to her ethical concerns. Although the thaumatrope is already captivating on account of "the figure itself, the intransitivity of the sign, the confidence-trickery of the turning word" (ibid: 112), for Jones, its significance is further enhanced in a practical direction on account of the cross-cultural image her particular toy combines.

> "There is something in all this that provides a kind of metaphor for cross-cultural scholarship. We blow – the afflatus confident – hoping to set in process a dialectic by which, in an act of consecutive easy encirclement, the self and the other will breezily combine, cultures discontinuous will appear continuous, the limitations of the image will be delimited and animated." (ibid: 112)

The thaumatrope thus presents the constitutive mechanism operated by both the impersonal West wind and one's intimate breath as different principle facilitators of the cross-cultural embrace.

In conclusion Jones notes how re/reading her initial fragment has led to the distinction between the removed general and personally involved principles of cross-cultural writing: "Yet I wonder, if one of the winds I wished to describe is really, at some level, the breath on the thaumatrope: the impelling exhalation, the fast-motioning embrace of that which wishes to reconvene, ideally and utopianly, the beautiful black woman with the small white baby." (ibid: 113) The socio-corporeal and cross-cultural embrace in her childhood memory is thus aptly figured by a toy she operates by breath. From this perspective, the thaumatrope demands a particular, socio-corporeally subjective deployment of its medial potential from the agent at work – and so, by analogy, for (ficto/critical) ethnographic reading and writing. It figures the fusion of horizons that is also constitutively effected in the act of reading and writing, which in the case of cross-cultural representation and communication, however, so often comes at the cost of a con/textual con/fusion of horizons.

With regards to the difference between constitutive filmic projection and the ideal of receptive filmic projection, the insightful contraption of the thaumatrope captures, firstly, the essential mechanisms of the post-auratic medium film, secondly, the principle driving forces of wind and breath as well as, thirdly, Jones's personal concern with the kind of embrace that we enact in our practices of cross-cultural representation and communication; as epitomised by traditional, academic anthropology. By way of its poetics, the toy condenses into a single image the figures of the cross-cultural embrace that is a general aim of anthropology and the possibility of a positioned and embodied stance in terms of one's particular breath. Jones's thaumatrope signals an approach that does not stifle its subject, but rather breathes life into it via a living and enacted relationship. By virtue of its threefold metaphorical combination, "Thaumatropes" develops ficto-*critical* edge when it manages to connect the im/mediate, self-reflexively performative interpellation of the *ficto*-critical vector and theoretical insights of the *ficto*-critical twist with Jones's personally motivated ficto-*critical* concerns and interests. Ingeniously, her layered structural metaphor of the thaumatrope encompasses all this.

For example, in Jones's depiction of the Aboriginal community's cross-cultural film reception we suddenly recognise the constitutive mechanism that we successfully abstract from in our cross-cultural practice of anthropology. Jones's *ficto*-critical insight in this respect then aims to conceive of the constitutive mechanism differently in order to better address, potentially even redress, her critical concerns. The mechanisms under critical consideration underlie both Jones's textual acts as well as those of her readers, thus connecting the experiential awareness triggered by the *ficto*-critical vector with the ethical concerns of the text. Thus im/mediately pointing out to the reader their own implication in the representational practices under critique amounts to a textual interpellation with tendentious interventionist potential.

Also, with particular regards to our generic practices of post-auratic reception Jones wonders, "How […] does the authority of the real real become firmly established over, and discernible from, the more various orders of fictions?" (ibid: 110) How come one model of representational practices dominates even though alternative (text) cultural practices are not only available, but in fact the subject of many such investigations? "If in other areas of scholarship we grant the interpenetration of different orders of disclosure (the 'fictive' and the 'factual'), why do anthropological topics so assiduously dissever them? Is the issue one of epistemology […] or of lexical poverty […]?" (ibid: 110) If post-auratic media allow for different modes of engagement and epistemological relating, even referentiality, then why is it that where the stakes are as high as they are in cross-cultural encounters we still insist on one-way practices that generically prevent reciprocal exchange?

At this stage of the present thesis, it is important that "Thaumatropes" in this manner identifies elements of classic and instituted anthropological practice that deploy the potential of post-auratic projection in a way of which Jones is critical. Her essay takes a turn to produce ficto-*critical* edge when it points out the way in which the constitutive mechanisms of post-auratic representation and communication – which are also the subject of her text's *ficto*-critical vector and twist – are employed to certain effects with which she disagrees.

Where texts intersect their aesthetics with a poetics of reading to ficto-*critical* effect, they feed the experience and insights of the *ficto*-critical vector and twist into the ethical concerns that they simultaneously raise constatively. Generally speaking, the ficto/critical trope presents a *ficto*-critical experience and understanding whose practical significance is given wider discursive implication by the text's other issues and concerns. It endows texts with ficto-*critical* edge. In this way, ficto/critical strategies that are motivated by experiences in specific contexts engage post/modern formal means to serve certain ethico-political agendas. Their mutual aim is to inscribe such textual structures as can lead their readers towards realising their own ficto/critical discourse analyses motivated by their respective idiocultural and con/textual positioning. Ultimately, the goal is to raise awareness of the reading self's agency and potential – if not responsibility – to transform certain textual and generic practices thus under ficto-*critique*.

After the intersection of *aesthetics* and *poetics* has been the detailed subject of the second chapter, this first section of the fourth chapter has now re/traced its further chiasmic intersection with ethics which allows ficto/critical texts to im/mediately, performatively, and self-reflexively address aspects of our textual practices presently under way as cultural techniques with detrimental effects. Highlighting to the reader their performative implication in the textual practices currently under constative critique is precisely ficto-*critical*. Notably, the realm of potential for this twofold intersecting, ficto/critical trope is thus pre/structured by its possible points of origin in the paradigmatic situation of our textual practices, which alone can be addressed *ficto*-critically.

4.2 QUALIFYING A COMPLETE FICTO/CRITICAL TEXT

Now that the two-step ficto/critical trope has been established across my readings of Stephen Muecke's "The Fall" and Gail Jones's "Thaumatropes" I would like to further substantiate these findings by turning to yet another highly-accomplished ficto/critical text. Katrina Schlunke's *Bluff Rock: Autobiography of a Massacre* (2005) presents this exceptionally rich textual structure. The following reading shall qualify it as an exemplary ficto/critical text that instantiates all the defining traits the present thesis proposes.

At the general level, *Bluff Rock* investigates the historiographic textual relation that allows local discursive entities to form, circulate, and effectively serve wider cultural functions. Her particular object of scrutiny is the discursive formation of The Bluff Rock Massacre that a leaflet presents to tourists travelling the New England Highway whose view conveniently leads onto the topological bluff in question from a distance (2005: 29-32).

Importantly, Schlunke's thorough examination of the leaflet's archive reveals not a singular and exceptional event, as the leaflet purports to commemorate, but a multiple scene of frontier violence that was part and parcel of early Australian settler society's mundane exploitation and expulsion of Aboriginal people. In response, she carefully researches how the official leaflet yet both documents and, at the same time, fictionalises The Bluff Rock Massacre into discursive existence. Furthermore, Schlunke also conducts something of a critical discourse analysis of her archive that assesses the mutual parameters of both its construction and her reception. In so doing, I want to argue, Schlunke turns her creatively critical discourse analysis into something more of a ficto/critical discourse analysis.

For example, from a local perspective Schlunke reads outside the texts proper in order to locate the discursive events in the landscape they imply (ibid: 92-4). On finding it impossible to map these textually mediated occurrences onto the geography of the bluff, she then sets the leaflet's pre/scribed reading situation on the highway in relation to the actual setting on the bluff, with the effect that the spatial intricacies at work in the textual relation of The Bluff Rock Massacre as a discursive event are thrown into relief. From a historiographic perspective Schlunke cross-reads the tourist leaflet, local stories, letters, diaries, and other records which, between them, allow her to carefully re/construct the con/texts – past and present – of each text's historical production and reception (ibid: 59-97, 135-87, 213-36). Thus, she emphasises to uncanny effect how our relation to the fictional history of The Bluff Rock Massacre has always been – and continues to be – a present textual relat*ing*.

Bluff Rock brilliantly exemplifies the characteristic pattern of the ficto/critical two-step with regards to historiography. Firstly, Schlunke pursues a general epistemological interest in the narratives of local history. Due to the particular archive of The Bluff Rock Massacre her initial question "How do we know the past?" (ibid: 11) soon becomes something more like: How do we know the past through text? The curious text-cultural detour of relating to the past *by way of* relating to text lets her envisioned epistemology of local history soon overlap almost to congruence with the epistemology of textual representation and communication. Schlunke's leading question now reflects the historiographic relation as a textual relat*ing*, which is how the *ficto*-critical perspective of *Bluff Rock* commences.

Secondly, however, these text-epistemological considerations arise out of Schlunke's ethical concern with our – personal, local, as well as national – relations to the past which always already imply the present and future. In this respect, her leading question is how the textual relation between our/selves and the past can affect present relations in the world. Schlunke's epistemological concern with historiography arises out of an ethical concern with present cultural relations in Australia. At the heart of *Bluff Rock*'s concern with the representation of exploitative and violent inter-cultural relations during Australia's past frontier conflicts lies the practically significant self-conception of each particular (local? white? Australian?) reader in the present, which collectively, effectively p/re/structure present and future Australian inter-cultural relations. This is how the central ficto-*critical* perspective of *Bluff Rock* commences.

Taken together, the ficto/critical two-step thus emerges because the perspective under which Schlunke is concerned with the historiographic relation has an ethical interest at heart. *Bluff Rock*'s *ficto*-critical interest in textual representation and communication is ficto-*critically* motivated. Firstly, the epistemology of historiography concerns the question of how the relation between a self and a text can both effect and affect the relation between a self and the past. Formulaically rendered this *ficto*-critical constellation is:

([self – text] – past)

Secondly, however, this epistemology of historiography may in turn affect present and future cultural relations between self and other because such wider discursive formations are p/re/structured by linguistic discursive formations of the past. This extended ficto-*critical* constellation is:

([{self – text} – past] – other)

Typically ficto/critical, Schlunke's ethical perspective on the epistemology of historiography locates the textual medium firmly at the centre of attention. Its p/re/structuring parameters and frame/work, after all, present the theoretical hinge for any ficto/critical two-step strategy.

Furthermore, *Bluff Rock* also creates potential for the realisation of a *ficto*-critical vector. Consider, for example, Schlunke's self-reflexive focus on her own reading and writing as only the latest – albeit interventionist – link in an ongoing chain of textual acts. This chain reaches back to letters, diaries, and records from the Australian frontier context which function as precursors to the tourist leaflet that she now reads and writes about in *Bluff Rock*. But the chain of textual acts does not stop there. Schlunke's programmatic scrutiny of particular textual acts – her subjects' as much as her own – forces upon her reader the sense that through their act of reading they, too, are implied in the text's subject of investigation. Before long it dawns on the perceptive reader that we now occupy her erstwhile recipient position, whose protocol of reading we now read in turn. In this manner, Schlunke's self-reflexive meta-commentary works to interpellate her reader *qua* reader, while read*ing*, as the next link in a chain whose constitutive mechanisms come under scrutiny while they are under way.

In other words, not dissimilar to the previously considered reverse *mis en abyme* structure of two mirrors facing each other, the foregrounded chain-like logic of textual production and reception indicates the underdetermined readerly position and thus brings the constitutive frame/work with its parameters into the picture. Only in reading can the reader realise her im/mediate linkage with the depicted chain of textual mediations. Our textual relat*ing*, which is the subject under scrutiny, is necessarily under way because it is the only means of access. The represented chain-like structure of textual acts can thus hit home as a *ficto*-critical vector. While there is a contingent historical beginning of the textual chain under consideration, the systemic nature of the analysis implies all our recipient acts to come. This *ficto*-critical reversal of direction does not point deeper into the transcendental realm of past textual re/presentation, but presently towards its non-transcendental frame/work of reception that is ongoing.

Note against this background how the fictocritical two-step in *Bluff Rock* lies condensed in the trope of the historiographic relation. The key insight is that the conceptualisation of the past by means of textual epistemology becomes an ethically significant act in the present with p/re/structuring relevance for the future. In Schlunke's words, "we shape ourselves through how we think about the past. We tell stories about where we come from and who we are." (ibid: 11) And because such stories structure present conceptions of identity, they also p/re/structure the realm of conceivable future action. Something purely linguistic-discursive here becomes in/formative of wider discursive, worldly structures.

Throughout *Bluff Rock*, Schlunke is acutely aware that there is something pressingly, albeit counter-intuitively, current in our seemingly backward-directed concern with history: "The art of the past is to remember that it is always told in the present. We are not what we were, and we cannot predict what we will become. As new ways of being open to us, so new ways of knowing become available, and these possibilities happen to us *here* and *now*." (ibid: 22, my emphases) Looking back onto history is thus a present activity directed at an essentially unknown future which is yet p/re/structured in the blind spot of this reverse outlook. This is also the gist of how Walter Benjamin's "Theses on the Philosophy of History" famously figure "the angel of history" (2007a: 257-8). Historiography, as Alasdair Gray alternatively puts it in *Why Scots Should Rule Scotland*, "bring[s] the past up to date" (2001: 76-7, 105) – albeit necessarily from a certain perspective and to certain effect. In other words, the re/presentation of past constellations is always simultaneously a re/configuring of notions in the present that can p/re/configure the realm of conceivable future constellations. And to mark *Bluff Rock*'s own potential as a textual moment of such p/re/structuring Schlunke deliberately deploys the deictic shifters "here" and "now" (2005: 22).

Because Schlunke is ethically concerned with present Australian inter-cultural relations, she analyses, in the form of The Bluff Rock Massacre, current textual formations of frontier violence against Aboriginal people. Partly she approaches her subject as an academically distanced, white, privileged, and thereby central cultural critic – albeit one who will still have reason to feel marginal/ised in Australian society as queer. But, partly, she is also aware of her proximity to The Bluff Rock Massacre as a local, which leads her to investigate her discursive familiarity with similar narratives she encountered growing up not too far from the bluff. Thus multiply situated, Schlunke's creative inquiry skilfully draws on her expertise as a cultural critic to make sense of her own potential complicity with a representational violence that is not only traditionally ripe, but presently ongoing in our textual relations to Australia's frontier past. Her academic project is thus personal from the outset and includes herself as – at least partially – a product of the mechanisms she is scrutinising (ibid: 234).

For example, Schlunke detects a connection between her childhood knowledge about the demise of local Aboriginal people and the fictive narrative of the tourist leaflet. In both cases the point was to seal off history from the present, and thereby to obscure the *present* significance of such historiographic relat*ing*.

Only in retrospect she now recognises the discursive function of what knowledge she had of frontier violence as a child. At the time, knowing "[t]hat Aboriginal people were killed was another way of saying Aboriginal people did not exist now" (ibid: 12). In this manner, a radical discontinuity in Australian inter-cultural relations with Aboriginal people was implied. Structurally, the question of a present and indeed future significance of these aspects of the past was effectively forestalled. As a result, the present and future that were p/re/structured by this kind of historiographic strategy did not have to be as affected by obvious guilt as would otherwise have been appropriate.

What particularly bothers Schlunke about this strategy and prompts her inquiry into The Bluff Rock Massacre is the discursive function that actual – yet actually significantly different – events have acquired. She is troubled that because of such historiography "historical deaths were part of the shutting down of a history, not of its continuous opening up" (ibid: 13). Adding insult to fatal injury, massacres of Aboriginal people were endowed with the ongoing discursive function to prevent practically meaningful engagement with them, paradoxically, *by our ways of knowing them*. Especially her childhood reflection on knowing about local frontier violence thus "isn't a complaint about knowing too little" (ibid: 14). As she puts it, "I always knew, but I also always knew *how* to know" (ibid: 14, original emphasis). The motivation for Schlunke's analyses thus derives directly from the ethical implications of not only what one knows, but of how one knows something to a certain effect.

Realising that at the time "knowing Aboriginal people died did not have the effect it should have" (ibid: 13), she lays her finger straight onto the crux of the matter: the ethical problem she investigates is also an epistemological problem. Additionally, this intersection of the epistemology of the past with the ethics of knowing the past becomes even more pressing when her investigation leads her to consider the epistemology of the past in terms of the epistemology of text. After all, text is just what she produces in protocolling her readings of the archive. In response to this self-reflexive realisation, Schlunke makes it her task not only to track down the actual deaths in her archive but also to re/trace the representational violence in writing that has encompassed the actual massacres as much as it has enabled their documentation to enhance the annihilation (ibid: 174-5).

What is decidedly uncanny about Schlunke's approach is that she lets her ficto/critical discourse analysis of these textual practices cut to the bone of her own as well as her reader's textual acts. She not only gives up generic academic distance by letting her subjective local perspective creatively contribute to her study, but by virtue of its self-reflexive text-practical focus her investigation furthermore collapses the medial distance for the reader. As Schlunke establishes that the mechanisms under scrutiny and critique are not only condensed in the particular contexts under investigation but constitutive of our communicative situation of textual representation, any pre-theoretically assumed innocence of the textual medium and our textual practices as such evaporates. As the reader is brought to realise this in reading, the *ficto*-critical vector hits home with ficto-*critical* edge.

In direct response to the awareness that *there* and *then* textual acts were instances of ethically charged practices in as much as they always happened – and continue to happen – *here* and *now*, Schlunke shifts her own textual conduct in at least two crucial respects. Firstly, she signals a strategically *ficto*-critical double vision in the following statement: "I am both writing a cultural history, and attempting a model of what writing a history might look like if it were constantly concerned with how the writer was able to write, and how that writing came into a particular form at a particular time." (ibid: 15-6) This strategy makes her project both particular and general in outlook. While she investigates the specific cultural history of The Bluff Rock Massacre, she also investigates the universally applicable frame/work of the textual acts she thus engages both as an object of study and as a writing subject. In this manner, her *ficto*-critical stance supplements an outward-directed, truthful re/construction of history with an inward-directed, critical assessment of the textual mechanisms and parameters that effect as well as affect such historiographic re/constructions. This latter, more inward-directed pursuit eventually leads her to the mutual conditions of im/possibility of both her archive and her own textual activity, as well as that of her readers.

Schlunke's investigation into the practices of her subjects thus yields both substantial knowledge on a particular Australian frontier context and murders of Aboriginal people there and then as well as a self-reflexive meta-commentary on the past and present textual practices of delivering this knowledge always here and now. In this twofold perspective she accounts for the parameters and practices that underwrite such text-discursive inventions as The Bluff Rock Massacre. In many ways, her ficto/critical textual form is motivated by a self-reflexive awareness of how the ethically charged communicative situation of textual representation she investigates implies her as a reader of her archival subjects and the writer of *Bluff Rock*. But Schlunke pursues an even wider emancipatory enlightenment impetus when – in addition to re/mediating our historiographic relation to The Bluff Rock Massacre and Australian frontier conflict in general to re/medial effect – she also endows her writing with a theory of textual practices that aims to empower the readerly position *per se*.

The curious double vision of simultaneously focusing on both a specific textual archive and its text-medial conditions of im/possibility alone makes *Bluff*

Rock an extraordinary textual mediation. But Schlunke furthermore lets the insights of this twofold investigation in/form her own textual conduct in terms of style and strategy. Her written critique thus self-reflects its insights into the textual acts she simultaneously analyses and produces. In response to her findings Schlunke is going out of her way to circumspectly mark and strategically counter aspects that could imply her own writing – *qua* text-cultural technique of historiography – in the representational violence she critiques. All the while, she steers her reader to consider the implications of her conception of the historiographic relation while exercising its relat*ing*.

Secondly, because of her acute ficto-*critical* concerns, Schlunke thus invests in writing that is already in/formed by the *ficto*-critical insights it investigates. Recognising how constitutive parameters of our text-cultural techniques seem to have favoured such ethically unacceptable representational violence as The Bluff Rock Massacre significantly complicates her own act of writing. Knowing that new practices lead to new epistemologies, she begins to experiment with textual strategies of counter-continuation in response to her awareness of the ethically problematic epistemology of the historiographic relation. She is keenly aware that her writing has to tread carefully in order to mark – if not altogether avoid – the potentially detrimental effects of its constitutive structures. Her strategy thus aims to both harness and critique, to both continue and counter the textual conditions of the im/possibility of historiography by generically *other* means. Schlunke's aiming to explode a generic mode of text by exploiting its power, by short-circuitously re/directing its distinct force, renders her writing strategically ficto/critical.

For example, Schlunke deploys such counter-continuation to the aforementioned shutting down of history, declaring "[t]o avoid the threat of 'resolution' that narrative has, I have chosen excess" (ibid: 16). Especially the section "Taking it personally, making it personal" (ibid: 199-202), in which she figures her textual intercourse with Edward Irby, one of her subjects, as the consumption of marriage forces a sense of epistemological and functional uncertainty onto her reader. As she anachronistically writes her present – white, female, queer, etc. – readerly context into a pre/post/erous fiction of the past frontier context, which she reads into existence via her archive, Schlunke cleverly takes Hans-Georg Gadamer's literary-hermeneutic notion of a "fusion of horizons" (1972) to the extreme. But she simultaneously highlights a constitutive mechanism of textual reception by so blatantly inserting her own con/text into the text she reads, which thereby precisely cons the text. The irony being, of course, that this is how we make sense of any text to begin with. It is simply what constitutes (a) reading – even, and especially, where this is not as strikingly apparent.

Additionally, a mysterious night parrot turns the textual exchange into a *ménage a trois*. Abducted from the poetry of Dorothy Porter (ibid: 202) the bird figures as a trope for historiography in Schlunke's fiction. She thus invests increasing estrangement rather than reductive familiarity in her textual p/re/scription of the past and its p/re/structuring capacity. This brilliantly outrageous passage of *Bluff Rock* presents a textual intervention that assertively re/deploys the criticised historiographic potential of textual invention for its own purposes. Forced to ponder which function this in(ter)vention serves, Schlunke conducts her reader towards the realisation that she continues to countering effect the same mechanisms she simultaneously critiques in the formation of the tourist leaflet. Her textual strategy is thus not so much one of distanced external critique, but one of involved engagement, of traitorously re/directing a constitutive potential from within.

When Schlunke states that "I want to unknit *how* we know something, I want to unravel how stories can both fix ideas (and so our ways of knowing) and intimately undo these certainties" (ibid: 14, original emphasis), she turns this stance ficto/critical by starting at home and letting her writing self-reflexively per/form this. In this sense, *Bluff Rock* presents an instructive texture of unknitting the weaving of knowledge in which it consists. But the ficto/critical formation of *Bluff Rock* is also the result of Schlunke's ethical motivation for this epistemological resolve. This is why her ficto/critical strategy ingeniously shifts from investigating the text-discursive invention of The Bluff Rock Massacre to investing in a pre/post/erous text-discursive in(ter)vention herself. It is also how *Bluff* Rock becomes a counter-continuation of historiography by ficto/critically other means. Such apotropaic counter-continuation is one hallmark of a ficto/critically traitorous strategy.

Effortlessly ticking the usual boxes of (unmarked) fictocritical writing – or (hyphenated) ficto-criticism, for that matter – *Bluff Rock* also perfectly fits the slightly more complex notion of (slashed) ficto/critical strategies the present thesis proposes. Crucially, *Bluff Rock* is pervaded by a ficto/critical understanding of our textual practices which in/forms both its *ficto*-critical and ficto-*critical* perspectives. Precisely this double writing, the twofold pursuit of mediating a message while making the underlying medium strange again, makes Schlunke's text strategically ficto/critical. In this sense, her own mediations in the textual formation *Bluff Rock* are perhaps best characterised by the words she reserves for the actual landscape feature that is Bluff Rock: "A message. A strange angel." (ibid: 20)

5. Towards a Ficto/critique

Around the time I began reading more ficto/critical texts for this study, a classmate reported back to our FUB *Colloquium für Examenskandidaten* from a post/colonial academic conference in which he had participated. Although I can neither remember the conference title nor its specific topic, Lyam's informal report to our little group stoked and formatively influenced my nascent thinking on ficto/criticism. He laid his finger on something that resonated strongly with an idea I was working on, something that I had only intimated the ficto/critical would implicitly address, but that I was as yet unable to formulate clearly. Hearing Lyam complain about goings-on at the conference suddenly threw into some relief for me where one particular virtue of the ficto/critical and its unusual itinerary lay in contrast to more established forms of academic critique. While he was still excited by the clever and pertinent papers that had been delivered, this nevertheless only compounded his simultaneous sense of resignation that, as he put it, all we ever do is write another paper. It's always and only ever yet another text. That's our response to all these pressing and depressing concerns. But no matter how well delivered, it mostly just doesn't seem to connect, he insisted.

In a short aside, Lyam considered this situation to be the reverse scenario from footage he had seen of a factory manager who, clipboard in hand, walks alongside his employees telling the camera about numbers and figures, production and sales, the necessity to restructure and lay-off, while the people he is talking about are standing *right there* next to him – but it just did not seem to connect. Whatever was written on that piece of paper on the manager's clipboard mattered greatly to the people present on the assembly lines, but the same text simultaneously facilitated the manager's staggering situational abstraction. Now, the reverse scenario with the papers at the conference – all of which were very much ethically aware and concerned about real people and real situations – was that these concerns remained theoretical, on paper, contained in, possibly even by, these texts. Engaging with real matters of concern in this way means first and foremost engaging text, to engage textually, which creates another arena entirely – paradoxically, even in abstraction from the one ostensibly at the centre of attention. It was almost, Lyam suggested to our little Po/co Research Forum, as though it were systemically preferable that all of these engaged and concerned academics, critics, and theorists were thus primarily engaged in and concerned with their own reading and writing rather than where it supposedly mattered.

A great deal of Lyam's frustration on that day would have been caused by the realisation that you cannot change things quickly, even when you see through plain (systemic) injustices and produce a compelling theory and pertinent critique to address these concerns, because the discourses under consideration are mostly at work in very different loops and bubbles from the ones into which our academic theorising and critiquing usually enter. Personally, I am fairly sure that thoughts to this effect cross every engaged and aspiring academic's mind at one point – Lyam, for one, was not amused. He vowed to take up a position in which he could really hands-on do something that matters. And for all I know that is precisely what he did, where he found purpose, and how he blossomed.

As for theorising the ficto/critical, however, Lyam's input gave my thinking a perspectival spin. As he had said, the point was not that academic theorists and critics weren't doing *anything*, but rather that precisely what they *were* doing – theoretical and critical reading and writing – seemed to be systemically implicated in ways that their theories and critiques neither reflected constatively nor countered performatively. The internal perspective of thus reading and writing is that you are doing this one thing and are *thereby* concerning yourself with another matter entirely. By contrast, the ficto/critical texts that enthused me at the time seemed to suggest otherwise. They seemed to address precisely the instituted gap between our frequent theories and critiques of reading and writing, on the one side, and our theories and critiques of other issues and concerns, on the other side. This is how Lyam led me towards a first blueprint of how indeed to theorise and critique our textual practices *in their role for* wider discursive practices that still ought to be theorised and critiqued *at the same time*.

This itinerary struck me as especially timely because while much academic writing delves straight into theorising and critiquing the first principles of its respective subjects, there are also practically relevant aspects to the first principles of thus engaging issues textually which may indeed happen to connect to the wider discursive issues under scrutiny. It also promised to be a particularly productive inroad to conceptualise some effects of the ficto/critical because the performativity of our reading and writing can hardly be denied in read*ing* and writ*ing* and thus presents an im/mediate basis on which to self-reflexively both address and engage individual agents in precisely the discursive circuit and bubble where their textual acts indeed matter. In this manner, I began to realise, the ficto/critical provides a response to the conundrum of what form of textual address to fashion if our textual practices are implied in – even systemically integrated into – the subjects under critique.

Lyam's schematic suggestion provided several more stepping-stones to the ficto/critical that I then expanded in my textual encounters. With regards to his perspective on critical practice, the issue was not only being preoccupied with reading and writing instead of getting hands-on involved, but it also pertained to how the performance of our textual practices would introduce, exercise, perpetuate, and naturalise elements and aspects ostensibly under critique. Likewise, with regards to the hitherto prevalent (unmarked) fictocritical or (hyphenated) ficto-critical perspectives on textual theory, the issue included not only discursively consequential rhetorical effects of dominant generic forms, but also the equally discursively consequential performative effects of our textual practices. Taking its cue from both these realisations, my approach of the (slashed) ficto/critical has narrowed its focus onto the intersection between textual theory and critical praxis by proposing a critical theory of our textual practices *in their relevance for* the wider discursive practices and effects under critique in our textual cultures. Rather than dropping the text-discursive side entirely, the ficto/critical thus addresses the only aspect in which it can indeed legitimately hope to intervene, namely our textual practices that are always already presently under way.

In this dimension, the ficto/critical problematises what much academic reading and writing takes for granted. Because our textual practices are so deeply ingrained in our textual cultures, precisely because reading and writing presents itself as the natural and ultimate academic tool, this may prevent even the inclined and engaged theorist or critic from reflecting them as potentially, even systemically, implied in their respective subjects under critique. Moreover, not only may particular text-cultural forms of reading and writing be part of the subject under critique, but indeed our cultural techniques of reading and writing *per se*, of which academia perceives itself as naturally the highest echelon. In this sense, the ficto/critical point is to avoid simply forging ahead with doing what we have always been doing in the same ways we have already been doing it. The point is no longer to simply aim for 'better' writing in the sense of writing specifically tailored to an agenda. Instead the ficto/critical suggests, firstly, to self-reflect the issues under critique in relation to the practices in which we participate and which we perpetuate in thus mounting our critique and, secondly, to create the same theoretical awareness for the recipient agent by letting the text interpellate them to ficto/critical effect – that is, by highlighting the *ficto*-critical and indicating the ficto-*critical*. Hence, the ficto/critical point is to aim for writing that can create both a self-reflexive meta-commentary and an im/mediate awareness of the practical implications of our textual performances.

If writing always and only ever yet another text is what we do, and if writing *qua* cultural technique is just as much part of the subjects under critique as it is our medium of critique, then the constitutive level of our textual practices ought to be included in the critique, so as to let it pre-emptively in/form both our textual form and practices in their relevance for the wider discursive issues under critique. If writing another theoretical or critical text in the academic circuit about something else cannot easily precipitate change in the wider discursive circuits with which it is thus concerned, it can still legitimately hope to do so in the academic circuit which comprises such acts. While wider discursive concerns are thus only addressed through a narrow focus on the complicity of our textual practices in them, this yet gains the precious advantage of im/mediately interpellating the agent at work. In this fashion, the transcendent medial fiction of the text is made im/mediately relevant for the mediating agent's textual conduct under way, which has the potential to short-circuit the distance of mediation on top of collapsing the distanced academic speaking position. Even our acts of reading and writing are ethically charged, which is what the ficto/critical can address in a novel way that endows it with a particular edge entirely alien to established forms of critique.

Although there is no neat congruence between the complex that so exasperated Lyam and the complexes to which fictocriticism initially was a response, his report still led me to pursue the following thoughts with regards to the (slashed) ficto/critical. Firstly, if fictocriticism deserves credentials as interventionist writing, then what could it meaningfully be said to intervene in other than our linguistic-discursive and textual practices? Secondly, if our textual practices were to be made the nexus between an im/mediately involving interventionist critique and the mediation of wider discursive issues of concern, then suddenly the distance between textual subject and object, between textual agent and textual concern would be short-circuited to im/mediately striking effect with counter-continuing intent. Thirdly, if literary studies are to mount theories and critiques beyond their realm, then it were preferable for their own (textual) conduct in so doing to self-reflect and implement the implications of these theories and critiques.

In other words, if the text-cultural techniques we engage and perpetuate are an integral part of our textual cultures under scrutiny, then they should by right pre-emptively instantiate the insights of our proposed theories and critiques. Theorising and critiquing wider discursive, cultural, and political practices needs to be recognised and reflected as discursive, cultural, and political practice itself – potentially even as implicated in the very practices under scrutiny. These points resonated productively with the primary texts I was reading at the time. Looking back, my study has thus – almost in response to Lyam's frustration – outlined the itinerary of the ficto/critical as follows.

The second chapter has proposed the counter-intuitive route of im/mediate *ficto*-critical reference. The *ficto*-critical vector was introduced as a trope whose performative self-reflexivity im/mediately interpellates the mediating agent at work on the text. It thus enables a kind of textual intervention that – unlike its generic academic counterpart – is not based on another gaping textual bridge towards its subject matter, but instead bridges the gap towards its textual agent short-circuitously. Ideally, this im/mediate experiential interpellation of the recipient is then accompanied by a structural metaphor that explanatorily illuminates what its *ficto*-critical vector illumines. This further tropical turn has been introduced as the *ficto*-critical twist, whose ultimate aim is to access and p/re/structure the textual agency at work on the text from within – that is, while at work on the text. The combination of frictioning conceptual work that highlights the textual frame/work under way at the same time as its aesthetics and poetics are inextricably intersected has been qualified as pre/post/erous because in the last instance it is geared towards p/re/structuring the mediating agent for post/erity.

With regards to Lyam's stance it is significant that the second chapter has transacted the following interrelated shifts in perspective that have already been anticipated in the introductory first chapter: from a writerly and textual focus towards the readerly perspective, from writerly or textual self-reflexivity towards readerly self-reflexivity, from textual performativity towards the readerly performance of the text, and from interpellation through mediation of experience towards interpellation through the im/mediate experience of our mediat*ing* – all of which, taken together, have precipitated a broader shift in perspective from the level of generic between towards the meta-generic level, on which the first principles of our textual practices come into focus. Both illumining and illuminating our textual frame/work necessarily under way in reading, *ficto*-critical strategies can legitimately hope to intervene where *it* matters. The crucial point is that the *ficto*-critical does not simply put its ideas out there, but brings them home to each individual reader by generating an im/mediate awareness of their, always presently enacted, textual implication and agency. In this manner, the *ficto*-critical activates unprecedented inroads for critical textual interventions.

At the same time, with regards to a potential general ficto/critique of our textual practices, the second chapter has heeded the initial call for a different thrust in our literary studies and textual analyses and provided a novel perspective which aspires to focalise the constitutive text-epistemological frame/work of reading and writing from within particular textual acts of read*ing* and writ*ing*. Importantly, the counter-intuitive route of the combined *ficto*-critical tropes thus delivers an equally evident and solid basis on which ultimately to theorise and critique the paradigmatic communicative situation of textual representation.

The third chapter has first refined the notion of the ficto/critical in a way that retains its potential for particular positions to resist detrimental generic patterns via counter-continuation. It has then juxtaposed two ideologically opposed text-practical interpretations of the constitutive frame/work of textual practices. Finally, it has re/formulated a theory of the ficto/critical in terms of artful thought-experimental writing. Firstly, both elements of the two-step ficto/critical trope have been analysed in order to focalise how ficto/critical practices harness their enlightening thrust towards readerly positional emancipation in the equation of textual work for their empowering notion of apotropaic counter-strategies. Secondly, the analysis of the polar academic and ficto/critical text-practical ideals has re/traced the ideological drive at work in the theoretical guidance of our text-practical conduct and has thereby identified this nexus' respective potential to either maintain or change (wider) discursive formations in which we participate. Thirdly, with its interrelated layers of meaning the notion of artful thought-experimental writing has ventured to capture both the strategic dimension and ideological stance of the ficto/critical in the precise way in which these have mutual conditions of im/possibility with their targeted genres of textual form and conduct – that is, first and foremost, with their academic other.

In response to Lyam's almost sinister intimation that our academically critical conduct might well be serving systemic purposes, the third chapter has effectively corroborated the sentiment evoked early on that there is nothing innocent about our allegedly disinterested and objective academic textual practices. Every single one of our textual acts has ethico-political potential that we always already performatively (re)mediate together with the constative mediations at the centre of attention. Most importantly, the realisation that different text-practical principles engage the same constitutive textual frame/work to very different (wider) discursive effects focalises the ideological bone of contention that is tacitly and continuously at stake in all our textual practices. And it is precisely at this point that ficto/critical writing as much as ficto/critical theory can legitimately hope to make a difference. Such is the ficto/critical lifeline that this study can offer Lyam to perhaps salvage his confidence in critical textual interventions.

Towards a general ficto/critique of our textual practices the third chapter has thus contributed the envisioned shift from textual analysis towards text-cultural analysis. Between the poles of generic fidelity and generic resistance, between conservative tradition and radical betrayal, as well as between perpetuation and counter-continuation it has brought the ideological dimension of our textual conduct into sharp focus. Its close readings have even come good on the promise of a different perspective for cultural studies by directing them towards the level of text-practical ideology. First and foremost, however, the third chapter has brought the present theory of the (slashed) ficto/critical into its own by substantiating the introductory outline of it as an im/mediately striking interventionist aesthetic of deconstruction in terms of artistic and artful thought-experimental writing that ultimately aims to precipitate equally artistic and artful thought-experimental reading responses.

While there may be different degrees of ficto/criticality pre/scribed by different texts, one crucial point of the third chapter has been that the ficto/critical is just as much a *readerly* as a writerly *stance* towards text. My study's focus on ficto/critical strategies and ideology has been at pains to ensure that the particular positioning of each textual agent remains underdetermined. In so doing, it has made palpable another perspective directed towards a general critique of the discursive effects that our textual practices introduce, exercise, and naturalise. Having formulated a theory of ficto/critical strategy and ideology against the background of a ficto/critical understanding of textual representation and communication, the general perspective of a ficto/critique of our textual practices has now indeed become a distinct possibility.

Furthermore, the course of the third chapter has implemented the anticipated transition from a concern with the concepts of judgement, interpretation, and representation to a post-generic understanding of the principle tropes of fiction, criticism, and theory. The deconstruction of this erstwhile generic triad has yielded an aporetic state in which the communication of a representation's *medial fiction* is necessarily primary to the secondary differentiation of its epistemological status as either fictional truth-constituting or non-fictional truth-representing. Iain Sinclair's enigmatic formulation "fictionalized through documentation" (2000: 7) aptly captures how either fictional or non-fictional facts *in writing* always already constitute a medial fiction. We always already encounter a medial fiction to which we then index either fictional or non-fictional significance.

In other words, *fiction*, which has previously been conceptualised as derivative of non-fictional language use, has now been re/conceptualised as the constitutive term within whose realm the tropes of *theory* and *criticism* identify the respectively idealising and manifesting principles of reading-writing. Fiction thus re/emerges both as the primary term in a deconstructed understanding of the traditional hierarchy between fiction and non-fiction and as the post-generic realm within which the principle directions of idealising theory and manifesting criticism unfold the frame/work between the object text and its medial fiction, the textual object.

The fourth chapter has finally supplemented the second step of the twofold ficto/critical trope. First, the generation of ficto-*critical* edge by way of harnessing the *ficto*-critical vector and twist for wider discursive issues and concerns has been exemplarily re/traced. Next, the motivational drive to write differently, ficto/critically, has been illuminated against this self-directed two-step trope. Because a ficto/critical awareness links the epistemology of our own textual practices to the wider ethical issues with which we concern ourselves textually, it generates the urge to break with current generic forms and practices. Our present textual cultures often play a part in wider discursive problems simply because our textual practices have gained systemic significance, because they are our culture-constituting techniques. In light of this, the ficto/critical thus presents a textual form of address that can legitimately hope to both intervene in our textual acts and deconstruct our conception thereof in order to work towards ultimately redressing wider discursive issues and concerns. Completing the scope of ambitions of this thesis, the fourth chapter has thus actualised the initially desired cultural studies perspective that focalises the ethical dimension of our textual practices.

So while Lyam, on that day, despaired at what he perceived as the futile path of academic critique, the ficto/critical itinerary that the present study has sketched out would suggest that another – im/mediately available – way out of this dead end is, in fact, through. The *ficto*-critical takes its cue from the one aspect that can indeed be im/mediately addressed textually, namely our practices of textual mediation. By making this inroad for text-practical intervention central to their wider discursive concerns, ficto-*critical* strategies thus seize the only sure-fire option for im/mediate readerly interpellation. Following these combined tropical turns, a broader picture of how both our constitutive and generic text-cultural practices impact on our cultural formations will hopefully emerge, eventually. What I have called a more general ficto/critique would then focalise those constitutive text-cultural effects that formatively affect our wider textual cultures, by which I mean cultures in which certain text-cultural practices have not only become pervasive but now actually function as foundational cultural techniques.

Whereas since the second half of the 20th century a succession of waves of critical perspectives have made different issues central to their approaches, their textual means and conduct of critique have hardly changed. In fact, more often than not they have maintained and strengthened the textual practices that they have in common with their subjects of critique. Meanwhile, the contingent and constitutive sides of our textual practices that would self-reflexively apply to our theorising and critiquing have hitherto not been fully included in the scope of analysis. Because textual practices are almost all-pervasive in our present textual cultures, however, this kind of ficto/critical thrust is highly pertinent and should, ultimately, be carried into all walks of life in which relating to the world, the other, and one/self is increasingly mediated textually, and in which these wider discursive formations are thus manipulated by the mechanics of textual meaning formation – more often than not in the blind spot of our ostensible intentions.

Bibliography

Arendt, Hannah (1979): "On Hannah Arendt", in: Hill (ed.): *Hannah Arendt: The Recovery of the Public World*, p. 303-339.

Acker, Kathy (1982): *Great Expectations*, New York: Grove.

— (1986): *Don Quixote: Which Was a Dream*, New York: Grove.

Alexander, George (1997): *Mortal Divide: The Autobiography of Yiorgos Alexandroglou / Γιώργος Αλεξανδρόγλου*, Rose Bay, NSW: Brandl & Schlesiger.

Anderson, Nicole/Schlunke, Katrina (eds.) (2008): *Cultural Theory in Everyday Practice*, South Melbourne, VIC: Oxford University Press.

Andrews, Bruce/Bernstein, Charles (eds.) (1984): *The L=A=N=G=U=A=G=E Book* (= Poetics of the New Series), Carbondale: Southern Illinois University Press.

Appiah, Kwame Anthony (1991): "Is The Post- in Postmodernism the Post- in Postcolonial?", in: *Critical Inquiry*, volume 17, number 2, p. 336-357.

Attridge, Derek (2004): *The Singularity of Literature*, London: Routledge.

Bartlett, Alison (ed.) (2009): *Outskirts: Feminisms Along the Edge*, volume 20: On Fictocriticism, May 2009, http://www.outskirts.arts.uwa.edu.au/1179626 (April 24, 2012).

Bellamy, Dodie (2004): *Pink Steam*, San Francisco: Suspect Thoughts.

— (2006): *Academonia*, San Francisco: Krupskaya.

Benjamin, Walter (2007): *Illuminations*, edited by Hannah Arendt, translated by Harry Zohn, New York: Schocken.

— (2009): *One-Way Street and Other Writings*, translated by J. A. Underwood, London: Penguin.

— (2009a [1928]): "One-Way Street", in: *One-Way Street*, p. 46-115.

— (2009b [1936]): "The Work of Art in the Age of Mechanical Reproduction", in: *One-Way Street*, p. 228-259.

— (2007a [1940]): "Theses on the Philosophy of History", in: *Illuminations*, p. 253-264.

Benterrak, Krim/Muecke, Stephen/Roe, Paddy (1996 [1984]): *Reading the Country: Introduction to Nomadology*, revised edition, South Fremantle, WA: Fremantle Arts Centre Press.

Bernardo, Susan/Carlson, Cindy/Mazzola, Robert (eds.) (2002): *Gender Reconstructions; Pornography and Perversions in Literature and Culture*, Aldershot, UK: Ashgate.

Brewster, Anne (1996a): "Fictocriticism: Pedagogy and Practice", in: Guerin/Butters/Nettelbeck (eds.), *Crossing Lines*, p. 89-92.

— (1996b): "Fictocriticism: Undisciplined Writing", in: Hutchinson/Williams (eds.), *Writing – Teaching, Teaching Writing*, p. 29-32.

Coetzee, John Maxwell (2003): *Elizabeth Costello*, London: Secker & Warburg.

Davis, Mark (1997): *Gangland Cultural Elites and the New Generationalism*, St. Leonard, NSW: Allen & Unwin.

Deleuze, Gille/Parnet, Claire (1996 [1977]): *Dialogues*, translated by Hugh Tomlinson and Barbara Habberjam, New York: Columbia University Press.

Deleuze, Gilles/Guattari, Felix (1987 [1980]): *A Thousand Plateaus: Capitalism and Schizophrenia*, translated by Brian Massumi, Minneapolis: University of Minnesota Press.

De Montaigne, Michel (2012): *The Complete Essays*, translated and edited by M. A. Screech. London: Penguin.

Dening, Greg (1996): *Performances*, Chicago: University of Chicago Press.

Derrida, Jacques (1982 [1972]): *Margins of Philosophy*, translated and annotated by Alan Bass, Chicago: University of Chicago Press.

— (1992): *Acts of Literature*, edited by Derek Attridge, New York: Routledge.

— (1998): *The Derrida Reader: Writing Performances*, edited by Julian Wolfreys, Edinburgh: Edinburgh University Press.

— (1982 [1972]): "White Mythology", in: *Margins of Philosophy*, p. 207-271.

— (1998 [1978]): "The *Retrait* of Metaphor", in: *The Derrida Reader: Writing Performances*, p. 102-128.

— (1992a): "'This Strange Institution Called Literature': An Interview with Jacques Derrida", in: *Acts of Literature*, p. 33-75.

— (1992b): "The Law of Genre", in: *Acts of Literature*, p. 221-252.

Didion, Joan (1990 [1979]): *The White Album*, New York: Farrar, Straus and Giroux.

Ellmann, Maud (1993): *The Hunger Artists: Starving, Writing, and Imprisonment*, Cambridge, MA: Harvard University Press.

Exploited, the (1981): *Punks Not Dead*, Secret Records.

Fairclough, Norman (1995): *Critical Discourse Analysis: The Critical Study of Language*, London: Longman.

Flavell, Helen (2004): *Writing-Between: Australian and Canadian Ficto-Criticism*, PhD thesis presented at Murdoch University, Perth, WA, http://research repository.murdoch.edu.au/53/ (June 4, 2013).

— (2009): "Who Killed Jeanne Randolph? King, Muecke or 'Ficto-Criticism'", in: Bartlett, *Outskirts*, volume 20, http://www.outskirts.arts.uwa.edu.au/volumes/volume-20/flavell (April 24, 2012).

Foucault, Michel (1984): *The Foucault Reader*, edited by Paul Rabinow, New York: Pantheon.

— (1984 [1969]): "What is an Author?", in: *The Foucault Reader*, p. 101-120.

Gadamer, Hans-Georg (1972 [1960]): *Wahrheit und Methode: Grundzüge einer Philosophischen Hermeneutik*, Tübingen: Mohr/Siebeck.

Game, Ann/Metcalfe, Andrew (1996): *Passionate Sociology*, London: SAGE.

Gibbs, Anna (1998): "The Gift", in: Kerr/Nettelbeck (eds.), *The Space Between*, p. 33-44.

Gibson, Ross (2008): *The Summer Exercises*, Crawley, WA: University of Western Australia Press.

Glück, Robert (2004): "Long Note on New Narrative", in: Mary Burger/Robert Glück/Camille Roy/Gail Scott (eds.), *Narrativity: A Critical Journal of Innovative Narrative*, http://www.sfsu.edu/~poetry/narrativity/issue_one/gluck.html (Aug. 02, 2013).

Gray, Alasdair (1997): *Why Scots Should Rule Scotland 1997*, Edinburgh: Canongate.

Guerin, Caroline/Butters, Philip/Nettelbeck, Amanda (eds.) (1996): *Crossing Lines: Formations of Australian Culture*, Proceedings of the Association for the Study of Australian Literature Conference 1995, Adelaide, SA: Association for Study of Australian Literature.

Hayles, N. Katherine (2002): *Writing Machines* (= Mediawork Pamphlet Series), Cambridge, MA: MIT Press.

Herk, Aritha, van (1990): *Places Far From Ellesmere: A Geografictione – Excavations on Site*, Red Deer, AB: Red Deer College Press.

Hill, Melvyn A. (ed.) (1979): *Hannah Arendt: The Recovery of the Public World*, New York: St. Martin's.

Hughes, John (2007): *Someone Else: Fictional Essays*, Artarmon, NSW: Giramondo.

— (2007a): "Preface", in: *Someone Else*, p. *xi-xviii*.

— (2007b): "Translations", in: *Someone Else*, p. 183-189.

Hutchinson, Jan/Williams, Graham (eds.) (1996): *Writing – Teaching, Teaching Writing*, Proceedings of the First Annual Conference of the Association of University Writing Programs, Sydney: University of Technology.

Jones, Gail (1997): *Fetish Lives*, South Fremantle, WA: Fremantle Arts Centre Press.

— (1998): "Thaumatropes", in: Kerr/Nettelbeck (eds.), *The Space Between*, p. 98-114.

Kaplan, Alice (1993): *French Lessons: A Memoir*, Chicago: University of Chicago Press.

Kerr, Heather/Nettelbeck, Amanda (eds.) (1998): *The Space Between: Australian Women Writing Fictocriticism*, Nedlands, WA: University of Western Australia Press.

Kerr, Heather B. (2001): "Sympathetic Topographies", in: *Parallax*, volume 7, number 2, p. 107-126.

— (2002): "Perverse Writing – Maternity and Monarchy: Fictocriticism and Exorbitant, Plural Bodies", in: Bernado/Carlson/Mazzola (eds.), *Gender Reconstructions*, p. 148-166.

Kinsella, John (1995): *The Silo: A Pastoral Symphony*, North Fremantle, WA: Fremantle Arts Centre Press.

— (1999): *Counter-Pastoral*, Sydney: Vagabond.

— (2000): *The Hierarchy of Sheep*, Highgreen, UK: Bloodaxe.

— (2001): *Auto*, Applecross, WA: Salt.

— (2005): *The New Arcadia*, North Fremantle, WA: Fremantle Arts Centre Press.

Krauss, Rosalind E. (1986): *The Originality of the Avant-Garde and Other Modernist Myths*, Cambridge, MA: MIT Press.

— (1986 [1980]): "Poststructuralism and the Paraliterary", in: *The Originality of the Avant-Garde*, p. 291-295.

Kristeva, Julia (1986): *The Kristeva Reader*, edited by Toril Moi, New York: Columbia University Press.

— (1986 [1983]): "Stabat Mater", in: *The Kristeva Reader*, p. 160-186.

Leiris, Michel (1992 [1939]): *Manhood: A Journey from Childhood into the Fierce Order of Virility*, Chicago: University of Chicago Press.

Lichtenstein, Rachel/Sinclair, Iain (2000 [1999]): *Rodinsky's Room*, London: Granta.

Lingis, Alphonso (2004): *Trust* (= Theory Out Of Bounds, edited by Sandra Buckley, Michael Hardt, and Brian Massumi, volume 25), Minneapolis: University of Minnesota Press.

— (2007): *The First Person Singular* (= Northwestern University Studies in Phenomenology and Existential Philosophy), Evanston, IL: Northwestern University Press.

Lucy, Niall (2010): *PoMo Oz: Fear and Loathing Down Under*, North Fremantle, WA: Fremantle Arts Centre Press.

Maddin, Guy (dir.) (2007): MY WINNIPEG, Everyday Pictures/Buffalo Gal Pictures.

— (2009): *My Winnipeg*, Toronto: Coach House Books.

Martínez, Manuel Ramos (2007): "Betrayed Borders: Double Agents and the Crisscrossing of Conflicts", in: *Sarai Reader 2007: Frontiers*, New Delhi: Impress, p. 256-263, http://www.sarai.net/publications/readers/07-frontiers (May 07, 2011).

Morris, Meaghan (2006): *Identity Anecdotes: Translation and Media Culture*, London: SAGE.

Muecke, Stephen (1992): *Textual Spaces: Aboriginality and Cultural Studies*, Kensington, NSW: New South Wales University Press.

— (1997): *No Road (Bitumen All the Way)*, Fremantle, WA: Fremantle Arts Centre Press.

— (2008): *Joe in the Andamans and Other Fictocritical Stories*, Sydney: Local Consumption Publications.

— (1996): "Bricolage", in: Benterrak/Muecke/Roe, *Reading the Country*, p. 168-72.

— (2002): "The Fall: Fictocritical Writing", in: *Parallax*, volume 8, number 4, p. 108-112.

— (2008a): "Introduction: There is No Heart", in: *Joe in the Andamans*, p. 10-16.

— (2008b): "The Fall", in: *Joe in the Andamans*, p. 18-25.

— (2008c): "A Chance to Hear a Nyigina Song", in: *Joe in the Andamans*, p. 80-93.

Nettelbeck, Amanda (1998): "Notes towards an Introduction", in: Kerr/Nettelbeck (eds.), *The Space Between*, p. 1-17.

Price, Richard/Price, Sally (1995): *Enigma Variations*, Cambridge, MA: Harvard University Press.

Probyn, Elspeth (1996): *Outside Belongings*, New York: Routledge.

Robb, Simon (2001): *Fictocritical Sentences*, PhD thesis presented at the University of Adelaide, SA.

— (1996): "Academic Divination Is Not a Mysticism: Fictocriticism, Pedagogy and Hypertext", in: Guerin/Butters/Nettelbeck (eds.), *Crossing Lines*, p. 97-101.

— (2001a): "Alien Sick", in: *Fictocritical Sentences*, p. 35-41.

— (2001b): "Greetings from Adelaide", in: *Fictocritical Sentences*, http://ensemble.va.com.au/tableau/simon (Dec. 17, 2010).

Schlunke, Katrina M. (2005): *Bluff Rock: Autobiography of a Massacre*, North Fremantle, WA: Curtin University Books.

— (2008): "Ethnografts", in: Anderson/Schlunke (eds.), *Cultural Theory in Everyday Practice*, p. 248-258.

Sebald, Winfried Georg (2007 [1995]): *Die Ringe des Saturn: Eine Englische Wallfahrt*, Frankfurt am Main: Fischer.

Shaviro, Steven (2007): *Doom Patrols: A Theoretical Fiction about Postmodernism*, New York: Serpent's Tail.

Shields, David (2010): *Reality Hunger: A Manifesto*, London: Hamish Hamilton.

Siegel, Don (dir.) (1976): THE SHOOTIST, Paramount Pictures.

Somerville, Margaret (1999): *Body/Landscape Journals*, Melbourne: Spinifex.

Stein, Gertrude (2004): *Look at Me Now and Here I Am: Writings and Lectures 1911-1945*, edited by Patricia Meyerowitz, London: Peter Owen.

Stern, Lesley (1999): *The Smoking Book*, Chicago: University of Chicago Press.

Stewart, Kathleen (2007): *Ordinary Affects*, Durham, NC: Duke University Press.

Taussig, Michael (2010 [1980]): *The Devil and Commodity Fetishism in South America*, Chapel Hill: University of North Carolina Press.

— (1992): *The Nervous System*, New York: Routledge.

— (1997): *The Magic of the State*, New York: Routledge.

— (2004): *My Cocaine Museum*, Chicago: University of Chicago Press.

— (2006): *Walter Benjamin's Grave*, Chicago: University of Chicago Press.

— (2009): *What Color Is the Sacred?*, Chicago: University of Chicago Press.

— (2006a): "Author's Note", in: *Walter Benjamin's Grave*, p. *vii-xi*.

— (2006b): "Walter Benjamin's Grave: A Profane Illumination", in: *Walter Benjamin's Grave*, p. 1-31.

— (2010a): "Preface to the Thirtieth Anniversary Edition", in: *The Devil and Commodity Fetishism in South America*, p. xi-xiv.

— (2010b): "The Corn-Wolf: Writing Apotropaic Texts", in: *Critical Inquiry*, volume 37, number 1, p. 26-33.

Wah, Fred (1996): *Diamond Grill*, Edmonton, AB: NeWest.

— (2000): *Faking It: Poetics & Hybridity – Critical Writing 1984-1999* (= The Writer as Critic, volume 7), Edmonton, AB: NeWest.